M000027711

Australian Aboriginal Words in English

Their Origin and Meaning

R. M. W. DIXON is Director of the Research Centre for Linguistic Typology at La Trobe University. Besides comprehensive grammars of the Dyirbal and Yidiñ languages from North Queensland, of the Boumaa dialect of Fijian, and of the Jarawara language from southern Amazonia, his books include *A Semantic Approach to English Grammar* (Oxford University Press, 2005), a general survey volume, *Australian Languages: Their Nature and Development* (Cambridge University Press, 2002), and a best-selling volume, *The Rise and Fall of Languages* (Cambridge University Press, 1997).

BRUCE MOORE is Head of the Australian National Dictionary Centre at the Australian National University. He edits the *Australian Oxford Dictionary*, the *Australian Concise Oxford Dictionary*, and the *Australian Pocket Oxford Dictionary*. His books include *Gold! Gold! Gold! The Language of the Nineteenth Century Australian Gold Rushes* (Oxford University Press, 2000).

W. S. RAMSON was the founding Head of the Australian National Dictionary Centre and the editor of the first edition of the *Australian National Dictionary*. He is the author of *Lexical Images: The Story of the Australian National Dictionary* (Oxford University Press, 2002).

MANDY THOMAS, by training an anthropologist, is currently Executive Director for Humanities and Creative Arts at the Australian Research Council. She is the author of *Dreams in the Shadows: Vietnamese-Australian Lives in Transition* (Allen and Unwin, 1999) and *Moving landscapes: National Parks and the Vietnamese experience* (Pluto Press, 2002).

The Australian National Dictionary Centre conducts research into Australian English and is jointly funded by the Australian National University and Oxford University Press. The Centre has editorial responsibility for the Australian range of Oxford dictionaries.

Australian Aboriginal Words in English

Their Origin and Meaning

Second edition

R. M. W. Dixon

Bruce Moore

W. S. Ramson

Mandy Thomas

OXFORD

UNIVERSITY PRESS

253 Normanby Road, South Melbourne, Victoria 3205, Australia

Oxford University Press is a department of the University of Oxford.
It furthers the University's objective of excellence in research, scholarship,
and education by publishing worldwide in

Oxford New York

Auckland Cape Town Dar es Salaam Hong Kong Karachi
Kuala Lumpur Madrid Melbourne Mexico City Nairobi
New Delhi Shanghai Taipei Toronto

With offices in

Argentina Austria Brazil Chile Czech Republic France Greece
Guatemala Hungary Italy Japan Poland Portugal Singapore
South Korea Switzerland Thailand Turkey Ukraine Vietnam

OXFORD is a trade mark of Oxford University Press
in the UK and in certain other countries

Copyright © R.M.W. Dixon, Bruce Moore, W.S. Ramson and Mandy Thomas 2006
First published 1990
Reprinted in paperback 1992, 1995
Second edition published 2006

This book is copyright. Apart from any fair dealing for the purposes
of private study, research, criticism or review as permitted under the
Copyright Act, no part may be reproduced, stored in a retrieval system,
or transmitted, in any form or by any means, electronic, mechanical,
photocopying, recording or otherwise without prior written permission.
Enquiries to be made to Oxford University Press.

Copying for educational purposes
Where copies of part or the whole of the book are made under Part VB
of the Copyright Act, the law requires that prescribed procedures be followed.
For information, contact the Copyright Agency Limited.

National Library of Australia
Cataloguing-in-Publication data:

Dixon, Robert M. W.
Australian Aboriginal words in English: their origin and meaning.
2nd ed.
Includes index.
ISBN 978-019554-073-4
ISBN 0-19-554073-5
1. English language—Foreign words and phrases—
Australian languages—Dictionaries. 2. Australian
Languages—Dictionaries. 3. Australian Languages—
History. 4. English language—Australia. I. Title.

499.1532

Typeset in India by diacriTech, Chennai.
Printed in Hong Kong by Sheck Wah Tong Printing Press Ltd

Contents

Guide to the English pronunciation of the borrowings

List of symbols used

Vowels		Diphthongs		Consonants	
i	heat	eɪ	hay	p	pat
ɪ	hit	oʊ	hoe	b	bat
ɛ	bet	aɪ	high	t	tap
æ	bat	aʊ	how	d	dot
a	part	ɔɪ	toy	k	cat
ɒ	hot	ɪə	tier	g	goat
ɔ	sort	ɛə	dare	f	fat
ʊ	put	ʊə	tour	v	vat
u	hoot			θ	thin
ʌ	hut			ð	that
ɜ	hurt			s	sat
ə	another			z	zap
				ʃ	shot
				ʒ	measure
				tʃ	church
				dʒ	joke
				m	mat
				n	not
				ŋ	ring
				l	long
				r	ring
				h	hang
				y	young
				w	way

Preface

Up until the late 1980s, all dictionaries of English—including the *Macquarie Dictionary* (1981)—included some words borrowed from the indigenous languages of Australia, but without stating their specific origin. For *kangaroo* from Guugu Yimidhirr in North Queensland, for *boomerang* from Dharuk at Sydney, for *budgerigar* from Kamilaroi in central New South Wales, and for all others, the etymology was simply given as 'native Australian' or 'Australian Aboriginal', without any attempt to identify which of the 250 or so distinct Australian languages a given word came from. This is rather like lumping together all loans into English from French, German, Spanish, Turkish, Hungarian, Russian, Greek etc. as 'European'.

In 1978, W. S. Ramson of the Australian National University announced a project to compile an *Australian National Dictionary* (*AND*), a 'dictionary of Australianisms on historical principles', to be published by the bicentennial year, 1988; I agreed to assist with the etymologies of words borrowed from Australian languages. Since it was known that many of the most important loans came from Dharuk, the Sydney language, Ramson employed linguistics student David Wilkins to work on these etymologies in 1980, using my comprehensive materials on the language.

Meanwhile, over in America, Random House was working on the second edition of their large 'unabridged' dictionary, and in June 1984 they requested my assistance in obtaining specific etymologies for a list of words claimed to be 'Native Australian'. About 35 of these were from Dharuk, for which etymologies had been provided by Wilkins. Utilising the files I had been building up since 1973 (with the assistance of grants from the Australian Research Grants Committee)—which gathered together all published and unpublished materials on each of the 250 Australian languages—Research Assistant Claire Allridge was able to trace the origin of a further 70 loans. I checked and corrected these etymologies, sending them off to Random House the following year (with a copy to Ramson for the *AND*). The *Random House Dictionary*, published in September 1987, thus became the first dictionary to include precise etymologies of loans from the Aboriginal languages of Australia.

In 1985, Ramson prepared a comprehensive list of about 400 loans from Australian languages for which there would be entries in the *Australian National Dictionary*. During 1985 and 1986, Linda Macfarlane and Lysbeth Ford, employed by the *AND* project, combed my files for the origins of these words, building on the earlier work of Wilkins and Allridge. The *AND*, published in September 1988, made this information available for the first time.

Soon after publication of the *AND*, Bill Ramson and I conceived the idea of the present book. Mandy Thomas, then an anthropology student, was employed by the Australian National Dictionary Centre to expand the *AND* entries on loans from indigenous languages (Chapter 3 of the present book) and to draft Chapters 1, 2 and 5; Ramson wrote the first draft of Chapter 4. All chapters were then thoroughly revised and rewritten by me, in consultation with Ramson and Thomas. In particular, I undertook a full reassessment of the etymologies in Chapter 3, making a fair few corrections and additions to the information given in the *AND*. A number of further loans were added in the course of this investigation. Most of the quotations included in Chapter 3 were taken from the *AND*, but a number were added, from additional sources, for the first edition of this work, which was published in hardback in October 1990 and reissued as a paperback eighteen months later (being reprinted in 1995).

Work on a topic such as this is cumulative, building on previous scholarship. We owe a considerable debt to such works as *Austral English: A Dictionary of Australasian Words, Phrases and Usages* by E.E. Morris (Macmillan, 1898) and *Australian Aboriginal Languages* by Barry Blake (Angus and Robertson, 1981), as well as the many handbooks on fauna and flora, anthropological texts, and grammars and dictionaries that we have consulted.

We have also depended on the help of many people. First of all, the foundational etymological research of Wilkins, Allridge, Macfarlane, and Ford. Then, a draft of the complete book was read by Barry Blake, Alan Dench, and Luise Hercus, and of Chapter 3 by Peter Austin and Gavan Breen, each of whom provided the most useful corrections and additions. Phil Rose gave assistance with the pronunciations of the words in English. Nicolas Peterson read the entire draft from the point of view of an anthropologist. We hope this book will appeal to a wide range of readers, including schoolchildren; Mary Besemeres read the draft as a sample member of the latter group, and her comments were really helpful.

Individual etymological queries and suchlike were answered by Paul Black, Neil Chadwick, Tamsin Donaldson, Wilf Douglas, Nicholas Evans, Kevin Ford, Ian Green, Jean Harkins, Mark Harvey, Jeffrey Heath, John Henderson, Tony Johns, John McEntee, Francesca Merlan, Frances Morphy, Alice Moyle, David Nash, Nick Reid, Bruce Rigsby, Alan Rumsey, Jane Simpson, Gerda Smith, and Dorothy Tunbridge.

Jeanette Covacevich, Senior Curator (vertebrates) at the Queensland Museum, read through the fauna section, and also had relevant parts read by other curators: Wayne Longmore (birds), Steve Van Dyck (mammals), Rolly McKay (fishes), and Geoff Monteith (insects). John Calaby, of the CSIRO Wildlife Division, read the entire fauna section and made the most valuable suggestions for improvement and addition, providing detailed historical information from his files. Tony Irvine, of the CSIRO Tropical Forest Research Centre (in Atherton, North Queensland), and Beth Gott, of the Department of Botany and Zoology, Monash University, read the whole flora section and made invaluable comments and corrections.

It is appropriate to undertake a revision of a standard reference work, such as the present volume, about every fifteen years. Bruce Moore (who took over as Director of the Australian National Dictionary Centre on Bill Ramson's retirement) and I have worked together and added another three dozen loans that appear to be in general usage, for which it has been possible to find etymologies. And further quotes have been added for many of the words already included. Chapter 6 (an enlargement of the list 'Aboriginal objects and concepts in English', on pages 211–16 of the first edition) has been added, and all the other chapters revised and updated by me, in association with Bruce Moore.

For this second edition, Peter Menkhorst, of the Victorian State Department of Sustainability and Environment, has provided critical comments on the fauna, and Tony Irvine on both flora and fauna sections of chapter 3; with their assistance, zoological and botanical identifications have been updated. Alexandra Aikhenvald provided comments on the entire manuscript. Information on loans into languages other than English came from Rik de Busser, Stefan Dienst, Ilya Itkin, Vladimir Plungian, and Dory Poa. New information on etymologies was supplied by Gavan Breen, Alan Dench, and Dorothy Jauncey. Comments were provided on a draft of Chapter 6 (added for this edition) by Barry Blake, Gavan Breen, Stephen Morey, Sarah Ogilvie, Nicolas Peterson, Bill Ramson, Mandy Thomas and Melanie Wilkinson. In addition, Sarah Ogilvie shared with us information from the ongoing revision of the *Oxford English Dictionary*, for entries from M to Pap.

We owe a tremendous debt to all of these friends and colleagues for the unstinting assistance they have provided in their area of special knowledge.

R. M. W. Dixon
Melbourne, October 2005

A note on pronunciation

Different languages have different habits of articulation, which must be clearly distinguished. On page vi, we give the phonetic symbols, in terms of which the pronunciation in English of the loans is shown for each entry in Chapter 3. The phonetic alphabet we use for representing the original forms of the words in Australian languages is described on pages 12–15 of Chapter 1.

One of the most important principles for the proper pronunciation of words in Australian Aboriginal languages is that every syllable should be clearly enunciated; there are, in most languages, no 'weak vowels' such as the schwa, /ə/, in English (as at the end of *data*, /deɪtə/ or in the middle of *kangaroo*, /kæŋgəru/). For example, the original word in Guugu Yimidhirr on which our *kangaroo* is based, *gaɲurru*, should be said almost as if it were three separate words with no gap between them, *ga-ɲoo-rroo*.

In most Australian languages, the first syllable bears the major accent or stress. It is most important to observe this, otherwise words may be pronounced in an unrecognisable way.

Plea for further information

We have attempted, in this book, to give accurate information concerning the major loans from Australian languages into English. There must surely be some things we have missed, and there may be additional words that could be included.

We invite our readers to send further data, and suggestions, to us at
  The Australian National Dictionary Centre
  The Australian National University
  Canberra, ACT 0200
  Australia

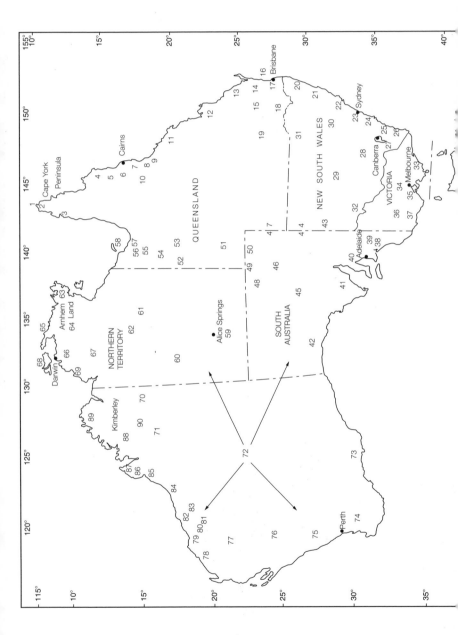

Key to the approximate locations of those Australian languages mentioned in this book

1
An introduction to Australian languages

As speakers of any language come into contact with strangers who show them new animals, plants, tools, and so on, they are likely to 'borrow' names for the new things from the strangers' language. (These are called 'borrowings' or 'loan words'.) Over the centuries, English has borrowed many words—*mosquito* comes from Spanish, *balcony* from Italian, *pyjamas* from Hindi, *ketchup* from Malay. Captain Cook returned in 1771 from his great voyage of exploration, and brought with him news of a quite unusual animal and the name it was called by Aborigines at the Endeavour River in New Holland. It was *kangaroo*.

When the First Fleet arrived at Sydney Cove in 1788, they soon adopted into English words from Dharuk, the local language—*dingo* for the native dog, *wombat* for a thick-set burrowing marsupial, *waratah* for a plant with remarkable red flowers, and *boomerang* for a weapon that they at first thought to be a kind of sword but was later discovered to be thrown in a curved path, to kill an animal. As new settlers came to Perth, Adelaide, Melbourne, and Brisbane, and then spread out into the interior of the continent, further words were borrowed from local languages into English.

Overall, however, a relatively small number of words have been taken from one or other of the 250 distinct Aboriginal languages into Australian English. Compare with Brazilian Portuguese, which has accepted well over a thousand words from the indigenous languages of that nation, or New Zealand English, which includes around 750 words of Maori origin. The first edition of this book told the story of about 400 words that have come into English from the native languages of Australia; a further three dozen have been added for this new edition. Some of the words have only local currency—a type of timber which grows in just one region—while others are in more general use. A fair few of these words have been adopted into the English spoken in Britain, America, and other countries. And a handful have found their way as loans into other languages. Five words feature in dictionaries of Dutch, French, German, Portuguese and Russian, cast into a phonological form appropriate for the language—*kangaroo, boomerang, koala, dingo* and *wombat*. (Next in order of popularity are *wallaby* and *kookaburra*, borrowed into, at least, French and Russian.) Tagalog, the major language of the Philippines, has just one loan that originated in an Australian language; there is no prize for guessing that it is *kangaroo*.

This first chapter gives a short account of the nature of Australian languages, and explains the ways in which we tried to determine which language each borrowing comes from, how it was pronounced, and what it meant in the original language. Chapter 2 provides short sketches of those languages from which the greatest number of borrowings have come. The central part of the book is Chapter 3, in which the loan words are arranged into sections such as 'fauna', 'flora', 'implements', 'dwellings', with a full account of each. Chapter 4 then describes the ways in which the borrowings were used in English. Chapter 5 provides a reminder that borrowing always takes place in two directions, and briefly mentions ways in which English words have been adopted into Australian languages. The final chapter shows how English words had their meanings extended, and were put together in new combinations, to describe objects, ideas and happenings associated with the indigenous peoples of Australia—as with *dreamtime, walkabout, outstation* and *dispersal* (when used with the meaning 'murder').

The native languages of Australia are highly developed instruments of culture, each possessing a wide vocabulary and an intricacy of grammatical forms. The apparent simplicity of the Aboriginal traditional hunting and gathering lifestyle is in sharp contrast to the elaborateness and complexity of their social and religious life, and to the richness of their language. These languages enable Aboriginal people to express subtleties of meaning in any aspect of their cultural lives, from complicated myths to detailed and precise information about the landscape. We hope that something of this richness will be apparent to our readers, as they follow the story of loan words from the original languages of Australia into the new language, English.

THE ABORIGINES AND THEIR LANGUAGES

The first discovery and settlement of Australia was made by Aborigines, at least 40,000 years ago. They soon spread out over the whole continent and probably numbered about one million by 1788. They were divided into about 700 separate groups, which have traditionally been called 'tribes'. Each had its own territory, its own political system and laws, and its own language and legends (though these were often interlinked)—just like the nations of Europe, but on a smaller scale.

The tribe-nations of Australia differed from political groupings in Europe and Africa in one important way—they did not have a single 'king' or 'chief', or a hierarchy of officers. No one was richer than anyone else, or had any right to order others around. Everyone in a tribe cooperated in the business of everyday life, and in artistic activity and ritual. Each person had certain obligations, depending on their age and sex, and on the particular kinship relations they bore to others.

The boundary of each group's territory was, in most cases, a natural barrier such as a mountain range or a strip of barren country. The size of the territory generally depended on the kind of terrain. Where food was scarce, as in many inland regions, the area of land occupied by a tribe was much larger than that in the rainforest or in a fertile river valley.

A tribe was divided into a number of 'local groups', each of which considered that it belonged to one part of the territory. Just south of Cairns, the Yidinyji tribe had a 'coastal group', associated with the country around what are now the towns of Edmonton and Gordonvale, and a 'mountain group', living for most of the year on the Atherton Tableland around what are now Yungaburra and Kairi. In the summer, when the weather is humid and unpleasant on the coast, the yellow walnut (*ganggi*) and a type of edible lawyer cane (*Calamus moti*, the species name being based on the Yidiny name *mudi*) would be ripe on the tableland, and the whole tribe would gather there. In the winter, when there might be frost on the mountains, the quandong (*murrgan*) and black walnut (*digil*) would be ready on the coastal flats, and the mountain people would come down to share in this feast. Ceremonies such as initiation would be performed at such times, when the whole tribe was assembled in one place because food was plentiful during that season.

Often, a tribal name is based on the name of the language the tribe speaks— the people speaking Yidiny are called the Yidinyji (literally: Yidiny-'with'). Just occasionally, a language name may be based on a tribal name—the Ngarinyin people in the Kimberley area of Western Australia speak the Ungarinyin language. Some names have a straightforward etymology (for example, some names of languages in south-east Queensland, such as Gabi-gabi, and some in Victoria, such as Wemba-wemba, just involve a doubling of the word for 'no' in that language, *gabi* and *wemba* respectively). For other names, no etymology is known.

Again, just like the nations of Europe, each Australian tribe is proud of having its own language. But sometimes the 'languages' (as speakers perceive them) of a number of neighbouring tribes may be mutually intelligible; as a linguist uses the term 'language', they are really dialects of one language. A similar situation applies in Scandinavia, where Danish and Norwegian are considered separate languages on political grounds, because they are associated with distinct nations, but in fact a Dane and a Norwegian, each speaking their own language, can understand each other fairly well, showing that these are dialects of a single language (if 'language' is defined on linguistic criteria).

At the time of first European contact, there were about 250 languages in Australia. Some were spoken by a single tribe; others had a number of dialects spoken over a group of adjoining tribes.

In other parts of the world, a group of languages can be linked together in one 'family tree', having developed in different ways from a shared ancestor. It has been shown that most of the languages of Europe, west Asia and north India are related and belong to what is called the Indo-European family. Their common ancestor, proto-Indo-European, is thought to have been spoken about six thousand years ago, between the Black Sea and the Baltic Sea.

Archaeologists believe that Aborigines, after their arrival in Australia, soon spread out to cover all habitable parts of the continent. This is likely to have taken between two and five thousand years; at the end of this period, the languages may well have been relatable in a 'family tree' diagram. There were then tens of thousands of years of what is called an 'equilibrium situation', during which the number of languages would have remained roughly constant. Aborigines were typically multilingual, and there were considerable trade and social links between adjacent groups. Each language borrowed some words, meanings and grammatical patterns from its neighbours, so that, within a given region, languages became more like each other in structural profile, while still remaining different enough to be considered separate languages (that is, not mutually intelligible). As a result, it is not now possible to put forward a 'family tree' linking all Australian languages, although a number of small trees are appropriate, for a number of small language families. For example, three languages from central New South Wales—see Chapter 2—Wiradhuri, Kamilaroi/Yuwaalaraay, and Ngiyambaa make up one genetic group.

A short book by R. M. W. Dixon, *The Rise and Fall of Languages* (Cambridge University Press, 1997), expounds the 'punctuated equilibrium' idea of language development. Dixon's longer monograph, *Australian Languages: Their Nature and Development* (Cambridge University Press, 2002), demonstrates with detailed maps and discussion how the indigenous languages of Australia constituted the longest-established 'linguistic equilibrium area' in the world (and also indicates which small, low-level 'family trees' can be established).

Finally, it must be stressed that no relationship has yet been discovered between the Australian language family and languages spoken elsewhere in the world.

HOW THE LANGUAGES HAVE FARED

During the more than 200 years of white occupation of Australia, there has been a steady loss of Aboriginal languages. Each decade, there are fewer languages spoken, and the total number of people speaking an Australian language has diminished.

There have been a number of reasons for this decline. In some cases, white people forbade the use of indigenous languages. In many missions and government settlements, children were separated from their parents at an early age and placed in boys' and girls' dormitories where only English was allowed; children heard speaking their native language would be punished (see Chapter 6). Sometimes it was by choice that Aboriginal people spoke to their children only in English, feeling that this was the best way to fit them for survival in what had become a white person's world. The influence of radio, TV, newspapers, magazines, and books—and church services—all in English, has also hastened the switch from Australian languages.

One way of killing a language is to get rid of all the speakers. In a few places in Australia, there were massacres of such severity that there were literally no speakers left to pass a language on to the next generation. There is known to have been a language called Yeeman, spoken around Taroom in south-east Queensland. That is all we know—its name. Not one word of the language was recorded before the entire tribe was wiped out in 1857.

About half of the original languages of Australia are no longer spoken or even well remembered, except in some cases through a couple of dozen words retained in the English spoken by descendants of the original tribe. Perhaps a hundred more languages are still spoken, but only by a small number of people, and few or no children are learning them.

There are just a dozen or so languages which are still in active use in most aspects of everyday life and are being learnt by children. Even these languages are at risk of dying out by the end of this century unless particular steps are taken to assist their speakers to retain them in an English-dominated world. These include the establishment and proper management of bilingual education programs in schools; the production of primers, dictionaries, written versions of traditional legends, videos, and radio programs; and, above all, the development of a feeling of pride in the languages. In order for a language to survive, it must continue to be used in everyday life as a medium of communication in the home. Once this has ceased, no amount of schooling will avail. (And once a language is gone, it can never be revived; to think otherwise can be a pleasant dream, but like all dreams it is but an illusion.)

KNOWLEDGE OF THE LANGUAGES

When Governor Phillip arrived in Sydney Cove, he carried a word list of the 'New Holland language', taken down by Sir Joseph Banks eighteen years before. This had actually been collected at the Endeavour River, two thousand miles north of Sydney, but Banks evidently believed that a single language must be spoken over the whole continent. Phillip was surprised that the local Aborigines recognised none of the words from Banks' list (for more details on this, see the entry on *kangaroo* at page 57 in Chapter 3).

The mystery was solved three years later when Phillip led a small expedition—including some members of the Sydney tribe—40 miles to the north-west. As Phillip wrote in a letter to Banks: 'It was a matter of great surprise to me when I first arrived in this Country, to find that the words used by the natives when you was [sic] here, were not understood by the present inhabitants, but in my last little journey, I found on the banks of the Hawkesbury, people who made use of several words we could not understand, and it soon appeared that they had a language different from that used by those natives we have hitherto been acquainted with ... I now think it very probable that several languages may be common on different parts of the coast, or inland ...'. Phillip realised, at last, that Aborigines in different parts of the continent spoke different languages.

The next advance in understanding came in 1841 when the explorer George Grey recognised recurrent similarities among the multitude of languages of the continent. First, as he put it, 'a general similarity of sound and structure of words in the different portions of Australia, as far as yet ascertained'; and secondly, 'the recurrence of the same word with the same signification, to be traced, in many instances, round the entire continent, but undergoing, of course, in so vast an extent of country, various modifications' (Grey's *Journal of Two Expeditions*, Vol. II, pp. 208–16). Just one of Grey's findings was that the word for 'water' at Adelaide was *kauw-ee*, and at Perth *gab-by*, but the people a dozen miles from Perth had *kow-win*, a word very similar to that used at Adelaide.

From about 1875 until 1910, there was a flurry of interest, with all sorts of people gathering information on Aboriginal culture and languages before—as they believed at that time—the Aboriginal race became extinct. In 1878, the Melbourne meteorologist and public servant R. Brough Smyth published a mammoth two-volume work, *The Aborigines of Victoria*; in 1879, the missionary George Taplin included forty-three Aboriginal vocabularies and much other information in *The Folklore, Manners, Customs and Languages of the South Australian Aborigines*; clergyman John Mathew had fifty vocabularies from all over the continent in his 1899 book on the origin of the Aboriginal race, *Eaglehawk and Crow*; and in 1886, Edward M. Curr, who had been a pioneer settler in northern Victoria, put out the four-volume work *The Australian Race*, including 250 vocabularies from all over the continent, sent in by policemen, mining wardens, station owners, and others.

Between 1897 and 1917, the Sydney surveyor R. H. Matthews published no less than 185 research papers in twenty Australian and overseas journals on the social organisation, kinship systems, and languages of Aborigines in New South Wales, Victoria, and southern Queensland; he often included short grammatical notes alongside basic vocabularies.

For many languages that are now extinct, all that we have is a couple of word lists from Smyth or Curr; for no less than ten languages, the only grammatical information is that recorded by R. H. Matthews. Unfortunately, these early recorders were not trained linguists, and wrote down Aboriginal words in terms of English sounds rather than in a phonetic alphabet. Just think what the result would be if a Russian wrote down English words as if he were hearing badly pronounced Russian! It is a task requiring considerable skill, to reconstruct the original pronunciation for a word from a now-extinct language, on the basis of records written down by amateurs in the nineteenth century.

Despite this activity before the First World War, most Australians had little idea of the nature of Australian languages. People tend to talk of European 'languages' but of Aboriginal 'dialects', expressing the general misconception that there must just be one Aboriginal language. In fact, the 250 languages of the continent are all as different as French and German; anyone knowing one language would not be able to understand another, but would have to learn it (see Chapter 6). (Many Aborigines are gifted linguists, and many, although not all, were multilingual, having reasonable proficiency in the languages of two or three neighbouring groups.)

Between 1920 and 1960, little work was done on Australian languages. There was Arthur Capell, teaching at the University of Sydney and doing fieldwork in Arnhem Land and the Kimberley, but only two or three others. Then the science of linguistics, already well-established in America and Europe, came to Australia.

Departments of Linguistics began to be established in Australian universities in the late 1960s, and many good students have now received professional training. During the past forty years, the majority of the languages that still remain—both those actively used and also many that are only remembered by a few middle-aged or old people—have received proper attention, with the preparation of grammars, dictionaries, and collections of traditional narratives (although only some of these have so far been published). During this period, the Summer Institute of Linguistics has been conducting missionary work in Australia, their aim being to translate the Bible into Australian languages. SIL members first make a thorough study of each language, and they have also been responsible for a good deal of useful linguistic description.

Perhaps the greatest loss to the complete study of Australian languages was the total annihilation of the original languages of Tasmania. There were, in 1803, at least eight separate languages in Tasmania, but only a few fragments were recorded before their speakers died or were killed. There appears to have been no contact between the people of Tasmania and those of the mainland since the Bass Strait was submerged around 14,000 years ago. Due to the sparseness of information available, it has not been possible to determine whether the languages of Tasmania were related to those of the mainland.

THE NATURE OF AUSTRALIAN LANGUAGES

A language consists of words and grammar. There are two parts to grammar—'morphology', which deals with the structure of words, and 'syntax', which describes the ways in which words are combined to make sentences.

Morphology is a study of how an ending can be added to a word to form another word, as in English where *'s* added to a simple noun makes it into a possessive (*John*, *John's*), *-en* added to an adjective makes it into a verb (*wide*, *widen*), *-ful* added to a noun makes it into an adjective (*beauty*, *beautiful*), *-er* added to a verb makes it into a noun (*build*, *builder*). Morphology also deals with things like all the different forms of a verb, such as *laugh, laughs, laughed, laughing*.

Syntax is concerned, among other things, with the order of words—in English, an adjective comes before a noun (*the round table*), but in French it generally follows the noun (*la table ronde*). Syntax is also concerned with grammatical relations like subject and object. The subject of a sentence is generally a person who does something, like *the girl* in the following sentences: *The girl laughed*; *The girl can swim*; *The girl stroked the cat*; *The girl is eating another biscuit*. The object of a sentence is a thing or person that something is done to—like *the cat* and *another biscuit* in the last two examples.

Some sentences have a subject and no object; they are called 'intransitive', and their verb is an intransitive verb (e.g. *laugh, swim*). Other sentences have both subject and object, and are called 'transitive'; their verb is a transitive verb (e.g. *stroke, eat*). One rule of English syntax is that the subject comes before the verb and the object follows it; other languages put subject, object, and verb in different orders.

Australian languages have a much more complicated morphology than English. They are rather like Latin and Greek, in that there are lots of different forms of the verb, and the noun has a number of different endings, called case inflections, showing whether it is subject, or object, or has another function in a sentence. But Australian languages are different from Latin and other familiar languages of Europe in the way they organise case marking. In most Australian languages, there is a special case ending just for the subject of a transitive sentence (this is called 'ergative case'). The subject of an intransitive and object of a transitive sentence are both marked in the same way, by having no ending at all. Let us look at two sentences from Nyawaygi, spoken to the south of Ingham in North Queensland (for pronunciation of the letters used here, see Table 1 on page 13).

Mujumuju waaji-ña	The woman is laughing
Jiwu mujumuju-ŋgu muja-ña	The woman is biting a plum

The first sentence is intransitive; it has an intransitive subject *mujumuju* 'woman', bearing no ending, and an intransitive verb *waaji-*, 'laugh', which has the present tense ending *-ña*. The second sentence is transitive, with the transitive verb *muja-*, 'bite', also, showing present tense ending *-ña*. Here the object *jiwu*, 'plum' (actually Burdekin plum, *Pleiogynium timorense*), has no ending, but the transitive subject *mujumuju*, 'woman', takes ergative case ending *-ŋgu*.

Most Australian languages have an ergative case inflection. In some languages, it is *-ŋgu*, in others *-lu*. A number of languages have both *-ŋgu* and *-lu*. Warlpiri, spoken to the north-west of Alice Springs, has *-ŋgu* on a noun consisting of two syllables (such as *kurdu*, 'child') and *-lu* on one of three or more syllables (such as *wawirri*, 'kangaroo'). Eastern dialects of the Western Desert language have *-ŋgu* on common nouns (like *wati*, 'man') and *-lu* on personal names which end in a vowel. This is an example of the kind of grammatical similarities and differences which are found between different languages.

In English, we show what is subject and what is object by word order (*Mary hit John* has a quite different meaning from *John hit Mary*). But in Nyawaygi and other Australian languages (as in Latin), subject and object in a transitive sentence are shown by case endings: *-ŋgu* on subject and no ending for object. The three words in the second Nyawaygi sentence can be arranged in any order, without changing the meaning: *Jiwu muja-ña mujumuju-ŋgu* or *Muja-ña jiwu mujumuju-ŋgu*, and so on. Australian languages have a more complex morphology than English, and as a result, the word order can be freer. (What happens is that Australian languages use word order to mark emphasis, with the most important word being put into a certain position in the sentence.)

Every language has pronouns in 'first person' (referring to the person speaking), 'second person' (referring to the person being addressed), and 'third person' (anyone other than speaker and addressee). English has a very limited set of pronouns—in the first person, we have singular and plural forms (*I* and *we*), but in the second person there is only *you*, used for both singular and plural. Australian languages show rich systems of pronouns, having separate forms for singular ('I'), dual ('we two'), and plural ('we all, more than two'). Many languages have separate inclusive and exclusive first person forms, that is, one which includes and one which excludes the addressee, as in the Warlpiri inclusive dual *ŋali*, 'me and you', and exclusive dual *ŋajarra*, 'me and someone else, not you'.

The forms of pronouns are often similar between languages in different parts of the continent, showing that they have developed in differing ways from one original form. For example, 'I' and 'you two' in the Warungu language of north-east Queensland are *ŋaya* and *yubala*, and in the Nhanta language of south-west Western Australia are *ŋayi* and *ñubalu* respectively.

A block of languages in the central far north have developed very complex word structures, with information about what is subject and what is object, and much more besides, being incorporated into the verb. In a language like Tiwi, spoken on Melville and Bathurst Islands, a sentence can consist of a single long verb, such as *neremenhthinepirnani*, 'I kept on hitting you'. This can be analysed into its component parts (see C. R. Osborne, *The Tiwi Language*, Australian Institute of Aboriginal Studies, 1974, p. 27).

ne +	re +	menh +	thine +	pirn	+ ani
subject	past	object	continuous	'hit'	repeated
'I'	tense	'you'	activity		action

Besides grammar, the other component of a language is its words, or vocabulary. Each language, in every continent, has a working vocabulary of quite a few thousand words. As is the case elsewhere, the languages of Australia have an abundance of words for describing objects and concepts that are culturally important for their speakers. There are thus many terms for referring to parts of animals, and there are many specific terms referring to seed types or to the stages of development that intervene between grub and beetle. There is typically a rich vocabulary for stars, colours of the sky, types of lightning, and other natural phenomena.

Speakers of Australian languages are sensitive to everything that goes on around them, and have many nouns for describing different kinds of noise. In Yidiny, just to the south of Cairns, these include: *dalmba*, 'the sound of chopping, or of a shellfish being bashed on a rock to break the shell'; *gaŋga*, 'the sound of someone approaching (feet on leaves or twigs, or a walking-stick being dragged along the ground)'; *yuyuruŋgul*, 'the shshing noise of a snake sliding through the grass'; and *duŋur*, 'a reverberating noise'.

Australian languages have specific names for each significant plant and animal, but also have a full range of abstract and generic terms, such as *miña*, 'any edible animal', and *mayi*, 'any edible plant', which recur in many languages. (Another noise term in Yidiny is *ñaŋgi*, 'any annoying noise'.)

Not only are there in Australian languages a large number of adjectives that refer to dimension and physical properties; there are also many that refer to the emotions which arise from a highly developed sense of social responsibility, relating to 'shame', 'pity', 'being offended', and 'longing for one's own country, relatives, traditions', etc.

Each language has a slightly different organisation of meanings. This can be illustrated from a conversation that R. M. W. Dixon had in July 1989 with Bessie Jerry, who speaks the Girramay dialect of Dyirbal. Over the preceding ten years, Dixon—with the help of Mrs Jerry and other Dyirbal people, and of Tony Irvine, a biologist with the CSIRO Tropical Forest Research Centre at Atherton—had compiled a list of 600 Dyirbal plant names together with their botanical classifications. About a third of these have edible parts, and Dixon was going through the list with Bessie Jerry, enquiring for each plant whether it 'could be eaten raw' or 'needed to be cooked'.

The way Bessie Jerry explained things, in Girramay, made Dixon realise that he'd framed the question in a very 'English' way. There is in Girramay an adjective *gunga*, which has three related senses: used of a fruit or nut that ripens naturally in the sun, it means 'unripe, green' (and here the opposite is *dungun* 'ripe'); used of meat or of any vegetable food that requires cooking, it means 'raw, uncooked' (here the opposite is *ñamu*, 'cooked'); used of a human or animal, it means 'alive' (being here the opposite of *buga*, 'dead, stinking'). Dixon changed the way he posed the question (and switched to using Girramay rather than English). As each new plant was considered, he now enquired: 'Can it be eaten when ripe or must it be cooked?' The operative meaning contrast in Girramay is between being brought to an edible state naturally, by the heat of the sun, or needing the heat of a fire to bring it into an edible condition. The English word *raw* just means 'uncooked', and can refer to something that is edible. The Girramay word *gunga*, used of food, may be roughly translated by 'raw', but it means 'not yet ready to be eaten'. It makes no sense, in terms of the semantics of Girramay, to ask if something can be eaten raw.

Traditionally, when a person dies, their name becomes 'taboo', and should not be pronounced for a considerable period. Not only that, but a noun, adjective, or verb which sounds similar to the dead person's name might also be tabooed. There is even an instance of the first person pronoun *ŋayu*, 'I', being tabooed in one dialect of the Western Desert language (in the 1950s) on the death of a man called Ngayunya. A tabooed word may be replaced by a new compound formation or by a word borrowed from a neighbouring language. Often, the original word will return to use after the period of mourning is over.

One aspect of Aboriginal life that has fascinated anthropologists and linguists is the complex kinship system. Aboriginal people are conscious not only of ties that bind them to close family, but also of their kinship ties with everyone else in the group. All members of their society are classified into one of about twenty kin categories, according to the rules of the kin system (principles like: 'mother's mother's sister's children are placed in the same category as mother's brothers and mother's sisters'). This system of classifying everyone as a relative determines the kind of social relationship that two people may have, and their obligations towards one another. It also determines the group of people from whom a wife or husband must be chosen.

In many communities, people in a certain kin relationship must follow 'avoidance behaviour'. A mother-in-law and son-in-law should never be alone together, and, even if others are present, should never look directly at one another. In some parts of the continent, there is even a special 'avoidance speech style', which must be used whenever someone like a mother-in-law or son-in-law is within earshot. These avoidance styles (sometimes called 'mother-in-law languages') have the same phonetics and grammar as the everyday language styles, but show different forms for some (in a few languages, for all) nouns, verbs, and adjectives. Some corresponding words in the two speech styles of Guugu Yimidhirr from North Queensland are:

	Everyday style	Avoidance style
'ear'	*milga*	*dhuba*
'egg'	*gundil*	*wurruun*
'crocodile'	*ganhaarr*	*wayin*
'sun'	*ŋalan*	*gandaganda*
'large black kangaroo'	*gaŋurru*	*daarraalŋan*

All Aboriginal groups have a system of beliefs that is reinforced by religious rituals and the passing on of traditional stories from generation to generation. These stories and songs are slightly different for each community, and often involve a description of the movement of dreamtime ancestors around significant places in the local environment during a time in the mythic past. The language of sacred songs used during ritual is often rather different from that of everyday speech, containing words from other languages, and special words that only occur in songs and have no independent meaning outside a song.

Whereas the avoidance speech styles and song styles were used by everyone in a community, there were in some places secret language styles used only between initiated men. These would be taught to boys at the time of initiation, and would only be used on ritual occasions. The most amazing secret language is Damin, used by the Lardil people on Mornington Island in the Gulf of Carpentaria; this has a whole range of sounds not found in everyday Lardil or in any other Australian language, including clicks (which are otherwise only known to occur in Zulu and nearby languages in southern Africa).

HOW TO PRONOUNCE AND WRITE AUSTRALIAN LANGUAGES

The alphabet has only been invented two or three times in human history. Speakers of one language tend to 'borrow' an alphabet used by some other language and adapt it for their own needs. The English alphabet was taken over from Latin (we still call it 'the Roman alphabet'), which was based on the Greek alphabet, which was in turn based on an alphabet that was probably invented in the ancient Middle East.

The pronunciation of English has altered a good deal over the past 800 years, but our alphabet has not been adjusted to keep up with this. *Knee* used to be pronounced with a 'k' before the 'n'; this dropped out of use a long time ago, but we still write a *k* at the beginning. There are many inconsistencies in English spelling (which make it hard to learn). A single sound may be written in different ways in different words; for instance, all of *beat, see, we, key, fiend* involve the same vowel, yet it is written as *ea, ee, e, ey, ie* (and in more ways besides).

Many Australian languages are now being written and used in newspapers and books. They use letters of the Roman alphabet, chosen so that each sound is always represented by the same letter or combination of letters.

Table 1   The consonants in Australian languages and letters used for them

active articulator	tongue tip	tongue tip turned back	blade of tongue	blade of tongue	back of tongue	bottom lip
passive articulator	gums behind teeth	roof of mouth	teeth	hard palate	soft palate	top lip
STOPS	*d*	*rd*	*dh*	*j*	*g*	*b*
NASALS	*n*	*rn*	*nh*	*ñ*	*ŋ*	*m*
LATERALS	*l*	*rl*	*lh*	*lʸ*		
RHOTICS	*rr*	*r*				
SEMI-VOWELS				*y*		*w*

Table 1 sets out the consonant sounds encountered in Australian languages and the letters used to represent them in the etymologies given in Chapter 3. For each consonant, one part of the tongue or lips (called 'the active articulator') is moved to come into contact with, or come close to, some part of the lips, teeth, gums, or top of the mouth ('the passive articulator').

Some of these sounds are pronounced in a very similar way to sounds in English—*d, g, b, n, m, l, y,* and *w*. Those written *dh, nh,* and *lh* are pronounced like *d, n,* and *l,* but with the blade of the tongue touching the teeth (often, the tip of the tongue is at the base of the bottom teeth). Those written *rd, rn,* and *rl* have the tongue tip bent back in the mouth; they are like the 'retroflex' sounds in Indian languages and in Indian pronunciations of English. The sound written *j* is much sharper than English *j,* being more like *d* and *y* pronounced simultaneously; *ñ* is like *n* and *y* pronounced simultaneously (as in Spanish, from where this symbol is taken, and a bit like the *n*-sound in *onion*); and *l^y* is like *l* and *y* pronounced simultaneously (like the *l*-sound in *William*).

In most Australian languages, *p* can be substituted for *b*, *t* for *d*, *k* for *g*, *th* for *dh*, *rt* for *rd*, and a sound that is like English *ch* (in *church*), only sharper for *j*, without any difference to the meaning of a word. Some people use *b*, *d*, *g*, ... (as we generally do here), while others prefer *p*, *t*, *k*, ...; either choice is satisfactory (so long as one series is chosen and consistently maintained). Thus, the name of the large black kangaroo in Guugu Yimidhirr (from which our loan word *kangaroo* comes) may be written either *kaŋ-urru* or *gaŋ-urru*. There is just a handful of Australian languages which do have two series of stop consonants, and here both *b*, *d*, *g*, ... and *p*, *t*, *k*, ... are needed (this applies to the South Australian languages Diyari and Adnyamathanha—see their entries in Chapter 2—and the south Queensland language Gunya, from which the tree name *yapunyah* comes, see pages 147–8).

While English distinguishes between *b* and *p* (but most Australian languages don't), Australian languages recognise a distinction between two kinds of rhotic or *r*-sound (which are treated as variants of one sound by speakers of English). There is a trill, written *rr*, similar to that used in Scottish English, and a liquid *r*, similar to that in other varieties of English, but with the tongue tip turned back a little. Substituting one rhotic for the other changes the meaning of the word (just as substituting *p* and *b* does in English)—in Nyawaygi *rrubi* is a noun, 'worm, maggot', and *rubi* is a verb, 'swallow'.

One quite tricky sound for English speakers to master is *ŋ* when it comes at the beginning of a word. English has this sound, but only at the end of a word, such as *bang* (where it is written as 'ng'). Australian languages have *ŋ* at the beginning of many words, including the most important pronouns; 'I' is often *ŋaju* or *ŋaja* or *ŋayu* or *ŋaya*. It only needs a bit of practice to say *ŋ* at the beginning of a word. Say *bang-ayu* (make sure you just say *ŋ*, as in *singer*, and not *ŋ* plus *g*, as in *finger*). Say *bang-ayu* a few times and gradually drop off the initial *ba-*. Thus, *baŋ-ayu*, *baŋayu*, *baŋayu*, *ŋayu*.

One interesting feature of Australian languages is that (leaving aside a handful of isolated exceptions) they lack any fricatives or sibilants, like English *f*, *v*, *th*, *s*, *z*, *sh*, *h*.

Most Australian languages have only three contrasting vowels, which are written as *u* (pronounced like the vowel in English *boot*), *i* (as in *bit*), and *a* (as in *bat*). Just a few languages have more vowels, most commonly *e* and *o* (pronounced like the vowels in *bet* and *bought*). If a vowel letter is doubled then it should be pronounced very long.

As mentioned before, a basic rule for the proper pronunciation of words in Australian languages is that every syllable should be clearly enunciated. Vowels in Australian languages are seldom reduced in quality, like *ə*, the final sound of English *banner* and *the* (or the middle vowel in English pronunciations of *kangaroo*); every vowel in each syllable is provided with a clear (non-reduced) pronunciation.

In most Australian languages, the first syllable bears the major accent or stress. It is most important to observe this, otherwise words may be pronounced in an unrecognisable way.

THE LOAN WORDS AND THEIR ETYMOLOGIES

The main criterion for inclusion in this volume is that a word should be in everyday use. We require at least two written examples of use in a general context, such as *jarrah* in 'A devil-may-care little locomotive, which ate jarrah wood for breakfast' (Norman Duncan, *Australian Byways, the Narrative of a Sentimental Traveler*, 1915, page 39). If the only written record of a word is of someone explaining how Aborigines named a certain thing, then it does not qualify for inclusion, as *toulah*, for which we have just 'The natives called my attention to an animal the size of a cat, which ran about in the branches of a tree. They called it toulah' (Carl Lumholtz, *Among Cannibals*, 1889, page 152).

For each of the loan words in Chapter 3, we give the most common spelling of the word as it is used in English, then the most usual pronunciation in an 'educated Australian' style (we have not attempted to cover all variant, regional pronunciations), and then alternative spellings. Following this, in square brackets, is information on the Australian language the word comes from, and its original form in that language (using the phonetic alphabet explained in the last section). The meaning in the original language is also given if it differs from the meaning of the loan word as it is used in English. There is then the meaning of the word in English and, at the end of this, a date in square brackets, e.g. [1788], which is the earliest written record (published or unpublished) we know of for the word. For most of the loans, we include one or more quotations to illustrate the meaning of the word. The interested reader will find further quotations for almost all the words in the *Australian National Dictionary*, and additional quotations for some of the most common words in the large *Oxford English Dictionary*.

When words are transferred from one language to another, they must be adapted to the phonetic system of the borrowing language. Sounds like *rd* and *dh* tend to become just *d* (or *t*) in English; thus, the burrowing rat kangaroo, called *burdi* in Nyungar, the Perth language (with a retroflex stop *rd*), becomes just *boodie* in English (with a plain *d*); and the deadly snake, called *dhayban* or *thaypan* in Wik-Mungkan (with a dental stop *dh* or *th*), is just *taipan* (with a plain *t*) in English. English doesn't generally have ŋ between two vowels, so a word like *kaŋurru*, from Guugu Yimidhirr, becomes *kangaroo*, pronounced /kæŋgə'ru/ in English, with the ŋ replaced by *ng*. This is the pronunciation an English speaker would expect, from the spelling—but note that the name for the monitor lizard, *bungarra*, is pronounced as /bʌŋərə/ (not as /bʌŋgərə/), with the ŋ of the original Nhanta form *baŋarra* preserved, and not replaced by *ng* (see page 100, below).

We mentioned above that Australian languages have many words starting with ŋ, a sound which cannot begin words in English. Because of this, there has been a tendency not to borrow words that begin with ŋ (less than two per cent of the loans listed in Chapter 3 come from a word with initial ŋ, whereas in most Australian languages five to ten per cent of words start with ŋ). Of the few ŋ-initial loans there are, some are written with *gn-* but pronounced just with an initial *n-* (see *gnamma hole*, on page 192); others are written and pronounced with initial *n-*, as with *nulla-nulla*, based on *ŋala-ŋala* in the Sydney language, Dharuk. The word *humpy* comes from *ŋumbi* in Yagara, the Brisbane language; here the initial ŋ may not have been heard by the first settlers, since it is completely missing from the English form.

Some words have been shortened in the process of being borrowed, such as *yabij*, 'freshwater crayfish' in Wemba-wemba from western Victoria, which has become just *yabby*. The three vowels found in Australian languages have been represented in writing, and had their pronunciation altered in many different ways. In some words, consonants are doubled in English spelling (as in *nulla-nulla*), simply because the English writing system often does have double letters, sometimes for no phonetic reason.

Meanings can also be changed in the adaptation of a word to a new language. *Bulʲa* meant 'sorcery' in the Perth language (see quotation on page 150), but was taken into English as *boylya* with the sense 'sorcerer'. In Nyawaygi, *burun* or *purun* was 'fighting ground', but has been adopted into the English used in North Queensland as *prun* (the first vowel has been omitted) with the meaning 'fighting corroboree' (see quotation on pages 158–9).

We have tried to include, in Chapter 3, all of the best-established loan words from Aboriginal languages into English. We have not included place names, which would be a major study in themselves, or plants, etc. named after places, e.g. *Barcoo grass, Barcoo rot* (see the entry for *Barcoo* in the *Australian National Dictionary*). We also exclude genus and species names assigned to fauna and flora which are based on an Australian language, unless these are also in common use (e.g. *Parinari nonda* for the nonda tree, page 116).

In trying to uncover the etymology for a word, we first examined the time and place of its first use in English, and then searched the materials available on languages in that area. Sometimes a number of languages share a certain word, and the date of first use gives the best clue to language of origin—*warli* is 'camp, hut' in many South Australian languages, but the early date of 1839 for the adoption of *wurley* into English suggests Gaurna, spoken around Adelaide, as the source. In other cases, it is the place of first use which provides the best clue—*bardi* is the word for 'grub' in many languages in Western Australia and South Australia, but the earliest mentions in print come from Perth, suggesting that the source language was Nyungar.

For some words, there is more than one possible source. The English word *nardoo*, for a fern with edible spores, could—on phonetic grounds—have been adopted from *ŋardu*, used in a number of South Australian and western New South Wales languages, or from *nhaadu*, used in Kamilaroi and other languages from east-central New South Wales. The written records indicate a South Australian origin, the first use of *nardoo* in print being in reports of the Burke and Wills expedition. But for *gundy* (page 197) and *currawong* (page 84), we cannot definitely tell which of two different forms in two different languages was the original source of the loan.

In the case of *kipper*, 'initiated man, initiation ceremony', it seems that the word was first adapted from *gibarra*, 'initiated boy' in Dharuk (from Sydney), during the 1790s, and then the borrowing was reinforced when Brisbane was settled in the 1820s, since in the Brisbane language *giba* is 'initiated boy'.

In some instances, where the same word was used in a number of Australian languages in a given area and we cannot be absolutely sure from which language the word was borrowed into English, we mention the most likely language, and comment that the word did have a fair geographical spread.

When searching for the first use of a word, one can, of course, only use written records. It is likely, in the case of some loan words, that they were used in spoken English for some years or even decades before they were written down. Although the first written record of *nardoo* was 1860, this name—for a plant whose food was widely known to Aborigines—may have been used by settlers well before that date. Where the same word occurred in a number of languages, it could well have been taken into spoken English more or less simultaneously at several different locations, perhaps with slightly different pronunciations, which would have gradually amalgamated into one accepted form as the word became better known and appeared in writing. In many cases, even the written records are patchy, and we may never be able to reconstruct more than a part of the whole story.

All etymologies given in earlier works (including those in the *Australian National Dictionary*) have been reassessed and, in many cases, revised for this book. For a number of words, an Aboriginal origin has been suggested, but this seems to us unlikely, e.g. *yate*, the name for a hard eucalypt found in the extreme south-west; and the pejorative term for an Aborigine, *boong*. For other words, etymologies have been given which are engaging but appear, on detailed investigation, to be without foundation, e.g. *jackeroo*. We have also had to question at least one etymology that has been suggested for a word within its source language. *Wandjina*, the name for a type of ancestral spirit, comes from Ungarinyin, spoken in the north Kimberley region, Western Australia. E. A. Worms (*Anthropos*, Vol. 50, p. 549, 1955) said that the word means 'near the water', while H. H. J. Coate and A. P. Elkin (*Ngarinjin–English Dictionary*, Vol. 2, p. 483, Oceania Linguistic Monographs, 1974) say that it is from '*warn*, across and *djina*, this one'. Alan Rumsey (the author of *An Intra-sentence Grammar of Ungarinjin*,

Pacific Linguistics, 1982) tells us he considers both etymologies to be incorrect—the word contains nothing like any of the forms for 'near' or 'water' in Ungarinyin, and it involves an *n*, whereas the word *warn* 'across' has a quite different sound, the retroflex nasal *rn*. Rumsey thinks that the word cannot be analysed within Ungarinyin.

We have been able to trace the origins of the great majority of words, but not all of them. There are still some words which *may* come from an Australian language (we cannot be absolutely sure of this), but if so, the language of origin is still to be discovered.

Finally, we should comment on the phonetic forms of the words in Australian languages which are given in Chapter 3 as originals for the loans. In some cases, professional linguists have worked with native speakers, and we can be fairly certain that the spellings they provide are correct. Many of the languages from which loans come are, however, extinct. In such cases, we have assembled the various spellings of a word found in old source materials (almost all written by people with no phonetic training) and, by judicious comparison, tried to work out what the original form was. Thus, the word for 'stone or rock' in the Sydney language was recorded as 'ke-bā' (Collins), as 'kibba' (Hunter), as 'kee-bah' (Southwell), as 'giber' (Hale), and as 'kiber' (Matthews); from these, we infer an original form *giba*.

In some cases, it is difficult to decide between two forms. For 'tame dog', Collins has both 'tein-go' and 'din-go', Hunter has 'tingo', while William Dawes wrote 'tain-go', making it impossible to decide between *din-gu* and *dayn-gu* (similarly for *wallaby*, see page 73, and *myall*, see page 171). In a fair number of cases, we cannot be absolutely sure of the exact original form of a word, and then state 'probably' before the most likely inference.

FURTHER READING

Australian Aboriginal Languages by Barry Blake (Angus and Robertson, 1981; a revised edition, University of Queensland Press, 1991) is one of the best introductory books on this topic. *Language and Culture in Aboriginal Australia*, edited by Michael Walsh and Colin Yallop (Aboriginal Studies Press, 1993), is also highly recommended.

Among the best anthropological texts, telling of the traditional culture and lifestyle of Aborigines, are Kenneth Maddock, *The Australian Aborigines: A Portrait of Their Society* (Penguin, 2nd edition 1982), R. M. Berndt and C. H. Berndt, *The World of the First Australians* (Ure Smith, 1964), and A. P. Elkin, *The Australian Aborigines* (Angus and Robertson, 3rd edition, 1954). A classic account of one tribal group, speaking a dialect of the Western Desert language, is Robert Tonkinson's *The Mardudjara Aborigines: Living the Dream in Australia's Desert* (Holt, Rinehart and Winston, 1978; for the second edition in 1991, 'Mardu' was used in place of 'Mardudjara').

2

Some important languages

This chapter provides short accounts of the most important Australian languages from the point of view of loan words into English (all languages which are thought to have supplied three or more loans are included). A brief account of the people who spoke each language, the kind of life they led, and the story of their contact with Europeans, is also given.

Many of the loan words came from languages of the state capital cities (Sydney, Perth, Melbourne, Adelaide, and Brisbane); all of these languages—except that of Perth—ceased to be actively spoken many years ago. Our accounts are thus based mostly on old records, which are acknowledged at the end of each entry.

As with hunter-gatherers on other continents, among Australian Aborigines it was the men who hunted large game, while the women would gather fruit, vegetables, seeds, grubs, small animals, and, if they lived on the coast, shellfish. All Aboriginal groups were nomadic, moving around within their territory according to the seasons to obtain food. Those living in well-stocked country on the coast or along major rivers would construct bark huts, in which they lived for some weeks or even months at a time. People living in the rainforest of North Queensland constructed large huts, to which they would return each wet season, for protection from the torrential downpours. People in the desert would in some seasons move on rather frequently in search of food, and their shelters would often be little more than windbreaks.

Every part of Australia was originally inhabited by Aboriginal people. As white settlement spread, there was almost always violent conflict between the two cultures. A settler would forbid Aborigines to come near the waterholes on his newly claimed 'run'. Banished from their traditional hunting grounds, the Aboriginal people might spear a sheep or a cow, and then be punished to the extent of some of their number being shot. Should the Aborigines retaliate by killing a white man or two, reprisals would be undertaken against a whole tribe, with scores of people being killed. For each language discussed below, we could repeat the story of dispossession, exploitation, and bloody murder. Instead, we ask the reader to bear in mind that this happened in every part of the continent, and is the reason why so much of this chapter is written in the past tense; many of the languages discussed here ceased to be spoken when there was no one left to speak them.

THE LANGUAGES OF NEW SOUTH WALES

There were originally about two dozen distinct languages spoken in what is now the state of New South Wales. Only one of these, Bandjalang, is still actively spoken, and that only by a handful of old people.

For some of these languages, very little information was recorded. All we have for Thawa, the language of Twofold Bay, is two word lists from August 1844, in the manuscript papers of George Augustus Robinson (held by the Mitchell Library, Sydney) and six words and one sentence in the manuscript notebooks of R. H. Matthews. We know that one language, probably called Ngarigo, was spoken right across from Canberra, through Cooma and the Monaro district, over the Snowy Mountains to Omeo in Victoria. There are about twenty short word lists of Ngarigo, but nothing whatsoever on the grammar beyond the pronouns 'I' and 'you'.

For a few languages, we have much fuller materials, often compiled by missionaries. In 1824, the Rev. Lancelot Threlkeld set up a mission at Lake Macquarie, just south of Newcastle. He published a grammar and spelling book of the Awabakal language. But, in the preface to his translation of the gospel of St Luke, Threlkeld said:

> Circumstances, which no human being could control, brought the mission to a final termination on December 31, 1841, when the mission ceased, not from any want of support from the Government, nor from any inclination on my own part to retire from the work, but solely from the sad fact that the aborigines themselves had then become almost extinct, for I had actually outlived a very large majority of the blacks, more especially of those with whom I had been associated for seventeen years.

He added: 'Under such circumstances, the translation of the Gospel by St Luke can only be now a work of curiosity—a record of the language of a tribe that once existed.'

Dharuk, the Sydney language

This language was spoken along the coast, from Port Jackson to the north side of Botany Bay, and inland at least as far as Camden and Penrith.

David Collins and John Hunter, officers with the First Fleet, published accounts of the early days of the colony, and they included useful word lists of the local language, quite well transcribed. Captain Watkin Tench, in *A Complete*

Account of the Settlement at Port Jackson (1793), mentioned that he had hoped to include an account of the language by Lieutenant Dawes, who had the best knowledge of it, but said that Dawes had left the colony.

William Dawes had gathered a great deal of linguistic information from Bennelong, an Aborigine who Governor Phillip had had captured. However, Dawes underwent a crisis of conscience when Phillip ordered him to take part in a punitive expedition after his gardener had been speared—this was to bring back the heads of six Aborigines (and they were given six bags to put them in). Dawes at first refused to go, but then he did go (no Aborigines were in fact encountered), and afterwards told Phillip he regretted having taken part. Faced with this insubordination, the Governor sent Dawes back to England.

Dawes' notebooks, labelled 'Grammatical forms of the language of N. S. Wales, in the neighbourhood of Sydney, in the year 1790', had long been thought lost, but came to light in 1972 in the library of the School of Oriental and African Studies in London. They give the beginnings of a grammar with many sentences and the forms of words set out on the Latin model (which is, as it happens, quite a good one for this language): 'I go, thou goest, he goes, we go, you go, they go; I did go ...; I shall or will go ...' and so on. Although Dawes' study was unfinished, it provides the fullest information we have on this language.

There was soon violent conflict between Europeans and Aborigines, and little more work was done on the language. The last recording was a short article on 'The Dharruk language' by the ubiquitous R. H. Matthews (pp. 155–60 of Vol. 35 of *Journal and Proceedings of the Royal Society of New South Wales*, 1901). 'Dharruk' was an inland dialect around Windsor, Penrith, and Campbelltown, but 'Dharuk' has nowadays been adopted as a name for the whole language. (For the people of Sydney, the name Iora or Eora was recorded in the 1790s, but this may just have been the name of a local group.)

Although they spoke dialects of the same language, the coastal and inland Dharuk had quite different methods of subsistence and distinctive social practices. For most of the year, the coastal Dharuk lived on seafood, which was supplemented by plant food and small animals when spring approached. They usually fished from canoes in pairs; the men used pronged fish spears, while the women employed bark-fibre fishing lines and hooks made from shell.

The inland group lived mostly on small animals and plant food as well as freshwater mullet and eels. They made fur cloaks from the skins of possum and kangaroo. The Iora are said to have referred to them as 'climbers of trees' since they could rapidly ascend the tallest trees to catch possums and collect honey made by the native bee. The coastal people also believed them to be highly skilled in medical practices, including the healing of deep skin wounds.

Even though little was recorded of the cultural life of Dharuk speakers, some things are definitely known about their religious life and their artistic practices.

There was ritual extraction of an upper incisor at an initiation ceremony as young men advanced to manhood. (By chance, Governor Phillip had the appropriate tooth missing, which helped him in his dealing with the Aborigines.) Elaborate burial ceremonies were noted by the settlers. The Dharuk people placed importance on creative art, which included body decoration and tree carvings; some of their carvings on rocks in the Sydney region can still be seen.

Within two years of the first settlement, there was an epidemic of smallpox, to which Aborigines had much less immunity than Europeans. Half of the Port Jackson tribe died, and it appears that the epidemic swept across most or all of the continent with similar results. This makes it difficult to estimate numbers of the original inhabitants; at every place other than Sydney, the population was already greatly reduced before white people came to settle.

For about fifty years, Dharuk culture continued to be passed on to young people, even thought it coexisted with the vastly different culture of the European invaders. However, by the middle of the nineteenth century, although a few bands still existed, much of the rich artistic and religious life was lost. Today there are still Dharuk descendants in the Sydney region, and some use a few words from this language in the English they speak, although the language ceased to be actively used many years ago.

As might be expected, Dharuk has supplied many loans (almost sixty are listed in Chapter 3), including some of the most widely-used words, such as *dingo*, *koala*, *wallaby*, *wallaroo*, *wombat*, *boobook*, *kurrajong*, *waratah*, *boomerang*, *nulla-nulla*, *waddy*, *woomera*, *corroboree*, *gin*, *myall*, *gunyah*, and *cooee*. Nyungar, spoken around Perth and Albany, has also been responsible for about sixty loans (see below), but these are less widely used than the words from Dharuk. (No other language has supplied more than a couple of dozen loans.)

There was a pidgin in use in the early days of settlement, described by David Collins as 'a barbarous mixture of English with the Port Jackson dialect'; it included *piccaninny*, 'child', taken from the pidgin spoken in west Africa and the West Indies (and ultimately deriving from Portuguese *pequenino*, the diminutive of *pequeno*, 'small'). As white settlers spread through the continent, they took this pidgin with them for talking to the new tribes they encountered. The settlers thought that they were talking 'the Aboriginal language', and the Aborigines were under the misapprehension that they were being taught the white man's language. In this way, a number of Port Jackson words (and some from other south-eastern languages) were spread far afield, and some, such as *yarraman*, 'horse', were borrowed from this pidgin into Australian languages spoken thousands of miles from Sydney. Other words from the pidgin, such as *bogey*, 'to bathe'; *pialla*, 'to talk'; *budgeree*, 'good'; *cabon*, 'big, great'; *murry*, 'very'; and *baal*, 'no', are listed in the section on 'Verbs', 'Adjectives and Adverbs', and 'Other' at the end of Chapter 3.

Some word lists taken down in diverse parts of the continent mingle words from a local language with words from this pidgin, perhaps on the assumption that it is 'all one language'; it is generally an easy matter to separate out the pidgin words.

SOURCE: J. L. Kohen and R. Lampert, 'Hunters and fishers in the Sydney region', pp. 342–65 of *Australians to 1788*, edited by D. J. Mulvaney and J. P. White, Fairfax, Syme & Weldon, 1987.

Wiradhuri

The Wiradhuri (or Wiradjuri) language was spoken, in a number of dialects, over a wide area extending from Hay to north of Gilgandra, down to Mudgee, then south-west to include Cowra, Yass, Tumut, Albury, and just over the border into Victoria. This country has abundant watercourses, and the people centred their lives around these; their diet included a plentiful supply of fish and birds.

In early summer each year, people travelled from all over Wiradhuri country into the territory of the Ngarigo people in the Snowy Mountains to partake of the bogong moth (page 102) amid festivity and ceremony. The Wiradhuri held regular rituals which had deep religious significance, as young boys would be initiated and also taught secret knowledge which was believed to have been handed down from the dreamtime. They had great respect for the dead and would carve trees at the graves of respected men.

European invaders intruded into the lives of the Wiradhuri in 1813, when Blaxland, Lawson, and Wentworth crossed the Blue Mountains. As settlers followed, there was a great deal of violent conflict, including such practices as using arsenic in the preparation of damper, which was then left around stations for Wiradhuri people to find and eat. On one occasion, a land grant of 500 acres was offered as reward for the capture, alive or dead, of the renowned Wiradhuri freedom fighter, Windradyne.

In 1830, the Church Missionary Society opened a mission station in the Wellington Valley under the Rev. William Watson; he was joined in 1837 by the Rev. James Günther. Annual reports of the mission complained of the bad effects of white settlement nearby, and described Aboriginal children as being 'cradled in prostitution and fostered in licentiousness'. Those were not the only difficulties—the missionaries quarrelled, and in 1838 Watson left to set up a rival mission just a few miles away; each establishment had only a dozen or so Aboriginal wards. Günther gave up in 1843, but Watson continued for a further seven years.

The first word list in Wiradhuri appears to be that taken down by John Oxley on 27 April 1817 (pp. 10–11 of his *Journals of an Expedition into the Interior of New South Wales*, 1820). Over the next ninety years, more than thirty further word lists, of varying length and quality, were gathered. James Günther compiled an extensive grammar and dictionary in 1840; the manuscript is in the Mitchell Library, Sydney, and it was published as pp. 56–120 of the Appendix to *An Australian Language*, edited by John Fraser, 1892. William Watson is said to have written a grammar, one copy of which was sent to Professor Max Müller at Oxford, but this has not been traced. Watson supplied a great deal of grammatical information to the American linguist Horatio Hale, published as pp. 479–531 of *Ethnography and Philology*, Vol. VI of the *Reports of the United States Exploring Expedition, under the Command of Charles Wilkes*, 1846. Although some Wiradhuri descendants today know a few words of the language, it is no longer actively spoken. Our etymologies have been inferred from old source material.

To the north of Wiradhuri, Ngiyambaa, a closely related language, was spoken, and Tamsin Donaldson was able to work with the last speakers of this language in the 1970s; her grammar, *Ngiyambaa: the Language of the Wangaaybuwan of New South Wales*, was published by Cambridge University Press in 1980. Information about the phonetic forms of words in Ngiyambaa, supplied by Donaldson, has been of assistance in our work on Wiradhuri.

About two dozen loan words come from Wiradhuri, including *billabong*; the names of a number of birds such as *corella*, *gang-gang*, and *kookaburra*; and names of a number of trees, including *quandong*.

SOURCES: P. Read, *A Hundred Years War: the Wiradjuri People and the State*, Australian National University Press, 1988; P. Read, '"Breaking up these camps entirely": the dispersal policy in Wiradhuri country 1909–1929', *Aboriginal History*, Vol. 8, pp. 45–55, 1984.

Kamilaroi and Yuwaalaraay

The Kamilaroi language is related to Wiradhuri and Ngiyambaa (as mentioned in Chapter 1, they form a small genetic family). It was spoken over a wide area of east-central New South Wales and along parts of the Weir and Moonie Rivers in southern Queensland. Kamilaroi territory went as far west as Coonamble, as far east as Goondiwindi and Tamworth, and extended over the Great Dividing Range into the Upper Hunter Valley, including the present town of Muswellbrook.

'Gamilaraay' would be the appropriate spelling according to the conventions followed in this book, but we retain 'Kamilaroi' since this is well-known from the pioneering study of Australian kinship systems, *Kamilaroi and Kurnai* by Lorimer Fison and A.W. Howitt (1880), and from the Rev. William Ridley's *Kamilaroi and Other Australian Languages* (1875).

Yuwaalaraay, spoken between Walgett and Lightning Ridge, and Yuwaaliyaay, between Lightning Ridge and Mungindi, are—on linguistic grounds—dialects of the same language as Kamilaroi. A good deal of Yuwaaliyaay culture and legends, and some words, were documented by Mrs K. Langloh Parker, especially in *Australian Legendary Tales* (1896) and *The Euahlayi Tribe* (1903). 'Euahlayi' was Mrs Parker's transcription of the name Yuwaaliyaay.

It appears that the Kamilaroi were, at the time of European invasion, gradually expanding their territory and were becoming a dominant influence over other groups in the Hunter region. Their social network was expanding as they began to intermarry with coastal groups and to influence religious ceremonies further afield.

The most sacred Kamilaroi ceremony was the bora ritual (the name *bora* is a loan into English from Kamilaroi) in which groups of boys were initiated into the secret rites and beliefs of the tribe; large numbers of Kamilaroi people would travel considerable distances to attend a bora. To reach a complete state of manhood was a long process involving at least five separate ceremonies over a number of years. The ceremonial site consisted of one or two cleared circles around which trees were elaborately carved and, in some cases, massive figures of raised earth were created on the ground. The last Kamilaroi bora ritual was held at Wee Waa in 1905.

In the mid-1970s, Corinne Williams, a student at the Australian National University, worked with speakers of Yuwaalaraay and Yuwaaliyaay (and on recordings made shortly before by Janet Matthews, who was married to a grandson of R. H. Matthews); her book, *A Grammar of Yuwaalaraay*, which includes an extensive vocabulary, was published in 1980 by Pacific Linguistics.

Kamilaroi is no longer actively spoken, although some of the older people do know a number of words. A *Gamilaraay/Yuwaalaraay/Yuwaalayaay dictionary*, compiled and edited by Anna Ash, John Giacon and Amanda Lissarrague, was published in 2003 by the Institute for Aboriginal Development; this includes a 'Learner's Guide', which is heavily based on Williams's grammar.

There are more than two dozen loans from Kamilaroi and Yuwaaliyaay listed in Chapter 3. Besides *bora*, they include *coolamon*, *bilby*, *brolga*, *galah*, *budgerigar*, and the names of a number of trees, including *coolibah*, *gidgee*, and *mulga*.

SOURCES: J. Ferry, *Aboriginal History of North Western New South Wales*, self-published, Armidale, 1978; W. A. Wood, *Dawn in the Valley: the Story of Settlement in the Hunter River Valley to 1833*, Wentworth, 1972.

Bandjalang

Bandjalang was spoken in at least twenty dialects over a large area in north-east New South Wales and south-east Queensland, from Beenleigh down to Ballina on the coast, south to Copmanhurst, and west to Warwick.

The first invasion of Bandjalang lands came in the 1840s from cedar cutters, with pastoralists following during the next decade. There ensued a guerrilla warfare in which Aborigines held their own for a while. But in 1859, gold was discovered in the Drake-Pretty Gully area, and the resulting flood of white prospectors, armed with guns, meant that the Bandjalang people were outnumbered and their cause lost.

The Bandjalangs' territory was uniformly rich in resources, but, even so, they frequently travelled to other areas when particular foods were plentiful; to Casino to eat wallabies when the casuarinas were in bloom; to Ballina for shellfish; and as far as Dalby to feast on bunya nuts about every third year (see page 109).

Although the myths and marriage rules of the Bandjalang were very different from neighbouring groups, there were similarities in some cultural practices. The Bandjalang held elaborate initiation ceremonies, and these were performed around a bora ring, as they were in other areas of northern New South Wales. Like the Kamilaroi, the Bandjalang mourned their dead over several months, during which time a number of ceremonies were performed to ensure that the spirit had a safe journey back to the ancestral world.

Bandjalang is probably the only language from New South Wales still actively spoken, although only by a dwindling number of old people. There have been a number of sound studies of varieties of the language: *A Description of the Yugumbir Dialect of Bandjalang* by Margaret Sharpe (née Cunningham) (University of Queensland, 1969), *Gidabal Grammar and Dictionary* by the missionaries Brian and Helen Geytenbeek (Australian Institute of Aboriginal Studies, 1971), and *The Middle Clarence Dialects of Bandjalang* by Terry Crowley (Australian Institute of Aboriginal Studies, 1978). The Crowley volume includes, as an appendix, the grammar, texts, and dictionary compiled by W. E. Smythe, who was a doctor in northern New South Wales during the 1940s, at a time when there were still a considerable number of people speaking Bandjalang.

In recent years, Margaret Sharpe has published *A Dictionary of Yugambeh, Including Neighbouring Dialects* (Pacific Linguistics, 1998). She has also self-published *Dictionary of Western Bundjalung, including Gidhabal and Tabulam Bundjalung* (second edition, 1995) and *An Introduction to the Yugambeh-Bundjalung Language and its Dialects* (revised edition, 1996). (Note that the spelling Bundjalung is requested by members of this ethnic group, even though the three vowels in the name have the same value, as shown in the older spelling Bandjalang, retained here).

About six loan words are thought to come from Bandjalang—the names of one insect and of four trees, including *carabeen* and *cunjevoi* (the plant).

SOURCES: M. C. Calley, Bandjalang Social Organisation, unpublished PhD thesis, University of Sydney, 1959 (copy held in the Australian Institute of Aboriginal and Torres Strait Islander Studies, Canberra); M. Oakes, 'The first inhabitants', pp. 187–205 of *Lismore: The Story of a North Coast City*, edited by M. Ryan, Currawong Press, 1979.

Dharawal and Dhurga

The Dharawal language (whose dialects included Wodi-wodi, Gurungada, and Gami) was spoken in the Illawarra region, from the southern shore of Botany Bay to Jervis Bay, including the modern towns of Wollongong and Nowra. It was most closely related to its southerly neighbour, Dhurga (with dialects that included Wandandian, Tharumba, and Walbanga), which went from Jervis Bay to Wallaga Lake. Both languages probably extended inland to the Great Dividing Range.

This was a region rich in resources—vegetables and animals in the rainforest, fish and shellfish in the sea. The forest began to be cleared when Europeans took up 'runs', from the 1820s. In the 1870s, mining commenced on the sacred mountain called Gulaga (christened Mount Dromedary by the settlers). Despite these intrusions, many aspects of traditional life continued, with the last initiation ceremonies being held in 1910.

In the 1970s, the Aboriginal people of the South Coast region demonstrated a growing political consciousness. When the Shoalhaven Shire Council tried to establish a football field on Aboriginal land in 1973, tents were erected on the site to halt construction. In 1978, the people from Wallaga Lake mounted a campaign to stop logging around a sacred site on Mumbulla Mountain, just north of Bega; and they won this fight.

Very little is known about the Dharawal and Dhurga languages, which have not been actively spoken for some generations. Diana Kelloway Eades recorded a few dozen words from elderly people in the early 1970s, and examined all old sources. Her book, *The Dharawal and Dhurga Languages of the New South Wales South Coast*, was published in 1976 by the Australian Institute of Aboriginal Studies.

In Chapter 3, we mention three loans which probably came from Dharawal— the *parma* wallaby and tree names *bangalay* and *bangalow*, and one from Dhurga—*douligah*, the name for a spirit-being. In addition, the local word for 'Aboriginal people', *Yuin*, is from these two languages.

SOURCE: D. Byrne, *The Mountains Call Me Back: a History of the Aborigines and the Forests of the Far South Coast of New South Wales*, Occasional Paper No. 5, NSW Ministry of Aboriginal Affairs, 1984.

Baagandji

There was a single language, Baagandji, spoken in the country on both sides of the Darling River from Bourke to south of Menindee, and then extending to the south-west into South Australia. There were perhaps ten dialects, which were very similar in vocabulary but differed in a number of points of grammar. One of the best-known dialects was Marawara (or Maruara), to the north of Wentworth.

Baagandji country encompasses a range of environments from fertile riverlands to dry scrub. The riverlands were usually occupied in summer, while the drier regions were visited in the winter when the Baagandji hunted game in the mallee. Water was obtained from the roots of the mallee tree during the hunting season. On the Murray and Darling Rivers, canoes as well as extensive stone traps were used for catching fish.

The elaborate trade system, extending across the whole continent, allowed the Baagandji to communicate with other groups by exchanging a reed they made into fishing nets for such items as ochre and pituri. Baagandji myths tell of heroes from the ancestral past making tracks into their neighbours' country. This highlights the importance of the relationship they had with the people who lived beyond their boundaries—people with whom they traded, made alliances, and occasionally feuded.

Europeans first arrived in Baagandji country in 1829, and began to graze sheep and cattle on the land soon after. Few Aborigines survived the resulting onslaught of disease and violence, and those who did were soon forced to live and work on pastoral stations and reserves.

Luise Hercus worked with the last speakers of this language in the late 1960s and the 1970s. Her book, *The Bāgandji Language* (Pacific Linguistics, 1982) contains grammar, texts, and dictionary, as well as a listing of earlier sources.

In Chapter 3, we mention three loan words that appear to come from Baagandji, including *carney*, 'a bearded lizard' and *tally-walka*, 'an anabranch' (part of a river that diverges from and then rejoins the main flow).

SOURCE: Bobbie Hardy, *Lament for the Barkindji: the Vanished Tribes of the Darling River Region*, Rigby, 1976.

THE LANGUAGES OF WESTERN AUSTRALIA

There were originally about forty languages spoken in what is now the state of Western Australia, with the major concentration being in a strip close to the coast, from Moora up to the Kimberley.

Colonisation of the Perth region in 1829 was by a private syndicate under agreement with the British government. A convict settlement had been placed at Albany in 1826, but the convicts were withdrawn after five years and the establishment then brought within the boundaries of the new state of Western Australia.

The white population grew very slowly; after twenty years, there were only 4,500 settlers and fewer than 5,000 acres under crop. (It was then that convicts were accepted at Perth as a labour force through which settlement could be expanded.) Portions of the state were the last parts of Australia to be occupied by Europeans. The Aborigines fought hard and long, but, as elsewhere, they lost the war simply because guns are more powerful than spears.

Much of the state is desert, which has no appeal to Europeans, and the lifestyle of Aborigines living there underwent the least disruption. Some Western Australian languages are still spoken, although only a handful are today being learnt by children. A number of linguists—notably Alan Dench, Peter Austin and Geoffrey O'Grady—have in recent decades recorded many of those languages, which are (or were) remembered by just a few elderly people; some have already ceased to be spoken or fully remembered.

Nyungar, the language of Perth and Albany

A single language, now called Nyungar, was spoken over a large area of fertile country in the south-west. The northern boundary went close to New Norcia and Merredin; it then turned south-east by Narembeen, Karlgarin, and Lake King, then almost due east to Port Dempster. The present-day towns of Perth, Northam, Bunbury, Albany, and Esperance all lie in Nyungar territory.

This was a region of rich vegetation, with a high rainfall and many rivers and lakes. Although they lived beside a variety of water sources, speakers of Nyungar did not possess any water craft. They preferred not to eat shellfish, even though it was plentiful, living primarily on products of the forest. The Nyungar people wore kangaroo-skin cloaks almost all year round, and when it was particularly cold they might carry smouldering banksia cones under their cloaks for added warmth. Fire was frequently used to keep back the encroaching forest.

After white settlement, and the inevitable dispossession and conflict, the Aboriginal survivors maintained a dual economy based on hunting and gathering alongside the use of European goods. Epidemics of influenza and measles caused many deaths during the later part of the nineteenth century. After 1880, social organisation began to break up and ceremonial practices declined; ceremonies were still performed on rare occasions until they ceased altogether about 1920.

There were at least a dozen tribes in this region, each of which spoke a distinct dialect. The dialects in the Perth area appear to have been conservative, maintaining an older form of the language, but those further south underwent an interesting change whereby the last two sounds of a word appear to have been switched around (the technical term for this is 'metathesis'). The word for 'grass' at Perth was *jilba*, but at Albany it was *jilab*; 'head' was *gada* at Perth and *gaad* at Albany; 'breast' was *bibi* at Perth and *biib* at Albany. The small bandicoot *Perameles bougainville* was *marla* at Perth, but *maarl* further south, and it is probably the latter form that is the origin for the English loan word *marl* (most other Nyungar loans are from conservative dialects in the Perth area). Dialects in the south-west, around Bunbury and Busselton, showed other differences; they had *jilba*, 'grass', and *gada*, 'head', but *biba*, 'breast', for instance.

The earliest settlers at Perth showed a keen interest in the local language, and the materials they collected are better than those from any other capital city. The explorer George Grey published a lengthy *Vocabulary of the Dialects of South-Western Australia* in 1839, and an expanded version the following year. In 1842, G. F. Moore, lawyer and farmer, put out a longer listing, which incorporated the information Grey had gathered, with due acknowledgment. (In 1845, the Very Rev. J. Brady published a vocabulary in Rome, but this was plagiarised from Grey and Moore without any acknowledgment. He was later suspended by Rome.)

There are, in all, more than 150 word lists of Nyungar dialects, including no less than thirty by Daisy Bates, the Irishwoman who lived for many years among Western Australian Aborigines, recording their customs and languages (always wearing a long skirt and starched white collar). The traditional form of Nyungar is no longer spoken, although a number of words are still remembered by some older people. *The Aboriginal Languages of the South-west of Australia* by the missionary-linguist Wilfrid H. Douglas (2nd edition, Australian Institute of Aboriginal Studies, 1976) is a fascinating account of the linguistic situation in modern times, including a phonetically reliable vocabulary.

Nyungar has supplied about sixty loans to English, about as many as Dharuk—although these are less widely used than Sydney loans such as *boomerang, koala, dingo,* and *wombat*—and far more than any other language. They include the names for a number of eucalypts that only grow in Nyungar territory and are valued for their timber—*jarrah, karri, mallett, marri, tuart,* and *wandoo*; the grub *bardi*; mammals such as *chuditch, dibbler, numbat, quokka,* and *woylie*; and *mia mia*. Some of the loans are used only in Western Australia, for example *kylie*; in other parts of the English-speaking world, the corresponding loan from Sydney, *boomerang*, is the word that is used.

SOURCES: W. C. Ferguson, 'Mokaré's domain', pp. 120–45 of *Australians to 1788*, edited by D. J. Mulvaney and J. P. White, Fairfax, Syme & Weldon, 1987; N. J. Green, *Broken Spears: Aborigines and Europeans in the southwest of Australia*, Focus Education Services, 1984; N. Green (ed.), *Nyungar—the People: Aboriginal Customs in the Southwest of Australia*, Creative Research, 1979; L. Tilbrook, *Nyungar Tradition: Glimpses of Aborigines of South-western Australia 1829–1914*, University of Western Australia Press, 1983.

The Western Desert language

A single language was spoken over about one-and-a-quarter million square kilometres (about one-sixth of the total area of Australia) of arid country, mostly in Western Australia, but also extending into South Australia and the Northern Territory. It went from the Great Gibson Desert at latitude 21° in the north to the Nullarbor Plain at latitude 31° in the south; and west from longitude 118°

to 132° in the Northern Territory, with a tongue of territory extending almost to Woomera, at 136°, in South Australia.

In traditional times, the Western Desert people travelled from waterhole to waterhole in small family groups, gathering seeds and other vegetable foods, and killing small desert animals. They would sometimes have to walk a considerable distance over hot sand to reach a new supply of food and water. On occasions, usually after rain, when there was plenty of food, they gathered into larger groups and it was then that religious rituals would be performed, marriages arranged, and the like.

The first white visitor to the desert was the explorer Ernest Giles in 1873. Over the next fifty years, the desert people only very occasionally saw Europeans, and had no intensive contact. During the past seventy years, speakers of the Western Desert language have gradually migrated to European-settled towns and stations on the edge of the desert, or into missions or settlements established by the government. There are today no people living a traditional nomadic lifestyle, although all communities still feel a strong attachment to their home country, with its sacred ties to the ancestral past. Some groups continue to hold religious ceremonies, follow the rules which determine who a person may marry, go on hunting expeditions, and gather some traditional vegetable food alongside the bread and beef brought in by Europeans.

There are many dialects of the Western Desert language, which differ a fair amount in vocabulary but have remarkably similar grammars. These include Mantjiltjara, Pintupi, Luritja, Ngaanyatjarra, Yankunytjatjara, and Pitjantjatjara (the last has sometimes been used as a label for the complete language).

In recent years, a great deal of sound linguistic work has been done on several dialects, and bilingual education programs are in operation at a number of communities. There is an excellent teaching grammar, *An Introduction to the Western Desert Language*, by Wilf Douglas (Oceania Linguistic Monographs, Oceania Publications, revised edition, 1964) and a number of other grammars. There are also some excellent dictionaries, including *An Introductory Dictionary of the Western Desert Language* by Wilf Douglas (Western Australian College of Advanced Education, 1988); *Ngaanyatjarra and Ngaatjatjarra to English Dictionary* (Institute for Aboriginal Development, 2003); *Pintupi/Luritja Dictionary* by Ken and Lesley Hansen (3rd edition, IAD, 1992); *Martu Wangka–English Dictionary*, compiled by James Marsh (Summer Institute of Linguistics, 1992) and *Pitjantjatjara/ Yankunytjatjara to English Dictionary* compiled by Cliff Goddard (IAD, 2nd edition, 1996).

There are about twenty loans from this language (none of which are amongst the most commonly used words of English), including *wiltja*, 'shelter', *marloo*, 'red kangaroo', and a number of other terms for animals, plants, and so forth.

SOURCES: R. M. Berndt and C. H. Berndt, *The World of the First Australians*, Aboriginal Studies Press, 1988; R. A. Gould, *Yiwara: Foragers of the Australian Desert*, Collins, 1969; R. Tonkinson, *The Mardudjara Aborigines: Living the Dream in Australia's Desert*, Holt, Rinehart, and Winston, 1978 (2nd edition in 1991 with 'Mardu' in place of 'Mardudjara').

Yindjibarndi and Panyjima

Yindjibarndi (spoken on the Lower Hamersley Range and the Fortescue River) and Panyjima (spoken further to the south, around Tom Price) show many similarities, but are probably not quite close enough to be considered dialects of one language.

Their speakers have an intricate kinship system which is reflected in the language. If a Panyjima person wants to say 'we two', they have to know what the other person's relationship is to them in order to know which pronoun to employ. For 'me and my brother', one would use *ŋali*, but for 'me and my father', the correct pronoun is *ŋajubarda*, for example. This indicates the way in which kin relationships regulate the social behaviour of Aboriginal people.

Europeans came into this area in the 1860s, and there followed more than fifty years of bloody conflict. The Yindjibarndi and Panyjima people then worked on cattle stations, in the pearling industry, and later in Pilbara goldfields, while retaining much of their traditional culture and language. Today Yindjibarndi is actively spoken by several hundred people, mostly living around Roebourne. There are a few dozen speakers of Panyjima, most of them living near Onslow, but many of them tend to mix Panyjima with Yindjibarndi.

There have been two professional studies: *The Yindjibarndi Language* by F. J. F. Wordick (Pacific Linguistics, 1982) and a grammatical sketch of Panyjima (plus vocabulary) by Alan Dench on pages 124–243 of the *Handbook of Australian Languages*, Vol. 4, edited by R. M. W. Dixon and Barry J. Blake (Oxford University Press, 1991).

About twelve of the loans listed in Chapter 3 probably come from Yindjibarndi or Panyjima, including *yandy*, 'winnowing dish', and *willy-willy*.

SOURCES: J. R. Gibson, The In-betweeners: a Study of Changing Values and Relationships in Roebourne, W. A. with Reference to Aboriginal School Children, unpublished MA thesis from the University of Western Australia, 1973 (copy held in library of the Australian Institute of Aboriginal and Torres Strait Islander Studies, Canberra); B. T. Haynes et al., *W. A. Aborigines 1622–1972* (an extract from *Themes from Western Australian History: A Selection of Documents and Readings*), History Association of Western Australia, 1972.

Nhanta

This is the original language of the Geraldton region, spoken along the coast from north of the mouth of the Murchison River, south at least as far as Dongara, and for some way inland. One interesting feature of the language is that an initial consonant has been dropped from many forms, producing words that begin with a vowel (something that is unusual in Australian languages); for instance, the original *bibi*, 'breast', is now *ibi*.

During the hot summer months, speakers of Nhanta wore few or no clothes, but in winter they donned garments made of kangaroo skin. The explorer George Grey noted 'this tribe was the most northerly one that I had seen wear the kangaroo-skin cloak' (*Journals of Two Expeditions of Discovery*, Vol. 2, p. 16, 1841). The Nhanta people had elaborate initiation ceremonies, but—unlike their neighbours to the east—they did not practise circumcision.

Juliette Blevins worked with the last speakers of this language for her book *Nhanda, an Aboriginal language of Western Australia* (University of Hawai'i Press, 2001). Earlier information includes two word lists by R. T. Goldsworthy and one by A. Oldfield, published in 1886 in Volume 1 of *The Australian Race* by E. M. Curr; four vocabularies by Daisy Bates; and some information recorded in the 1950s by Geoffrey O'Grady.

Six of the words listed in Chapter 3 are thought to come from Nhanta, including *weelo*, 'curlew'; *bungarra*, 'monitor lizard'; and *adjigo*, 'yam'.

SOURCES: R. M. Berndt, 'Traditional Aboriginal life in Western Australia: as it was and is', pp. 3–27 of *Aborigines of the West: their Past and Present*, edited by R. M. Berndt and C. H. Berndt, University of Western Australia Press, 1979; H. A. Crake, *'Carridena': a History of the Three Springs Shire Area*, Three Springs Shire Council, 1979.

THE LANGUAGES OF VICTORIA

There were about twelve distinct languages spoken in what is now the state of Victoria, showing quite significant differences, both from each other and from the languages spoken in neighbouring regions.

In 1803, Britain was concerned that France might attempt to establish a colony in Port Phillip Bay, and a convict settlement was established close to Sorrento, on the Mornington Peninsula, chosen because it afforded a good view across the bay. Within six months, this was abandoned and the convicts moved to Tasmania.

When the next attempts at settlement came they were from Tasmania. In 1834, Thomas Henty brought cattle, seed, and fruit trees from Launceston and settled in Portland Bay. The next year, a party led by John Batman settled at what is now

Melbourne, and 'purchased' from the local Aborigines by mock treaty 600,000 acres of land in return for 'blankets, knives, looking-glasses, tomahawks, beads, scissors, flour, etc.', together with the promise of a yearly tribute.

Europeans spread quickly, and within fifteen years had taken over all of the rich land of the colony. The discovery of gold in 1851 then brought a deluge of new arrivals. Those Aborigines who had not succumbed to European diseases or been murdered were removed from their traditional lands and taken to government settlements such as Framlingham (near Warrnambool) and Lake Tyers (in Gippsland).

George Augustus Robinson, who had earlier rounded up the last Tasmanians, served as Chief Protector of Aborigines from 1838 until 1849, and his manuscript journal includes word lists, of variable quality, from many parts of the colony. In 1881, the pastoralist James Dawson published *Australian Aborigines: the Languages and Customs of Several Tribes of Aborigines in the Western District of Victoria, Australia* (reissued, Australian Institute of Aboriginal Studies, 1981), which included much carefully researched information on Kuurn Kopan Noot and other dialects of the language from the Portland/Warrnambool area (later referred to, erroneously, as Gunditjmara). There were, however, few people as concerned as Dawson. Within two or three decades, some languages had died, with only a couple of word lists to remember them by (for all we know, others may have vanished without being recorded at all).

Just after Christmas 1961, a boy from Framlingham came to Melbourne to stay with Luise Hercus, a teacher of the ancient Indian language Sanskrit. He mentioned that a few old people still remembered bits of the traditional languages. Hercus began an investigation, and wrote to Arthur Capell at the University of Sydney to ask whether the languages of Victoria had all been fully documented. Capell replied that little had been done, and nothing at all since 1910.

For the next six years, Luise Hercus spoke with almost every elderly Aborigine in Victoria (and further afield). For some languages, just a few words were remembered; these were recorded and provided with an accurate phonetic transcription. For three dialects of the language we call Wemba-wemba (see below), she was able to record narrative texts and get useful grammatical information. Her book, *Victorian Languages: a Late Survey*, was published in 1969, and a revised edition issued (by Pacific Linguistics) in 1986.

Wuywurung, the Melbourne language

There were three dialects of the language we call Wuywurung—Bun-wurung, spoken to the north of Westernport; Wuy-wurung proper, from Melbourne and the Yarra River north to Seymour; and Thaga-wurung, from the Goulburn River across to Bendigo. (Note that all three names end in *-wurung*, which means 'mouth' or 'language'.)

This area was richly endowed with varied resources of seafood and forest animals, as well as an abundance of bird life. Shellfish were available for most of the year on the rock platforms, sandy beaches, and mudflats around Port Phillip Bay and Bass Strait. The Wuywurung traded their prized greenstone axe heads for the possum-skin cloaks and spears of other Aboriginal communities who lived nearby.

Wuywurung culture and language had no chance of survival as Europeans poured into their land; for forty years, beginning with the gold rush of the 1850s, Melbourne was the largest city in Australia. In the 1960s, Luise Hercus was able to record a few dozen words said to be Wuywurung, but there was no one left who could construct a complete sentence.

Our information on this language comes from old sources—an 1851 vocabulary by the gardener Daniel Bunce; a long word list and grammatical notes compiled in 1862 by William Thomas; three pages of grammar by R. H. Matthews in 1902; and a dozen other word lists. A reconstruction—as far as the sources will allow—of the language and culture of the Wuywurung, by Barry Blake, is on pages 1–122 of the *Handbook of Australian Languages*, Volume 4, edited by Dixon and Blake (Oxford University Press, 1991).

There appear to be about ten loans from Wuywurung into English, including the name of that most ingenious weapon the *weet-weet* (page 182–3).

SOURCES: R. Broome, *Coburg. Between Two Creeks*, Lothian, 1987; P. Corris, *Aborigines and Europeans in Western Victoria*, Australian Institute of Aboriginal Studies, 1968.

Wathawurung

The Wathawurung language was spoken on the west side of Port Phillip Bay, including the present towns of Geelong and Bacchus Marsh, and probably extending inland as far as Ballarat.

When the first European settlers came to this country, there was an interpreter already available. In 1803, William Buckley had escaped from the short-lived convict settlement near Sorrento, and for the next thirty-two years he lived with the Wathawurung people, joining in on hunting expeditions, sharing their food, and even accepting a wife (although she soon ran away). *The Life and Adventures of William Buckley*, by John Morgan, was published in Hobart in 1852, but unfortunately contains almost nothing on the language.

There is in fact very little recorded of Wathawurung—a word list and bits of grammar written down in 1840 by the missionary Francis Tuckfield; a five-page grammar published in 1904 by R. H. Matthews; and a few other word lists. When Luise Hercus commenced her researches, in 1962, there was no one remaining who acknowledged knowing even a few words of the language.

Half a dozen English words appear to come from Wathawurung, including *borak*, 'nonsense, rubbish'; *merryjig*, 'very good'; and the name of the mythical monster, *bunyip*.

Wemba-wemba

The Aboriginal tribes of western Victoria and an adjoining portion of New South Wales—from Bendigo and Ballarat in the east to the South Australian border in the west, from Balranald and Mildura in the north to Hamilton and Chatsworth in the south—spoke what appear to have been dialects of a single language. They included Wemba-wemba from south of Moulamein; Madhi-madhi from around Balranald; Latji-latji from south of Mildura; Wergaia from Dimboola to Lake Hindmarsh; Jabwurung from south-east of Ararat; and Jajawurung from the Maryborough area. There was no general name for this complete language (as a linguist would use the term), and here we employ Wemba-wemba, the name of the dialect about which most is known, as a designation for the language. Wemba-wemba is closely related to Wuywurung and Wathawurung, the three languages making up a small genetic family.

Speakers of Wemba-wemba lived in a region which provided them with a rich and varied supply of food. They hunted kangaroos, smaller animals and eels, and gathered a large variety of vegetables. The sweet insect secretion called *lerp* (this is a loan from Wemba-wemba) was consumed in great quantities during a six to eight week season in late summer. The seeds of the nardoo plant made a staple food, which was ground into a pulp to be eaten as a porridge or cooked into a cake.

Wemba-wemba people built permanent stone huts, generally close to a stream, and occupied these camp sites for extended periods. Hundreds of Aboriginal mounds can still be seen in the area; these are up to 40 metres across and up to a metre and a half in height, and were oven sites used over hundreds of years. These contain ash, bone, teeth, shell fragments, and sometimes Aboriginal skeletons. In times of flooding, families would live on the mounds, and burials were sometimes performed there.

There are at least 150 accounts (published and unpublished) of the various dialects of the Wemba-wemba language. *Victorian Languages: a Late Survey* (2nd edition, Pacific Linguistics, 1986) by Luise Hercus includes grammars, vocabularies, texts, and songs in the Wemba-wemba, Madhi-madhi, and Wergaia dialects.

There are about a dozen English loan words from Wemba-wemba, including *mallee* and *yabby*.

SOURCE: F. Tucker, *Aboriginal Prehistory and History: Swan Hill Area*, Swan Hill Education Resources Centre, 1985.

THE LANGUAGES OF SOUTH AUSTRALIA

There were about fifteen languages spoken in what is now South Australia, most of them quite closely related.

When plans were made for colonising South Australia, it was advertised by the South Australian Company in London as containing large tracts of 'unoccupied lands'. The Colonial Office insisted that notice be taken of the native people. Land should be bought from Aborigines, if they would voluntarily sell. Should they refuse to sell their land, it would be the duty of the appointed Protector of Aborigines 'to secure to the Natives the full and undisturbed occupation or enjoyment of their lands and to afford them legal redress against depredators and trespassers'.

It was hard for the government in London to police what happened on the other side of the world. They would lay down rules of behaviour to which the intending colonists agreed, but then conveniently forgot about on the boat out. On arrival at Adelaide in 1836, the new settlers simply usurped the rights of the original owners.

In 1842, a bill was passed in the British parliament specifying that fifteen per cent of all moneys obtained from the sale of land should be spent on the native peoples in the new colonies. The South Australian government at first resolved to spend ten per cent of land revenues on looking after the Aborigines, but when copper was found, land prices skyrocketed, and it was decided that the Aborigines should have not even ten per cent, but just 'what was absolutely necessary'.

Most of the centre and north of the state is arid land which was not coveted by Europeans; languages spoken in those parts survived longer than those in the south, but many of these have recently become extinct or will be soon, when the last old speakers pass on.

During the last fifty or so years, the South Australian government has had a somewhat more constructive attitude to Aborigines than the governments of other states. Aborigines have been granted title to parts of their original territories, and bilingual education programs have been established where a language is still in use (this applies mostly to dialects of the Western Desert language, in the far north).

SOURCE: Henry Reynolds, *The Law of the Land*, Penguin, 1987.

Gaurna, the Adelaide language

Gaurna (or Kaurna) was spoken in a coastal strip from Cape Jervis to the head of the Gulf of St Vincent (bounded on the east by Mount Compass, Mount Barker, Gawler, and Clare), and then an inland tract up to Crystal Brook.

Speakers of Gaurna fished along the coast in summer, and in winter camped on the wooded plains and foothills, where they lived in shelters thatched with stringybark and grasses. They decorated their bodies for religious ceremonies and wore ornaments of bunches of kangaroo teeth and possum-hair headbands. Aboriginal graves have been found throughout the Adelaide peninsula, and there is recorded information to suggest that they practised elaborate burial rituals as part of their rich religious life.

The first European contact was with sealers, who came to Kangaroo Island (not then inhabited by Aborigines) and the adjacent mainland in 1801. They kidnapped Aboriginal women and passed on venereal disease, which quickly spread through the local tribes and often led to infertility. In the 1820s, hundreds of Gaurna people died in a smallpox epidemic (there had been at least one earlier epidemic, originating from Sydney). When the official colonists arrived in 1836, they displaced those Gaurna who still survived, and placed them on small 'reservations'.

In 1840, Lutheran missionaries C. G. Teichelmann and C. W. Schürmann published *Outlines of a Grammar, Vocabulary and Phraseology of the Aboriginal Language of South Australia Spoken by Natives in and for some Distance around Adelaide*. Our etymologies are based on this, on an 1839 vocabulary by William Williams, a 1920 vocabulary by J. M. Black (in the *Transactions of the Royal Society of South Australia*, Vol. 44, pp. 76–85), and on a further dozen short word lists.

About a dozen loan words have been traced to Gaurna, including *condolly*, 'whale blubber'; *pinkie*, 'bandicoot'; and *wurley*, 'shelter'.

SOURCES: R. Edwards, *The Kaurna People of the Adelaide Plains*, South Australian Museum, 1972; H. Groome, *The Kaurna, First People in Adelaide*, Tjintu Books, 1981.

Yaralde

A single language was spoken from Encounter Bay, past the mouth of the Murray River, along to the end of the Coorong, and inland as far as Bordertown. The people along the Coorong were called the Tangane, those to the east of Lake Alexandrina were the Yaralde, and those at Encounter Bay the Ramindjari (inland groups had further names). Yaralde is generally employed as a name for the whole language, although some writers follow Taplin in using Narrinyeri, which is the word for 'man'.

Tribes on the western side of the Mount Lofty Range, including Gaurna, practised circumcision, whereas tribes on the eastern side, including Yaralde, did not. The Mount Lofty Range was also a considerable linguistic demarcator—Gaurna, at Adelaide, shows more similarities with Nyungar, spoken over 2000 kilometres away at Perth, than it does with Yaralde, a mere 50 kilometres distant over the hills. Yaralde has similarities with a group of four languages spoken up the Murray River, from Murray Bridge to Mildura, and is very different from the other languages of South Australia, and of Victoria.

A main source of food was the large fish called in English *mulloway* (this is a loan from Yaralde *malowe*). A man would wade a fair distance into the river and stand absolutely still, holding his spear at an oblique angle ready to strike. Mulloway would swim around him and he would bring the spear down with a quick and powerful thrust. Fish would also be speared from a bark canoe which had a fire smouldering in the middle, ready to roast them without delay. An alternative method of catching fish was with a net. (Although people in other parts of Australia employed the hook and line, the Yaralde are said to have adopted these only after contact with Europeans.) Swans, geese, ducks, and other birds, which are plentiful on Lake Alexandrina, were caught with a noose at the end of a long stick; and women would dive into the lake for shellfish and crayfish.

The first linguist to work on Yaralde was also the best. In 1843, the Lutheran missionary H. A. E. Meyer published *A Vocabulary of the Language Spoken by the Aborigines ... in the Vicinity of Encounter Bay, Preceded by a Grammar*. The vocabulary was quite extensive and the grammar full and illuminating. A few other short word lists were published, and then, in 1879, George Taplin, Anglican missionary at Point Macleay, included a vocabulary and grammar in his book *The Folklore, Manners, Customs and Languages of the South Australian Aborigines*. Taplin criticised Meyer, but in fact he simply copied a great deal of Meyer's vocabulary and some of the simpler parts of his grammar. Some of the Yaralde people living today at Point Macleay and elsewhere know some words from the language, but it is no longer actively used.

There are about eight loans which come from Yaralde, including *toolache*, 'grey wallaby'.

SOURCE: H. A. E. Meyer, *Manners and Customs of the Aborigines of the Encounter Bay Tribe, South Australia*, 1846.

Adnyamathanha and Guyani

Adnyamathanha was spoken around the Flinders Ranges, to the east of Lake Torrens. Guyani, another dialect of the same language, was located to the north-west, between Lake Torrens and Lake Eyre. In Adnyamathanha-Guyani (and in Diyari, to the north), there is a contrast between voiced and voiceless stop consonants, *d* versus *t*, and *rd* versus *rt*, something which is unusual in Australian languages.

There are red-ochre quarries at Parachilna and Beltana in Adnyamathanha country which were once the centre of a huge trading network involving the Lake Eyre people and others to the south.

One notable feature of these people is their kinship system, and the intricate rules governing who one can marry. There are up to fifteen forms for a single pronoun (such as 'you two' or 'we all') depending on the relationships between the people referred to.

The explorer Edward John Eyre was the first European to meet the Adnyamathanha, when he travelled through the Flinders Ranges in 1840. Pastoralists followed in the 1850s and took over traditional hunting grounds. The Aborigines then camped around stations and police posts, subsisting on an unbalanced diet of European foods.

In recent years, the Adnyamathanha have been granted leases for two pastoral properties in their territory. They continue to be deeply involved in the custodianship of their land and their sacred sites, and in the continuation of the language.

Bernhard Schebeck published *Texts on the Social System of the At^{y}n^{y}amata̲na People with Grammatical Notes* (Pacific Linguistics, 1974). J.C. McEntee, of Erudina Station, worked with language speaker Pearl McKenzie to produce a most worthwhile dictionary, with careful phonetic representation (this is self-published). Dorothy Tunbridge has had a hand in three books: *Artefacts of the Flinders Range, an Illustrated Dictionary of Artefacts used by the Adnyamathanhas* (Pipa Wangka, Port Augusta, 1985), *Flinders Range Dreaming* (Aboriginal Studies Press, 1988) and *The Story of Flinders Range Mammals* (Kangaroo Press, 1991).

Chapter 3 includes four loans from this language, including *witchetty*, *euro*, and the name of the plant *parakeelia*.

SOURCE: P. Brock, *Yura and Udnyu: a history of the Adnyamathanha of the North Flinders Ranges*, Wakefield Press, 1985.

Diyari

Diyari was spoken in a region of scrub and hummock grasslands to the east of Lake Eyre (north of Adnyamathanha-Guyani). This is a harsh environment of extreme heat and meagre rainfall. As food was limited, speakers of Diyari lived for most of the year in small groups consisting of just a few families; groups would come together whenever food became more plentiful, and it was then that ceremonies were performed. The Diyari constructed low, domed huts, made of leaves and sand placed over a wooden frame, to protect them from the extreme climate.

J. G. Reuther, a missionary among the Diyari at the end of the nineteenth century, left copious manuscript notes, which included a grammar and dictionary (these were translated from the German and published in microfiche form by the Australian Institute of Aboriginal Studies in 1981). There is a profusion of linguistic material on this language by a number of other missionaries. Peter Austin worked with the last speakers in the 1970s; his book, *A Grammar of Diyari, South Australia* (Cambridge University Press, 1981), also includes a vocabulary.

About nine loans can be traced to Diyari, including the name of the large monitor lizard, *perentie*.

SOURCE: I. McBryde, 'Goods from another country: exchange networks and the people of the Lake Eyre basin', pp. 252–73 of *Australians to 1788*, edited by D. J. Mulvaney and J. P. White, Fairfax, Syme & Weldon, 1987.

Arabana and Wanggang015uru

Arabana was spoken to the west of Lake Eyre, and Wangganguru to the north, in the Simpson Desert (extending into the Northern Territory) and along the Lower Diamantina. These are dialects of one language.

Like other Australian tribes, the Arabana and Wangganguru had legends telling of ancestors who fashioned the landscape. In their travels, they followed the same pursuits and went along the same paths as Aborigines of recent times. Only occasionally did they have to resort to supernatural means—for example, being lifted up by a whirlwind to cross Lake Eyre, and crawling underground below one of the driest parts of the Simpson Desert on which there are no recognised soakages.

In 1867, the Lutherans established a mission at Killalpaninna, to the east of Lake Eyre, at which many Arabana, Wangganguru, Diyari and other people lived. This was closed during the First World War (since the people who ran it were German) and the Aborigines moved to the towns of Marree and Port Augusta or to pastoral properties in the region.

There are a handful of old vocabularies, but the major work on this language has been done by Luise Hercus, who worked for twenty years with the last old people who remembered it. Her book, *A Grammar of the Arabana-Wangkanguru Language, Lake Eyre Basin, Australia*, was published by Pacific Linguistics in 1994.

The loans into English from Arabana and Wangganguru are *mickery*, 'soak'; *pirri*, an engraving tool; *tula*, a wood-working tool; and the names of two mammals, *mulgara* and *yallara*.

SOURCE: L. Hercus, 'Arabana and Waŋgaŋuru traditions', *Oceania*, Vol. 42, pp. 94–109, 1971.

THE LANGUAGES OF QUEENSLAND

A Queensland language contributed the first—and the most widely-known—Australian loan into English. *Kangaroo*, from Guugu Yimidhirr, came into English in 1770 when Captain Cook had to spend six weeks at the Endeavour River repairing damage his vessel had sustained on the Great Barrier Reef.

About 90 distinct languages were spoken in what is now the state of Queensland, with the greatest concentration in the north (there were at least 55 languages spoken in Cape York Peninsula, north of a line from Townsville to Normanton).

The first permanent occupation by Europeans was in 1824 with the establishment of a convict settlement at Brisbane. The area was opened for the sale of land to free settlers only in 1842. Meanwhile, rich grazing land had been discovered around the Condamine River, in what is now called the Darling Downs, and intensive settlement of the region began in 1840. (Bigambil, the original language of the Darling Downs, appears to have disappeared from use by about the end of the nineteenth century, and is known only from four short word lists). There was, at first, closer European occupation of the inland parts of south-east Queensland than of the coastal country, because of better pasture, but by the 1850s the whole region had been taken over.

After the Burke and Wills cross-continental expedition failed to return in 1861, search parties set out from the east coast. They discovered tracts of good country in western Queensland, which pastoralists soon took up. In parts of North Queensland, European occupation was triggered by the discovery of gold, from the late 1860s.

All parts of the state saw warfare between white and black. In some areas, Aboriginal resistance was powerful enough to restrain settlement for a while, with some stations being temporarily abandoned. But, as is well-known, the invader returned, backed by the strength of firearms.

The only languages actively spoken today are a handful in the far north: the two languages from the Torres Strait islands (the western one, Kala Lagaw Ya, shows some features characteristic of an Australian language, but the eastern Torres Strait language has a quite different structure), Wik-Mungkan at Aurukun, Guugu Yimidhirr at Hopevale, Kuku-Yalanji at Bloomfield River, and perhaps one or two more. These Aboriginal groups, with some assistance from missionaries and the federal government, are now doing what they can to ensure that their languages are passed on to future generations.

Yagara, the Brisbane language

This language had a number of dialects. That spoken at Brisbane, probably extending up to Caboolture, was called in the old sources Durubul, Turrbal, or Thoerwel. From Ipswich south to Boonah and inland perhaps to Laidley, there was the Yagara dialect. The dialect spoken on North Stradbroke Island was Moonjan, and that on South Stradbroke was Jandai. Yagara is generally used as a label for the whole language. A separate language, Gowar, was spoken on Moreton Island.

Speakers of Yagara had a rich diet of seafood and vegetables that was supplemented with the meat of kangaroos and reptiles. Their territory contained semi-tropical rainforest, which supplied them with a variety of birds to eat, as well as honey, obtained from the nests of native bees, often high up in the tall forest trees. The Yagara held long religious ceremonies for which people travelled a considerable distance; initiation rituals would last for up to a month. The Yagara were famous among Aborigines of the region for their songs and for the way that they decorated their bodies with vivid vegetable paints and colourful bird feathers. They were renowned for being brave in war and dexterous in combat.

Very little was recorded of this language. There are about twenty word lists, all quite short. The Rev. William Ridley (in *Kamilaroi and Other Australian Languages*, 1875) stated that the grammar was complicated, but just gave the inflections of one noun, one pronoun and one verb (three pages in all). The only texts we have are short passages of Bible translation by Ridley. The original Yagara forms, for the etymologies in Chapter 3, have been inferred from the spellings in old sources.

About seventeen loans are thought to come from Yagara, including *humpy*, *dilly* (as in 'dilly bag'), *bung* (as in 'go bung'), the *bunya* pine, and the *piccabeen* pine.

SOURCES: C. C. Petrie, *Tom Petrie's Reminiscences of Early Queensland* (*dating from 1837*), 1904; A. Queale, *The Lockyer – its First Half Century*, Gatton and District Historical Society, 1978; J. G. Steele, *The Explorers of the Moreton Bay District, 1770–1830*, University of Queensland Press, 1972.

Gabi-gabi

Gabi-gabi was spoken from just north of Caboolture up to Childers, and inland to the Jimma Range and the Urah Range; its territory included Fraser Island (where the Bajala dialect was spoken) and probably also Bribie Island. To the north of Gabi-gabi, around Bundaberg, Gureng-gureng was spoken, and to the west, in an area roughly bounded by Toowoomba, Biloela, and Condamine, was Waga-waga.

The Rev. John Mathew described the daily life of Gabi-gabi people in his *Two Representative Tribes of Queensland* (1910). Vegetable staples were fern roots, the core at the top of the cabbage palm, a few wild fruits such as quandongs, native plums and native limes, plus yams and the root of the *cunjevoi*—'the juice, being poisonous, had to be expressed from the roots, which were then roasted before being eaten'. He mentioned that

> it was the recognised duty of the women to dig the yams (*Dioscorea transversa*) for family use. They were regularly provided with a yam-stick for this purpose, a staff about five feet long, the thickness of a stout walking stick, and pointed at both ends. It served another purpose equally well, being the women's fighting weapon. They used it like a single stick with great deftness in their feminine encounters.

Their 'most esteemed' food was the seeds of the bunya pine (see pages 109–110).

There are a couple of dozen word lists on this language, some quite extensive, and short grammatical sketches by the Rev. William Ridley (who called the language Dippil) and by John Mathew.

There are three loans known definitely to be from Gabi-gabi: the names of the stinging tree, *gympie*; the pine, *cooloolah*; and the banksia, *wallum*.

Dyirbal

A single language was spoken by a number of neighbouring tribes extending from Cardwell to beyond Innisfail along the coast, and inland to Malanda and Herberton. These included Dyirbal (for which the language is named) along the upper Tully River, the Millstream, and the Wild River; Ngajan, along the Russell River; Mamu, along the Johnstone River; and Girramay, along the Murray River.

Most of this territory was tropical rainforest with a wide variety of fauna and flora. Each noun in Dyirbal falls into one of four gender classes: masculine, feminine, edible, and neuter. The edible class contains only vegetable foods (meat and fish are 'neuter'), and is known to include at least 200 names for trees, herbs, vines, ferns, and roots, all of which have parts that can be eaten.

W. E. Roth, who was Chief Protector of Aborigines at Cooktown, wrote in 1903 (*North Queensland Ethnography*, Bulletin 5, p. 22) that the Mallanpara people on the lower Tully River, speaking the Gulngay dialect of Dyirbal, did not recognise 'sexual connection as a cause of conception'. This was a common misunderstanding among Europeans at that time. The Dyirbal people would have been unwilling to talk to Roth about this (as would people in Victorian England), but they were certainly aware of the physical origin of babies. There is even a verb, *bulmbiñu*, 'be the male progenitor of', which refers to the act of copulation that induces a conception.

When R. M. W. Dixon began work on this language in 1963, he counted about one hundred speakers; today there are no more than five. His book, *The Dyirbal Language of North Queensland* (Cambridge University Press, 1972), contains a grammar and a short vocabulary; a comprehensive dictionary is now being prepared for publication. Dixon collaborated with musicologist Grace Koch on a volume, *Dyirbal Song Poetry, the Oral Literature of an Australian Rainforest People* (University of Queensland Press, 1996).

There are eight loans that come from Dyirbal or a nearby language. These include the names of the bird, *chowchilla*, and four rainforest trees with millable timber, the most important being *jitta* (*Halfordia scleroxyla*), the hardest tree in the forest.

SOURCE: Bob Dixon, 'Words of Juluji's world', pp. 147–65 of *Australians to 1788*, edited by D. J. Mulvaney and P. J. White, Fairfax, Syme & Weldon, 1987.

Warrgamay

This language was spoken (to the south of Dyirbal) up the Herbert River as far as the Herbert Gorge, on the coast by Halifax, and on Hinchinbrook Island and Dunk Island.

E. J. Banfield had contact with speakers of Warrgamay when he lived on Dunk Island, and includes some account of their lifestyle, with a few words from the language, in *Confessions of a Beachcomber* (1908) and later books.

Carl Lumholtz, a Norwegian zoologist, lived from August 1882 until July 1883 at an abandoned cattle station on the Herbert River and had close contact with the Warrgamay people. His book, *Among Cannibals* (1889), presents a vivid picture of the break-up of tribal life in the face of European contact. But Lumholtz did not learn the language, and the vocabulary he recorded has only 120 words.

Soon after Lumholtz left, most members of the Warrgamay tribe were hunted and killed by the Queensland Native Police (Aborigines from a distant tribe who were given guns and told to shoot on sight; see Chapter 6). When R. M. W. Dixon began to study the language in the 1970s, there were just three people who remembered bits of Warrgamay, all of them born before 1900 (all are now dead). Dixon's 'Warrgamay', pp. 1–144 of the *Handbook of Australian Languages*, Vol. 2, edited by Dixon and Blake (Australian National University Press, 1981), contains a grammatical sketch and a vocabulary of about 900 words.

Three English loans may come from Warrgamay, the most notable being *boongarry*, recorded by Lumholtz for 'tree-kangaroo'. (The original Warrgamay form was *bulŋgarri*; Lumholtz couldn't hear the *l*.)

LANGUAGES OF THE NORTHERN TERRITORY

More than sixty languages were originally spoken in what is now the Northern Territory. This is an area of great linguistic diversity, including languages with very complex word structures that include prefixes (over most of Australia, there are only suffixes).

Dutch explorers mapped the north coast of Australia long before Captain Cook was born; they named Arnhem Land in 1623. The first British settlements in the north were simply to guard against any part of the continent being claimed by another European power. A garrison was established at Fort Dundas on Melville Island in 1824, but transferred to Raffles Bay on the mainland four years later, only to be abandoned in 1830, leaving behind herds of water buffalo which had been imported from Timor. Then, following rumours that the French were fitting out an expedition at Toulon to take possession of some part of north Australia, a town was established at Port Essington, close to Raffles Bay, in 1838, only to be again abandoned after eleven years.

The town of Darwin dates from 1869. Many people then came to the northern territory—pastoralists, miners following the gold lure, indentured labourers from China and Singapore working on the cable link to Britain—but few stayed long. Many of the cattle properties failed to pay their way.

Aborigines were affected by the spread of diseases such as smallpox, tuberculosis, and leprosy, but in some areas their traditional pattern of life was left undisturbed until the middle of the twentieth century. In recent years, they have been granted title to portions of their own lands in many parts of the Territory.

Most of the original languages are still spoken, although fewer than half are now being learnt by children (this is still the largest concentration of Australian languages in the continent). There are bilingual education programs at a number of schools, but more are needed.

Aranda

The name of this language is spelled Aranda or Arunta in the voluminous anthropological literature but is now spelled Arrernte in the practical orthography used by its speakers. It is spoken over 200,000 square kilometres in the southern part of the Northern Territory (just extending into South Australia and Queensland), which includes Alice Springs. There are a number of dialects, including Alyawarra (centred on the Sandover River), Anmatjirra (around Tea Tree), Western Aranda, Southern Aranda, Lower Aranda, Eastern Aranda, and Central Aranda. This language has undergone a change whereby initial consonants were lost, so that many words now begin with a vowel. When spoken in isolation, a word in Aranda ends in a central vowel like the one in the English word *the*, which can be written as 'e' or omitted, since it is predictable.

For a hundred years after white occupation of Australia, it was said that Aborigines had no indigenous religion. At the turn of the century, the Aranda were chief subjects of a remarkable study, *The Native Tribes of Central Australia* (1899), by Baldwin Spencer, Professor of Biology at the University of Melbourne, and Francis Gillen, postmaster at Alice Springs. These two authors described for the first time the Aboriginal view of the universe as created in the dreamtime; the fundamental properties of the belief system they uncovered were later found to apply all over Australia. They wrote about a whole range of religious practices among these desert people, providing information on secret-sacred rites, and beliefs concerning conception and death.

A Lutheran mission for the Aranda people had been established in the 1870s at Hermannsburg; the writings of Pastor Carl Strehlow contain illuminating descriptions of life and language, complementing those of Spencer and Gillen. His son, T. G. H. Strehlow, was brought up speaking Aranda, and also wrote extensively on language, songs, and traditions.

At least five dialects of Aranda are widely spoken today. Yeperenye School and the Institute of Aboriginal Development (IAD) (both in Alice Springs) have produced bilingual teaching materials. IAD is continuing to put out a wealth of fine publications on this language, including *Alyawarr to English*

Dictionary, compiled by Jenny Green (1992) and *Eastern and Central Arrernte to English Dictionary*, compiled by John Henderson and Veronica Dobson (1994). Amongst the multitude of earlier work on this language, *Aranda Phonetics and Grammar* by T. G. H. Strehlow (Oceania Monographs, 1944) and *Alyawarra, an Aboriginal Language of Central Australia* by Colin Yallop (Australian Institute of Aboriginal Studies, 1977) are particularly recommended.

There are about nine loans into English from Aranda, the most important being the religious terms *alcheringa*, 'dreamtime', and *churinga*, 'sacred ceremonial object'.

THE LANGUAGES OF TASMANIA

Little information is available on the extinct languages of Tasmania. What is known suggests that there were at least eight distinct languages, perhaps more. It is not possible to say whether or not these were related to languages spoken on the mainland.

It is thought that the Tasmanians were a group of Australian Aborigines cut off from the mainland when sea levels rose at the end of the last ice age, about 14,000 years ago. The dingo, which entered Australia only about 4,000 years ago, was not in Tasmania, suggesting that there had been little or no contact across the Bass Strait.

The Dutch navigator Abel Tasman was the first European seen by Tasmanians, in 1642. There followed a number of encounters with explorers, including the French expedition under D'Entrecasteaux, in 1792/3, which took down several vocabularies. Then came the first convict settlement, removed from Port Phillip Bay in Victoria to Hobart in 1804 (see above).

It seems that some of the most hardened criminals in the British Empire were sent to Tasmania. The Aboriginal people defended their traditional land with intensity. Amid such bitter warfare, the side that succumbed lost most resoundingly. By 1830, there were only 300 Tasmanians left out of a population estimated to have numbered about five thousand. These people were gathered together—with false promises—by George Augustus Robinson and placed on an island in the Bass Strait. Truganini, the last full-blood Tasmanian and pretty certainly the last person with full command of a Tasmanian language, died in 1876.

Pitifully little information was gathered on the lifestyle, subsistence activities, residence patterns, implements, religious practices, kinship system, and languages of the Tasmanians. *A Word-list of the Tasmanian Aboriginal Languages* by N. J. B. Plomley (published by the author, 1976) collates the known vocabularies and the handful of sentences recorded. 'Tasmanian' by Terry Crowley and R. M. W. Dixon, pp. 394–421 of the *Handbook of Australian Languages*, Vol. 2, edited by Dixon and Blake (Australian National University Press, 1981) is a linguistic assessment of this data, attempting to reconstruct the phonetics and the forms of some words. (Almost nothing is known about the grammar of any Tasmanian language.)

The number of words taken into English from languages spoken around the mainland capital cities varies from around sixty at each of Sydney and Perth to about ten at each of Melbourne and Adelaide. The extensive list of established loans in the next chapter includes just three that are thought to be from a Tasmanian language—the names of the trees *canagong* and *boobialla*, and the word *lubra*.

SOURCES: N. J. B. Plomley, *Friendly Mission, the Tasmanian Journal and Papers of George Augustus Robinson, 1829–1834*, Tasmanian Historical Research Association, 1966; L. Ryan, *The Aboriginal Tasmanians*, University of Queensland Press, 1981; Vivienne Rae-Ellis, *Black Robinson: Protector of Aborigines*, Melbourne University Press, 1988.

3

The words that were borrowed

In this chapter, we examine the words that have been borrowed from Australian languages and become part of Australian English. The process of establishing the origin of these words is described at the end of Chapter 1, on pages 15–18. The words are grouped under the following headings:

Each word has an entry rather like that in a dictionary. Most are based on the entries in the *Australian National Dictionary*, but have been modified to suit the purposes of this book or revised in the light of research undertaken in its preparation. Some new entries have been added. Each entry has a number of parts, in this order: the word, in its most usual spelling; the most usual pronunciation(s) in an 'educated Australian' style; alternative spellings; in square brackets: the source language, the word's phonetic form in that language, and its meaning if this differs from the English meaning (or as much of this as is known); a definition, followed in square brackets by the date of the earliest known written record (published or unpublished); and, in most cases, a quotation or set of quotations illustrating the word's use. When a word is used in more than its main sense, the secondary senses are 'strung on', as in a dictionary entry.

FAUNA

Aboriginal people traditionally placed great importance on the ability of men to hunt and kill animals. Even though women provided most of the food by collecting small animals and vegetable material, game, which was eaten less regularly, was considered to be a more valuable food item. Knowledge about hunting and skill with weapons were important markers of manhood. Sometimes the hunting of a large animal was part of a boy's initiation ritual, which enabled him to enter into adult society. Hunting ability did not rely solely on prowess, but also required a deep knowledge of the animal world, such as that needed in the expert examination of the tracks of animals. There were many ingenious techniques for capturing animals that included imitating their calls and using decoys and snares.

Animals and animal behaviour are central to the myths and legends of Aboriginal people. Frequently an animal is of particular importance to a section of a community which has the animal as their 'totem'. Animal totems provide a way of using the differences in the animal world to explain the differences between groups of people. People with the same totem are often not allowed to marry. Occasionally, if an animal is ritually important to a group, they may not be permitted to kill it. At certain times, such as during pregnancy, women should not eat animals that are considered dangerous to them. There are generally some animals, those quite easy to secure, which only the old people are allowed to catch and eat; this has been described as a bit like an old age pension.

The first white settlers named some local animals after old world species, like *native cat* or *native dog*, and called others after species in other countries to which they showed superficial resemblances. Thus, our word *goanna* is based on the American term *iguana*, borrowed from Spanish, which in turn took it from *iguana* in the Taino language (of the Arawak family), spoken in what is now Puerto Rico. Our *possum* is based on *opossum* in American English, which comes from *opassom*, meaning 'white dog' in the Virginia Algonquin language. Our *bandicoot* was given a name based on a rat-like animal in India, related to the name *pandi-kokku*, 'pig-rat' in the Dravidian language Telugu. The word *emu* comes from the word for 'cassowary' in Portuguese, *ema*. *Dugong* is based on the Malay *duyong*, while *cockatoo* reached us, via Dutch, from the Malay *kakatua*.

There were some animals on this continent that were unlike anything found in other parts of the world, and for these the name was most frequently adopted from an Australian language.

Mammals

bettong /ˈbɛtɒŋ/
[Dharuk, Sydney region *biduŋ* for *Bettongia gaimardi*.]
The genus name *Bettongia*, covering rat-kangaroos, is based on this Dharuk name; five of the species in the genus (and one outside it) are described as types of *bettong*.

The *southern bettong* (or *eastern bettong*), *Bettongia gaimardi*, inhabits dry, grassy open forest. The *burrowing bettong*, *Bettongia lesueur*, lives in arid and semi-arid country; it is called *boodie* in Western Australia and *tungoo* in Central Australia. The *brush-tailed bettong*, *Bettongia penicillata*, was once widespread in dry habitats; it is called *woylie* in Western Australia. There are also the *northern bettong*, *Bettongia tropica*, in North Queensland, and the *rufous bettong*, *Aepyprymnus rufescens*, down the east coast. The *Nullarbor dwarf bettong*, *Bettongia pusilla*, is known only from skeletal remains found in caves. [First written 1802]

> **1972** *Sunday Mail Magazine* [Brisbane], 3 September, 4. Bettongs, which occur in many parts of Australia … are the 'nest-making rat-kangaroos' and use their long flexible tails for the transport of nesting materials.

biggada /ˈbɪɡədə/
[Ngarluma, Roebourne region, Western Australia (and neighbouring languages) *bigurda*.]
A Western Australian name for the *euro*, *Macropus robustus*. [1863]

> **1977** H. BUTLER, *In the Wild with Harry Butler*, 58. The Biggadas dig, exposing the fresh water table, and all the other animals that need water know about it.

bilby /ˈbɪlbi/
Also **bilbi**.
[Yuwaalaraay, north New South Wales *bilbi*.]
Either of two bandicoots of the genus *Macrotis*. The larger one, *Macrotis lagotis*, a burrowing marsupial of woodlands and plains of drier parts of mainland Australia, has rabbit-like ears and a long, pointed snout. It is called *greater bilby*, *rabbit-eared bandicoot* or *rabbit bandicoot*. The name *dalgite* is used in Western Australia and

pinkie in South Australia. The *lesser bilby*, *Macrotis leucura*, was only found in desert country and is now believed to be extinct. [1855]

> **1984** *Australian* [Sydney], 12 July, 3. It might sound like something from Tolkien, but the bilby is real.

Recently, the Easter Bunny, reputed to bring gifts at Easter, has been accorded a more Australian name, the **Easter Bilby**.

bobuck /ˈboʊbʌk/
[Possibly from a language of the New South Wales or eastern Victorian coast.]
The possum *Trichosurus caninus* of mountain forests in south-east mainland Australia; also called *mountain brushtail possum*. [1953]

> **1994** K. HUENEKE, *People of the Australian High Country*, 127. That wild bush country carried a good many possums, especially that high country carried what the native local people called the Bobuck possum.

boodie /ˈbudi/
Also **boody**, and **boordee**.
[Nyungar, Perth–Albany region *burdi*.]
The *burrowing bettong*, *Bettongia lesueur*, formerly widespread in arid and semi-arid regions, then confined to islands off the coast of Western Australia, now being reintroduced on the mainland. Also called *tungoo* in Central Australia. See also *bettong*. [1842]

> **1857** W. S. BRADSHAW, *Voyages to India, China, and America, with an Account of the Swan River Settlement*, 114. Many of the animals of the forest … are very good for food, namely, the opossums, bandicoots, boodies.

boongarry /ˈbʊŋɡəri/, /ˈbʊŋɡæri/
[Warrgamay, Herbert River, North Queensland *bulŋgarri*.]
Lumholtz's tree kangaroo, *Dendrolagus lumholtzi*, now restricted to rainforest north-west of Cardwell, north-east Queensland. Also known as *mapi*. [1889]

> **1913** *Bulletin* [Sydney], 5 June, 15. The boongarry was long thought an aboriginal myth, like the bunyip; but it isn't and the Melbourne Zoo has a couple to prove it.

brumby /ˈbrʌmbi/
Also **brumbee**, and **brumbie**.
The origin of this word, meaning a wild horse, is obscure. It may possibly come from a language in southern Queensland or northern New South Wales. One possibility is that the name came from that of a Lieutenant Brumby, who let some horses run wild, but this has not been confirmed. (See E. E. Morris, *Austral English*, 1898, p. 58.) [1880]

2001 P. THOMSON, *Whitefella Wandering*, 16. We left Paul behind to catch a wild brumby with his cousins and meet us at the beach.

chuditch /'tʃudɪtʃ/
Also **chudice**. Used mainly in Western Australia.
[Southern dialect of Nyungar, Perth–Albany region *judij*.]
The *western quoll, Dasyurus geoffroii*, a native cat which had quite a wide distribution across the continent but is now found only in the south-west corner; also called *western native cat*. [c. 1842]

> **c. 1842** H. M. WHITTELL, 'John Gilbert's Notebook on Marsupials', *Western Australian Naturalist*, 4 (1954), 105. Dju-tytche K.G.S. [King George's Sound] … It lives in hollow stumps, hollow trees or in holes in the rock from which they issue at night in quest of food consisting for the most part of birds and the smaller quadrupeds. It is said to occasionally feed on insects; a gentleman informed me he found its stomach completely filled with the White Ant. It is a very destructive species in the farmyard attacking indiscriminately Ducks, Geese, Turkeys or Fowls.

dalgite /'dælgaɪt/
Also **dalgyte**, etc.
[Nyungar, Perth–Albany region *dalgaj*.]
A Western Australian name for the *greater bilby, Macrotis lagotis*. [1840]

> **2004** *Landscope*, Spring, 23. Dalgytes zigzag their way through the vegetation; their long pink noses high in the air sniffing for scrumptious larvae, fruit or bulbs.

dargawarra /dagə'wɒrə/
Also **tarkawarra**.
[Western Desert language, *darrga-wara*, literally 'bone-long']
The hopping-mouse *Notomys alexis* of arid western and central Australia. It is coloured light brown above, with greyish-white below. It obtains all the water it needs by feeding on seeds, shoots, and insects. Also called *spinifex hopping-mouse* and *long-tailed hopping-mouse*. [1935]

> **1998** *Landscope*, Autumn, 34. Stomach contents of a feral cat—four tarkawarra (spinifex hopping-mice) and two mingkiri (sandy inland mice).

dibbler /'dɪblə/
Chiefly used in Western Australia.
[Southern dialect of Nyungar, Perth–Albany region, probably *dibala*.]
The small insectivorous marsupial *Parantechinus apicalis*, which used to be found in the extreme south-west, but is now almost extinct. [c. 1842]

1986 *Australian Geographic*, April, 23. The dibbler, so named by Aborigines at least a century and a half ago, averages 14 centimetres in length, has a sharp, foxy face and a curious speckled appearance due to white flecking in its fur.

dingo /ˈdɪŋɡoʊ/

[Dharuk, Sydney region probably *din-gu* (or possibly *dayn-gu*) for 'domesticated dingo'] The wolf-like dog, *Canis lupus dingo* of mainland Australia, typically tawny-yellow. Although Aborigines have been in Australia for more than 40,000 years, the dingo came here only about 4,000 years ago. The dingo is also called *warrigal* in English, but in the Sydney language, *dingo* referred to the domestic dog as distinct from *warrigal*, the wild dog. [1789]

1790 J. WHITE, *Voyage to New South Wales*, 280. [A dingo or dog of New South Wales. Plate. Description by J. HUNTER.] It is capable of barking, although not so readily as the European dogs; is very ill-natured and vicious, and snarls, howls, and moans, like dogs in common.

The word **dingo** has been used in several other ways.

1. As a term applied to a person who displays characteristics popularly attributed to the dingo, especially cowardice and treachery.

1966 A. HOPGOOD, *Private Yuk Objects*, 21. You bloody dingo … Ya could've given him a chance.

2. In combinations:

dingo's breakfast

1976 W. N. SCOTT, *Complete Book of Australian Folk Lore*, 380. A dingo's breakfast is a pee and a good look round.

dingo fence, a fence erected to exclude dingoes.

1998 M. KEENAN, *The Horses too are Gone*, 207. Yet Sal had a quick eye for beauty and when we crossed the dingo fence and entered the rangelands she instantly fell in love.

dingo hunter

1985 C. NEWSOME, *Dingo Howlers*, 1. My Uncle Cliff's ability as a great Dingo hunter and shooter were enhanced by many instinctive attributes.

dingo-hunting

1997 S. DINGO, *Dingo: The Story of Our Mob*, 5. Before his dingo-hunting, that is dogging, days, Dingo Jim … had been a tracker for the police.

dingo pack

1964 'E. LINDALL', *Kind of Justice*, 22. The sheep station had gone down to the dingo packs.

dingo-proof

> **1988** R. BRECKWOLDT, *A Very Elegant Animal Dingo*, 215. But rivers had to be crossed and major roads intersected where special gates or dingo-proof grids had to be installed. There were even dingo grids across railway lines.

dingo scalp

> **1998** G. ALLEN, *Gun Ringer*, 69. Always on their own except the few times a year they rode into Karungie to cash their dingo scalps and fill up the tucker packs.

dingo scalper

> **1963** W. E. HARNEY, *To Ayers Rock and Beyond*, 40. He was one of those tough and wiry types, who as 'doggers' or 'dingo scalpers' helped to open this land.

dingo slut, a female dingo.

> **1899** *Bulletin* [Sydney], 4 February, 14. When a dingo-slut produces a litter of pups she leaves them in charge of a mate.

dingo stiffener, one employed to eradicate dingoes.

> **1945** *Bulletin* [Sydney], 31 January, 14. The rewards hung up for dingo-stiffeners. Northern Territory offered a measly seven and sixpence per head.

dingo trap

> **1998** A. CHAMBERS, *Battlers of the Barkly*, 17. Joe was gathering dead eucalyptus leaves to kindle a fire for his quart pot and chanced to catch his fingers in a dingo trap.

dingo trapper

> **1986** *North Queensland Register*, 6 March, 9.
>
> > In a lonely bush-built humpy in a region bleak and drear,
> > Dwelt an ancient dingo trapper who had reached his hundredth year.
> > He drove into the nearest town, thro' gibber stones and scrub,
> > Climbed stiffly from his dusty cart and clumped into the pub.

3. As a verb, meaning 'to behave in a cowardly manner'.

> **1960** R. S. PORTEOUS, *Cattleman*, 161. 'Lay orf … I'm done.' The man who had backed Ben for a fiver yelled, 'Don't let 'im dingo on ya, mate. Finish 'im off!'

dunnart / ˈdʌnat/

[Nyungar, Perth–Albany region *danard* probably *Sminthopsis griseoventer*, grey-bellied dunnart.]

Any of the small narrow-footed carnivorous marsupials of the genus *Sminthopsis* of all states. There are nineteen *Sminthopsis* species, each called a type of dunnart; these include *white-footed dunnart*, *common dunnart*, *fat-tailed dunnart*,

Gilbert's dunnart, chestnut dunnart, Kakadu dunnart and *Julia Creek dunnart.*
[1910]

> **2003** *Canberra Times*, 6 October, 1. The Kapalga experiment found that many
> small native mammals, such as bandicoots and dunnarts, were especially sensitive to
> frequent fire, and populations had declined in areas that were burned every year.

euro / ˈyuroʊ /

Formerly also **euroo**, **uroo**, and **yuro**. Chiefly used in South Australia and Western
Australia.
[Adnyamathanha, Flinders Ranges, South Australia (and a number of neighbouring languages) *yuru, thuru.*]
The reddish, short-haired macropod *Macropus robustus.* Although more difficult
to hunt than a kangaroo because they live mostly on rocky outcrops, euros were
a very common food item for Aborigines. Also called *common wallaroo* or *eastern
wallaroo.* [1855]

> **2002** *Victor Harbor Times* [South Australia], 31 October, 18. The week also saw
> another two kangaroo joeys come into care. One is a little Western Grey boy who is
> not yet furred … the other is a little female euro from the north of the state.

jumbuck / ˈdʒʌmbʌk /

Formerly also **dombock**, **dumbug**, **jimba**, **jombok**, and **jumbick**.
The origin of this word, meaning a sheep, is not known. It may possibly be
from an Australian language (*dhimba* in Kamilaroi has been suggested, but this
cannot be confirmed) or else an alteration of an English phrase ('jump up' has
been suggested). A possible origin is *domba* 'sheep' in Malay; the first sheep were
brought to Australia from Cape Town, where the language of commerce was
Malay. *Jumbuck* was a prominent word in the pidgin used by white settlers to
communicate with Aborigines, and was thence borrowed into many Australian
languages as the name for an introduced animal, the sheep. [1824]

> **1854** W. HOWITT, *A Boy's Adventures in the Wilds of Australia*, 129. He did not know
> what jumbucks were, he candidly said so. 'Why, sheep man, sheep! They are jum-
> bucks in this country.'

> **1998** *Daily Telegraph*, 27 June, 47. Shearers and shed hands still work much as they
> have for decades, at the exhausting jobs of fleecing the jumbuck of its valuable coat
> and pressing the wool tightly into bales.

kaluta / kaˈlutə /

[Ngarla, Pilbara region *garlurdu* 'mouse (any kind)'. The same name may be used
in the neighbouring language Nyamal, but we have not been able to confirm this.]
The small marsupial *Dasykaluta rosamondae* found in areas of woolly spinifex in
the Pilbara region of Western Australia. It was not described until 1964, and was

then regarded as an antechinus and named *Antechinus rosamondae*. It was reclassified in 1982 and accorded the present generic name. Also called *little red kaluta*, *little red antechinus*, and *spinifex antechinus*. [1982]

> **1982** M. ARCHER, *Carnivorous Marsupials* II, 435. For *rosamondae*, I propose the generic name *Dasykaluta*. *Dasy* refers to dasyurid and means hairy. *Kaluta* is the name given to *rosamondae* by the peoples of the Nyamal linguistic group of the Pilbara region including the area involving Woodstock Station … The name would be pronounced Dásé kálútà.

kangaroo /kæŋɡəˈruː/

[Extended use of Guugu Yimidhirr, Cooktown, North Queensland *gaŋurru* 'a large black or grey kangaroo, probably specifically the male *Macropus robustus*'.] Any of the larger marsupials of the chiefly Australian family *Macropodidae*, having short forelimbs, a tail developed for support and balance, long feet and power- ful limbs, enabling a swift, bounding motion. Loosely, *kangaroo* can refer to any or all of the members of the macropodid family of kangaroos, wallaroos, and wallabies. Kangaroos were the most frequently eaten large game animal of tradi- tional Aboriginal societies. The plural is now *kangaroos* but *kangaroo* was also used formerly. The word is abbreviated sometimes to **kanga** and often to **roo**. [1770]

This is the first and best-known borrowing of an Aboriginal word into English. In 1770, when Cook was forced to make repairs to the 'Endeavour' in North Queensland, he and his party saw a number of large marsupials. He described one in particular, a peculiar animal 'of a light mouse Colour and the full size of a Grey Hound, and shaped in every respect like one, with a long tail, which it carried like a Grey Hound; in short I should have taken it for a wild dog but for its walking or running, in which it jump'd like a Hare or Deer.' Cook elicited *kangaroo* or *kanguru* as the name for the animal, which was wrongly taken to be the name for any species of kangaroo or wallaby, and became widely used.

In 1820, Captain Phillip P. King visited the Endeavour River and took down a vocabulary that agreed with Cook's, except that, instead of *kangooroo*, he was given a word transcribed as 'min-ār', 'mee-nuah', or 'mēn-ū-åh'. Some people sug- gested that Cook and Banks had made a mistake, and it was even suggested that, when asked the name of the animal, a Guugu Yimidhirr person had said 'I don't know', this being the true meaning of *kangaroo* (as if any Aborigine would not know the name for the animal!).

The pioneer ethnologist W. E. Roth wrote a letter to the *Australasian*, published 2 July 1898, pointing out that *gang-oo-roo* was the name in Guugu Yimidhirr for a species of kangaroo, but this newspaper correspondence apparently went unnoticed by lexicographers. Finally, the observations of Cook and Roth were confirmed when, in 1972, the linguist John Haviland began an intensive study of Guugu Yimidhirr and again recorded *gaŋurru*. Haviland also pointed out that the word recorded in 1820 must have been *minha* 'edible animal'. King probably pointed at several species of kangaroo other than the large black variety, and the Guugu Yimidhirr might not have connected his pronunciation /ˈkæŋɡəˈruː/ with the word /ˈɡaɲurru/ or /ˈkaɲurru/.

Joseph Banks gave Governor Phillip his vocabulary of the 'New Holland language', and Phillip mistakenly thought that it must have been taken down at Botany Bay. Members of the First Fleet employed the word *kangaroo* in talking to the local Aborigines, and must have used it in connection with a variety of marsupials. The Iora people thought they were being taught the English word for 'edible animal'; when cattle were unloaded the Aborigines enquired whether they were *kangaroo*.

The story doesn't end there. When Europeans settled along the Darling River, the English word *kangaroo* (an original loan from Guugu Yimidhirr) was taken over into the Baagandji language (with the form *gaaŋgurru*) as the name for the introduced animal 'horse'.

> **2001** *Coober Pedy Regional Times*, 26 April, 17. When a kangaroo is killed on the road many people know to check if the kangaroo has a joey in its pouch; if there is, it is given to these ladies to be looked after.

The word **kangaroo** is used in a number of other ways.

1. With a distinguishing word:
antelope kangaroo, the kangaroo *Macropus antilopinus* of north Australia; **brush kangaroo**, or *brush wallaby*, a small kangaroo with coarse, dark, reddish fur; **bush kangaroo**, a medium-sized kangaroo; **eastern grey kangaroo**, the kangaroo *Macropus giganteus*, of eastern Australia, having silvery-grey fur; **(great) grey kangaroo**, the *eastern grey kangaroo* or the *western grey kangaroo*; **hill kangaroo**, the wallaroo; **Kangaroo Island kangaroo**, the kangaroo *Macropus fuliginosus fuliginosus*, also called *sooty kangaroo* because of its brown colour; **red kangaroo**, or **red plain kangaroo**, the large kangaroo *Macropus rufus*, widely distributed in drier inland Australia, having red to blue-grey fur above and white below (the name **red kangaroo** can also refer to any of several other red macropods); **rock kangaroo**, any of several forms of euro or wallaroo; and **western grey kangaroo**, the kangaroo *Macropus fuliginosus* of semi-arid southern Australia.

2. Figuratively, to mean:
a. an Australian, especially a member of the armed services or one representing Australia in a sport; Australia as so represented. In plural form, the name of the Australian international Rugby League team.

> **1898** *Truth* [Sydney], 23 January, 3. The English team of cricketers, lately badly walloped by the kangaroo.

b. In the phrase, **to have kangaroos in the top paddock**, to be crazy or eccentric.

> **1908** *Australian Magazine* [Sydney], November, 1250. If you show signs of mental weakness you are either balmy, dotty, ratty, or cracked, or you may even have … kangaroos in your top paddock.

3. In the names of flora and fauna:

kangaroo acacia, see *kangaroo thorn*.

kangaroo apple, any of several shrubs chiefly of southern and eastern Australia, especially *Solanum aviculare*, *Solanum laciniatum* and *Solanum vescum* (see *gunyang*), bearing an egg-shaped fruit edible when completely ripe (the fruit has the same name).

kangaroo bush, either *punty* or the 'sandhill wattle' (*Acacia burkittii*).

kangaroo fish, either the 'Burnett salmon' or 'Lungfish', *Neoceratodus forsteri*, found chiefly in Queensland, or the 'mudskipper', a small amphibious marine fish of tropical northern Australia and elsewhere.

kangaroo fly, a small and intensely irritating fly, probably any of several species.

kangaroo grass, the tall, tussocky, perennial grass *Themeda triandra*, widely distributed throughout Australia and occurring elsewhere; or, loosely, any of several other similar grasses.

kangaroo mouse, any of the very small species of the genus *Microdipodops*.

kangaroo paw, any plant of the genera *Anigozanthos* and *Macropidia*, perennials of the south-west of Western Australia, having distinctive elongated, paw-like flowers, especially the red-and-green flowering *Anigozanthos manglesii*, floral emblem of Western Australia.

kangaroo prickly acacia, see *kangaroo thorn*.

kangaroo rabbit *obsolete*, see *kangaroo rat*.

kangaroo rat, any of the small wallabies, including the bettong and potoroo, most species of which have a fast hopping gait and construct a nest with material carried in the tail (these are always referred to by zoologists as *rat-kangaroos*).

kangaroo thorn, the prickly shrub *Acacia paradoxa*, of all mainland states, but not the Northern Territory, naturalised in Tasmania and often planted as a hedge.

kangaroo tick, either of two ticks having the kangaroo or wallaby as chief host, the tick *Ornithodoros gurneyi* of arid inland Australia, the bite of which can severely affect a human, and the tick *Amblyomma triguttatum*.

4. In the following combinations:

kangaroo bar, also known as *roo bar* or *bull bar*, a strong metal bar or frame mounted at the front of a vehicle to reduce damage to the vehicle in the event of a collision with an animal, particularly a kangaroo.

> **1975** R. BEILBY, *Brown Land Crying*, 274. His vehicle was a late-model bone-white station wagon with plenty of chrome and massive kangaroo-bars forming a protective grid in front of the radiator grille.

> **2001** R. SMOLKER, *To Touch a Wild Dolphin*, 22. The kangaroos are such a hazard that most vehicles travelling outside of city limits are equipped with a 'roo bar' to protect the front of the car from damage should a roo be hit, as is practically inevitable.

kangaroo bone, a bone from a kangaroo, used by Aborigines as a tool or as an item of personal adornment.

1933 J. E. HAMMOND, *Winjan's People*, 31. The 'bouka' was worn with the fur inside, and clasped around the neck like a shawl and fastened in front with a kangaroo bone as a pin.

kangaroo camp, a place where kangaroos usually congregate.

1946 *Service Publication No. 6* [School of Public Health and Tropical Medicine], 258. Specimens that he had found in what he considered their natural habitat, a kangaroo camp about twenty miles north of Tibooburra.

kangaroo cloak, a cloak made from kangaroo skin.

1830 S. H. COLLINS, *A Geographical Description of Australasia*, 17. Most of them wore kangaroo cloaks, which were their only cloathing [sic].

kangaroo closure

1936 H. D. INGHAM, *Australasian Secretarial Principles*, 75. A method adopted in Parliamentary committees by which the chairman is permitted to select what amendments he considers are relevant to the question and 'jump over' those he thinks are not worth considering.

kangaroo corroboree, see *kangaroo dance*.

1898 D. W. CARNEGIE, *Spinifex and Sand*, 331. The kangaroo-corroboree, in which a man hops towards the musicians and back again, to be followed in turn by every other dancer and finally by the whole lot, who advance hopping together, ending up with a wild yell, in which all join.

kangaroo court, an improperly constituted court having no legal standing. Often one that disregards or parodies established principles of law or moral rights.

1988 *Age* [Melbourne], 4 March, 7. But Mr Gallagher said he would not 'turn up at any hearing for a kangaroo court which has the whole aim of destroying the BLF'.

kangaroo dance, an Aboriginal ceremonial dance in which the dancers' movements represent the movements of a kangaroo.

1988 *Royal Commission into Aboriginal Deaths in Custody*, 225. What sort of dance do you do? … There's Kangaroo dance, emu dance, crocodile dance, shake a leg.

kangaroo dog (bitch, hound), a dog used for hunting the kangaroo; (specifically) a breed of dog evolved in Australia from the Scottish deerhound and the greyhound for this purpose.

2001 B. MARSH, *Great Australian Shearing Stories*, 191. Now, I don't know if you've ever seen one of these kangaroo dogs or not, but they're built for speed, as you might imagine, with them having to catch kangaroos.

kangaroo drive, an operation in which kangaroos are herded, trapped and slaughtered, or otherwise hunted.

1930 *Aussie* [Sydney], 15 May, 14. One of the preliminaries was a kangaroo drive. A patch of country was encircled by the hunters, who gradually closed upon a narrow valley. There they rushed upon the hunted, and the yelling, dancing lines, the flying and clattering of spears and boomerangs, so confused the animals that dozens were easily killed.

kangaroo feather, (in the war of 1914–18) a jocular name for an emu plume worn on the hat of a member of the Australian Light Horse.

1937 R. FAIRBRIDGE, *Pinjarra*, 189. A good many young women had lost their hearts to some fine upstanding young man with a 'Kangaroo feather in his hat'.

kangaroo fence, a fence made to exclude kangaroos.

1988 *Townsville Bulletin*, 28 March, 3. At $920 a kilometre, farmers may find a Melbourne University-developed kangaroo fence expensive … It consists of sloping electric wires at the bottom and plain wire at the top.

kangaroo flesh

1848 *The Emigrant's Friend; or Authentic Guide to South Australia*, 26. The colony at first suffered great hardships, so much so, that eighteen-pence per pound was given for kangaroo flesh.

kangaroo fur

1842 *Colonial Observer* [Sydney], 23 March, 198. The officer … obtained from them a belt composed of small kangaroo fur, commonly worn by the natives of this coast.

kangaroo ground, a place where kangaroos gather.

1861 'AN OLD BUSHMAN', *Bush Wanderings of a Naturalist*, 19. There is a good kangaroo-ground up by the Yarra.

kangaroo hedge *obsolete*, a hedge of kangaroo thorn.

1882 E. B. BAYLY, *Alfreda Holme*, 67. 'Here our place begins,' said Mr Raymond, pointing to a dark line of kangaroo hedge on their right.

kangaroo hide, the skin of the kangaroo.

2000 D. MALOUF, *Dream Stuff*, 16. His most prized possessions were a pair of scuffed riding boots … and a belt of plaited kangaroo hide.

kangaroo hop, *kangaroo start*.

1979 J. J. MCROACH, *Dozen Dopey Yarns*, 75. She … rushes past us … and into a Volkswagen. She starts it, jumps it forward about eight feet, stalls, starts again and kangaroo hops.

kangaroo hunt

> **2001** *Koori Mail*, 7 March, 11. He told the court he had participated in a kangaroo hunt with Possum in 1989 during which he ate kangaroo intestines and drank kangaroo blood, giving him a skin name and certain status within Possum's tribe.

kangaroo jack, a heavy-duty, lever-action jack, used especially to lift logs and stumps.

> **1977** J. DOUGHTY, *Gold in Blood*, 209. A kangaroo jack, one of those huge, box-like affairs that weigh about a hundredweight and will lift anything.

kangaroo joey, a young kangaroo.

> **1957** *Bulletin* [Sydney], 27 November, 16. In outback Queensland we reared dozens of kangaroo-joeys, with few fatalities.

kangaroo knapsack, a knapsack made from kangaroo skin.

> **1984** G. BLAINEY, *Our Side of the Country*, 33. The shearers from Tasmania wore tall hats and carried everything in kangaroo knapsacks known as Derwent drums.

kangaroo land, Australia.

> **1900** *Western Champion* [Barcaldine], 24 April, 7. The Boers, appearing to be struck with panic, bolted into the ravines, hoping the Australians would rush in after them and be slaughtered, but the men from kangaroo land declined the invitation.

kangaroo leap, a sudden or jolting bound (also used figuratively).

> **1966** J. ALDRIDGE, *My Brother Tom*, 171. There was no dramatic dog fight, no picture of Tom tearing apart the northern skies with his kangaroo leaps from star to star.

kangaroo leather

> **1998** *The Land* [North Richmond, NSW], 23 July, 83. Handbags, wallets, portfolios, bumbags, purses, key cases, dilly bags, golfing gear, caps, travel bags, all made from the strongest leather in the world, Kangaroo Leather!

kangaroo mat, a floor rug made from kangaroo skin.

> **1972** *Bulletin* [Sydney], 15 January, 25. In one of the 30 or so souvenir stops … are three Tokyo tourists, flapping kangaroo mats and stroking koalas.

kangaroo meat

> **1960** *Countryman* [Perth], 28 July, 12. Jumping steak, as some cynics call kangaroo meat, has become big business in Australia.

kangaroo net, a net used by Aborigines to snare kangaroos.

> **1870** E. B. KENNEDY, *Four Years in Queensland*, 80. Kangaroo nets, some of them forty yards long, and in mesh and substance like a cricket net, were rolled up in bundles.

kangaroo route, a name for the Sydney–Singapore–London air route.

> **2000** *Qantas: Australian Way*, November, 73. Qantas was no different. On December 1, 1947 it began the first regular 1/2 weekly service through to London on the now-famous Kangaroo Route, a journey which then took four days.

kangaroo rug, a rug made from kangaroo skin.

> **1878** R. BROUGH SMYTH, *The Aborigines of Victoria*, I, 123. When evening arrives … the leader … stops, throws down his kangaroo rug (*Mogra*), sticks his spears in the ground, and at once commences important duties.

kangaroo scalp

> **1885** *Bulletin* [Sydney], 5 December, 10. Kangaroo-scalps are paid for at the rate of 9d. each.

kangaroo sinew, a kangaroo tendon used for binding or tying, or for personal adornment.

> **1832** J. BACKHOUSE, *A Narrative of a Visit to the Australian Colonies* (1843), 84. They also wear necklaces formed of Kangaroo-sinews rolled in red ochre.

kangaroo skin

> **1892** J. FRASER, *The Aborigines of New South Wales*, 47. A kangaroo skin, with the hair worn inwards, is a favourite kind of cloak in wet weather.

kangaroo soup

> **1837** *South Australian Record* [London], 11 November, 14. A tureen of kangaroo soup, is a dish that you would relish even in London.

kangaroo spear *obsolete*, a spear used by Aborigines to kill kangaroos.

> **1886** R. HENTY, *Australiana*, 9. He was one of my instructors in the mysteries of Australian bush life, such as throwing … the kangaroo spear.

kangaroo start (of a motor vehicle), a jerking start, as with a worn clutch or an inexperienced driver (also as a verb); cf. *kangaroo hop*.

> **1971** D. IRELAND. *The Unknown Industrial Prisoner*, 308. The Mercedes made a few kangaroo starts and then lurched off up the road.

kangaroo steak, a piece of kangaroo meat cut and cooked in the manner of beef-steak.

> **1836** *Historical Records of Victoria* (1982), I, 71. Kangaroo steaks also 'smoked upon the board' occasionally, but as they require a great deal of seasoning and cooking I do not think them so good as English beef steaks.

kangaroo steamer, a stew made from kangaroo meat.

> **1864** *The Colonial Cookbook* (1970), 70. Kangaroo Steamer … Take the most tender part of the kangaroo … chop it very fine, about the same quantity of smoked bacon (fat); season with finely-powdered marjoram, pepper, and a very little salt. Let it 'steam', or 'stew', for two hours; then pack or press tight in open-mouthed glass bottles.

kangaroo stew

> **1881** E. DAVIES, *The Story of an Earnest Life*, 132. Around the camp-fire were several men preparing kangaroo stew, and cockatoo pie and damper.

kangaroo tail, the tail of a kangaroo as an article of food, especially **kangaroo-tail soup**.

> **1989** *Countryman* [Perth], 6 November, 14. Emu patties, freshwater lobster and kangaroo tail soup were on last week's conference dinner.

kangaroo tooth, the tooth of a kangaroo, as used for personal decoration.

> **1833** W. H. BRETON, *Excursions in New South Wales, Western Australia, and Van Dieman's Land*, 210. The only ornament that I procured was a string of kangaroo teeth.

Kangaroo Valley, a name given to Earl's Court, a district of London.

> **1965** H. PORTER, *The Cats of Venice*, 108. Londoners call Earl's Court—you can readily imagine the tone of voice—Kangaroo Valley. That's because it's the address of the Australians, the invaders, the temporary, the hit-and-run, cut-and-come-again yahoos, the colonial vagabonds, the loud-mouthed and light-fingered rowdies, the uncouth, irreverent, cock-sure, yankee-ized and so on and so forth so-and-sos.

5. As a verb, meaning 'to hunt the kangaroo' or 'to leap in a manner resembling that of a kangaroo'.

> **1968** D. O'GRADY, *Bottle of Sandwiches*, 136. Kangarooing our way up the track in half-mile jumps. Stop, swear, fill, drive.

The word has also been used figuratively to mean 'to squat over (a lavatory) with one's feet on the seat'.

> **1964** A. H. AFFLECK, *The Wandering Years*, 74. Please don't kangaroo the seat, our breed of crab can leap six feet.

koala /koʊˈalə/

Formerly also **coola** and **koolah**.

[Dharuk, Sydney region *gula*, *gulawañ*. The early spellings *coola* and *koolah* were gradually replaced by the tri-syllabic *koala*, probably because of a scribal error.]

The tree-living, mainly nocturnal marsupial of eastern Australia, *Phascolarctos cinereus*, having a stout body, thick, grey-brown fur with a pale underside, large round furry ears, a leathery nose, and strong claws. It feeds largely on the leaves of certain eucalypts, and is the faunal emblem of Queensland. The koala has also been called *monkey bear*, *native bear*, *tree-bear*, and *koala bear*. It is sometimes said that *koala* is a word in 'the Aboriginal language' meaning 'doesn't drink'; this is entirely erroneous. (The name for koala was *gurrborra* in the Melbourne language, Wuywurung, and *dumbirbi* in the Brisbane language, Yagara.) [1798]

> **1886** D. M. GANE, *New South Wales and Victoria in 1885*, 171. In admitting that we shot this koala, we must inform our readers that it was not for the mere satisfaction of bringing it down, but principally for the acquisition of its skin.

kowari /kəˈwari/
[Diyari, Lake Eyre region, and Ngamini, about Goyder's Lagoon, South Australia *kawiri*.]
The brushy-tailed carnivorous marsupial, *Dasyuroides byrnei*, yellow-brown in colour with a striking black brush on its tail. It occurs in the sparsely vegetated stony deserts of the Lake Eyre basin. Also known as *Byrne's pouched mouse*. *Cowarie station* (on the Birdsville track) is named after this animal. [1873]

> **1985** V. SERVENTY, *The Desert Sea*, 104. The kowari … looks something like the mulgara, but has a more prominent black brush tail and lives in a hole in the ground during the day.

kultarr /ˈkʊlta/
[Gerard Krefft recorded the name in 1857 from Aborigines (probably speaking the Yitha-yitha language) at Gol Gol near Mildura; they said the animal was rare but thought it was called *kultarr*. W. D. L. Ride revived the name in his *A Guide to the Native Mammals of Australia*, 1970.]
The long-legged marsupial mouse, *Antechinomys laniger*, which bounds rapidly from short forelegs to long hind legs. This gait enables it to pivot on its forefeet and quickly change direction to escape a predator. Also called *wuhl-wuhl*. [1857]

> **1983** R. STRAHAN. *Complete Book of Australian Mammals*, 73. Once considered to be the marsupial equivalent of hopping-mice, the Kultarr was long known as the Jerboa-marsupial.

kumarl /ˈkʊmæl/
Also **goomal**. Chiefly used in Western Australia.
[Nyungar, Perth–Albany region *gumal*.]
The common brushtail possum, *Trichosurus vulpecula*. [1831]

1912 D. BATES, *Native Tribes of W.A.*, 120. One day while the wild cat was away hunting, an opossum (goomal) came along and made indecent proposals to the emu.

mala /ˈmalə/
Also **maala**, and **marla**.
[Western Desert language *mala*.]
The small *rufous hare-wallaby, Lagorchestes hirsutus*, which was abundant in the sandhill country of west and central Australia but is now found only on Bernier and Dorre Islands off Shark Bay, Western Australia. [c. 1842]

> **1990** O. NOONUCCAL, *Australian Legends and Landscapes*, 88. The Mala, or rufous hare wallaby, was once common throughout western central Australia and provided both a regular food source and one of the principal totemic associations for the clans that hunted there.

mapi /ˈmapi/
Also **mabi**, and **mapi-mapi**, which is the plural form in the Australian languages.
[Dyirbal and Yidiny from the Cardwell–Cairns region, North Queensland *mabi*.]
A name for *Lumholtz's tree kangaroo*, also called *boongarry*. An area of complex notophyll vine forest (which this tree kangaroo inhabits), on the Atherton Tableland, North Queensland, has recently been named **Mabi Forest**. [1895]

> **c. 1934** R. M. CROOKSTON, 'The unseen tragedy of the Aborigines' (Lutheran Church archives, Adelaide), 2. An expert tree-climbing native came with us into the scrub to spot, climb for, and chase down Mapi, the tree-climbing 'roo, from his perch on the branches sixty or seventy feet up till he jumped and gave us a chance to catch him by the tail.

mardo /ˈmadoʊ/
Used in Western Australia.
[Nyungar, Perth–Albany region *mardu*.]
The yellow-footed marsupial mouse, *Antechinus flavipes leucogaster*, which lives in dry forest and woodland. It eats insects, nectar, and small birds, and often pilfers food from suburban gardens. [1839]

> **1998** *Landscope*, Spring, 6. The nest boxes are for species, such as brush-tailed possums, brush-tailed phascogales, mardos and bats, which need tree hollows.

marl /mal/
Chiefly used in Western Australia.
[Nyungar, Perth–Albany region *maarl* and *marla* (dialectical variants).]
The small *western barred bandicoot, Perameles bougainville*, light grey-brown above and white below, with a striped rump, originally occurring across much of

arid southern Australia, but now only on Bernier and Dorre Islands, Shark Bay, Western Australia. [1840]

> **1983** F. HADDON & T. OLIVER, *The Gould League Book of Australian Endangered Wildlife*, 27. The reason for the marl being so vicious towards each other in captivity is that in the wild they defend their territories against animals of their own species.

marloo /ˈmalu/
Also **merloo**.
[Western Desert language *marlu*]
A Western Australian name for the *red kangaroo, Macropus rufus*. [1910]

> **1984** W. W. AMMON et al., *Working Lives*, 149. The big red roos, the marloo, keep to the plain country.

mingkiri /ˈmɪŋkəri/
Also **menkie**.
[Western Desert language, *min-giri*.]
The mouse, *Pseudomys hermannsburgensis*, of sandy spinifex country from the Pilbara through to central Queensland. Also called *sandy inland mouse*, and *Hermannsburg mouse* (from Hermannsburg Mission in the Northern Territory, where it was first described). [1923]

> **1923** F. WOOD JONES, *The Mammals of South Australia*, 319. This little mouse has a wide distribution in the Centre. The original specimens came from Hermannsburg, Central Australia, where it is known to the natives by the name 'Menkie'.

> **1996** *Landscope*, Autumn, 25. The good season, with abundant grass seed, meant that large numbers of tarrkawarras (spinifex hopping-mice) and mingkiris (sandy inland mice) were also captured.

monjon /ˈmɒndʒɒn/
[Wunambal, North Kimberley, Western Australia, *monjon*.]
The smallest rock wallaby, *Petrogale burbidgei*, which is restricted to rugged, inhospitable parts of the Kimberley region, Western Australia. It was only identi-fied in 1978, and initially was called *warabi*, which was thought to be its name in Wunambal. This animal was renamed, in 1990, as *monjon*, which is its name in Wunambal. [1990]

> **2000** M. KEENAN, *Wild Horses Don't Swim*, 266. Species at risk in the area include the orange leaf-nosed bat, pygmy long-eared bat, yellow-lipped bat, Carpentarian dunnart, monjon, Lakeland Downs mouse, nabarlek, scaly-tailed possum and golden-backed tree rat.

mulgara /ˈmʌlgərə/, /məlˈgarə/
[Probably Wangganguru, north South Australia *mardagura*.]
The small carnivorous marsupial, *Dasycercus cristicauda*, which inhabits burrows in sandy regions of drier Australia. [1923]

> **1941** E. TROUGHTON, *Furred Animals of Australia*, 33. A rat which provided a meal for three hungry Mulgaras was skinned as by a skilled taxidermist, no bones being left attached to the skin which was inside-out and almost perfect.

mundarda /mʌnˈdadə/
Chiefly used in Western Australia.
[Nyungar, Perth–Albany region, probably *mandarda*.]
The *western pygmy possum*, *Cercartetus concinnus*, which resembles a minute ball of soft, red-brown hair. [1840]

> **1840** G. GREY, *A Vocabulary of the Dialects of South Western Australia*, 89. Mundar-da—a small species of mouse, which is generally found in the tops of Xanthorrhea [grass trees].

nabarlek /ˈnabəlɛk/
[Gunwinygu, central Arnhem Land *na-barlek* (*na-* is the masculine gender prefix).]
The *little rock wallaby*, *Petrogale concinna*, which occurs in the Kimberley region of Western Australia (this habitat just crossing the border into the Northern Territory) and in eastern Arnhem Land. It only appears after dark in the dry season, but in the wet may bask in rocks for some hours after dawn. *Nabarlek* has been adopted by Queensland Mines as the name of a mine. [1970]

> **2000** *Wild: Australia's Wilderness Adventure Magazine*, April, 60. The mammals were not so easy to spot. We did see a northern nail-tailed wallaby and euros and the odd rock wallaby (nabarlek) but failed to catch any glimpse of smaller animals such as quolls, possums and Antechinuses as we had hoped.

nanto /ˈnæntoʊ/
Also **nanta**, **nantah**, and **nantu**.
A horse. [1839]
[Gaurna, Adelaide region (and many other languages of South Australia) *nhandu*, which means 'male kangaroo'. The horse was originally called in Gaurna *bindi nhandu*, literally 'European kangaroo'. *Bindi* ('habitation of souls before birth and after death') had been extended to mean 'European'.]

> **1924** F. J. MILLS, *Happy Days*, 8. 'That ain't much of a lookin' nanto,' said one, indicating a large chestnut horse.

noolbenger /'nulbɛŋgə/
Chiefly used in Western Australia.
[Southern dialect of Nyungar, Perth–Albany region, probably *ŋulbuŋgur*.]
The tiny *honey possum*, *Tarsipes rostratus*, which has a long snout and brush-tipped tongue. [1840]

> **c. 1842** H. M. WHITTELL, 'John Gilbert's Notebook on Marsupials', *Western Australian Naturalist*, 4 [1954], 112. Nool-boon-goor, Aborigines of King George's Sound. This little creature inhabits the smaller trees from the blossom of which, like the Meliphagidae, it is constantly extracting honey and minute insects.

numbat /'nʌmbæt/
[Nyungar, Perth–Albany region *numbad*.]
The small, termite-eating marsupial, *Myrmecobius fasciatus*, now occurring only in south-west Western Australia and rare. It has red to grey-brown fur with light stripes across the back and rump, and is sometimes called a *banded anteater*. [1842]

> **2000** A. GOODE, *For Love of the Land*, 236. It takes 400 years for a mallee tree to grow a hollow in it big enough for a numbat to live in.

pademelon /'pædimɛlən/
Also **paddymelon** and formerly with much variety, as **pademella**, **paddymalla**, and **paddymellon**.
[Probably from Dharuk, Sydney region *badimaliyan*, altered by folk etymology to *paddy-melon*. *Paddymelon* is also a name for a plant (p.143).]
Any of several small, compact-bodied wallabies of the genus *Thylogale*, inhabiting dense vegetation in moist forests of eastern Australia, including Tasmania, and New Guinea. The *red-legged pademelon*, *Thylogale stigmatica*, is found in forests on the coast of Queensland and northern New South Wales; the *red-necked pademelon*, *Thylogale thetis*, is found further south, from southern Queensland to central New South Wales, while the *rufous-bellied* (or *red-bellied*) *pademelon*, *Thylogale billardierii* is now restricted to Tasmania. A **paddymelon stick** (*obsolete*) was an Aboriginal weapon used as a missile in hunting small game. [1802]

> **1977** W. A. WINTER-IRVING, *Bush Stories*, 91. What we called the pademelons, small kangaroo rats … were numerous and … would explode from a scrubby bush, hopping in panic to escape a passing rider and sometimes collide with the horses.

parma wallaby /'pamə wɒləbi/
[Dharawal, Illawarra region, New South Wales, probably *bama*.]
The greyish-brown wallaby, with a white throat and white cheek stripe, *Macropus parma*, first reported from the Illawarra region and then believed to be extinct in Australia. However, Sir George Grey had introduced it to Kawau Island,

New Zealand, where it has thrived. And it has recently been reported (in small numbers) in wet forest along the Great Dividing Range north of Sydney. Formerly also called *parma kangaroo*. [c. 1842]

> c. 1842 H. A. LONGMAN, 'John Gould's Notes for John Gilbert', *Memoirs of the Queensland Museum*, VII (1922), 291. Three kinds of wallaby run in the brushes of Illawarra, viz., *Halmaturus ualabatus*, *H. Tithys* (the common pademellan, a red-necked kind), and a nearly allied species called 'Pama' by the natives. Of this latter, which is very like *Derbyanus*, I wish as many specimens and crania as convenient.

pinkie /'pɪŋki/
Also **pinky**.
[Gaurna, Adelaide region *biŋgu*.]
A South Australian name for the *greater bilby*, *Macrotis lagotis*. [1840]

> 1926 A. S. LE SOEUF et al. *Wild Animals of Australasia*, 299. White men in the bush usually refer to the species as the 'pinkie' or the 'bielby'.

pitchi-pitchi /'pɪtʃi-pɪtʃi/
[Western Desert language, *btjibiji*.]
The long-legged marsupial mouse, *Antechinomys laniger spenceri*, a sub-species of *Antechinomys laniger* (see *kultarr*), with scattered populations in central and western Australia. [1937]

> 1987 *Woman's Day*, 19 January, 105. This pretty little animal is called a wuhl-wuhl or a pitchi-pitchi. It is a marsupial-carnivore.

potoroo /pɒtə'ru/
[Probably from Dharuk, Sydney region *badaru*.]
Any small, long-nosed, nocturnal animal of the genus *Potorous*. Also known as *rat-kangaroo*. Both a zoological genus (*Potorous*) and a family (Potoridae) have been named after it. The *broad-faced potoroo*, *Potorous platyops*, from the south-west, has been extinct for more than a hundred years. The *long-footed potoroo*, *Potorous longipes*, and *Gilbert's potoroo*, *Potorous gilbertii*, are confined to very small areas in the south-east and south-west respectively. The *long-nosed potoroo*, *Potorous tridactylus*, is common in Tasmania, but now rare in coastal woodlands on the mainland. [1789]

> 1989 *Age* [Melbourne], 29 September, 18. Hawthorn had interesting characters, modest men like John Kennedy junior. He inhabited the same landscape as his father and observed the same laws, but there, it seemed, the similarities ended. The old man dominated the sky like a wedge-tail eagle, the son was content to lope along the ground like a potoroo.

quenda /ˈkwɛndə/
Chiefly used in Western Australia.
[Nyungar, Perth–Albany region *gwerndi, gwernda* (dialectal variants).]
The short-nosed southern brown bandicoot, *Isoodon obesulus*. [1831]

> **1968** *Western Australian Naturalist*, 178. Many mammals dig burrows as heat refuges, but the Quenda typically builds a mound-like nest of grass and litter. I have observed released animals taking refuge under the skirt of needle-like leaves surrounding low-growing Blackboys, and inspection of a number of these trees in the Roleystone area revealed scratchings underneath which suggested that they were frequented by bandicoots.

quokka /ˈkwɒkə/
Formerly also **quagga**.
[Nyungar, Perth–Albany region, probably *gwaga*.]
The small, *short-tailed wallaby*, *Setonix brachyurus*, of south-west Western Australia (common on Rottnest and Bald Islands), having long, greyish-brown fur. [1831]

> **1968** V. SERVENTY, *Southern Walkabout*, 150. It is the famous quokka, one of the pademelon wallabies, which creates most interest. It was this wallaby, mistaken by a Dutch visitor Vlaming for a large rodent, which led to the island's name, Rottnest or 'Rat's Nest'.

quoll /kwɒl/
[Guugu Yimidhirr, Cooktown, Queensland *dhigul* for *Dasyurus hallucatus*.]
Any of the several carnivorous, long-tailed, spotted marsupials of the genus *Dasyurus* of Australia, including Tasmania, and New Guinea. Originally called *native cat*; the name *quoll* was recorded on Captain Cook's voyage, but was not adopted until the middle of the twentieth century. The *northern quoll, Dasyurus hallucatus*, was formerly found across northern Australia, but has now contracted; the *spot-tailed quoll, Dasyurus maculatus*, occurs near the east and south-east coasts, and in Tasmania; the *western quoll, Dasyurus geoffroii* (also called *chuditch*) was in the centre and west; and the *eastern quoll, Dasyurus viverrinus*, is probably extinct on the mainland, but common in Tasmania. [1770]

> **1770** J. BANKS, *The Endeavour Journal of Joseph Banks, 1768–1771*, II (1962), 117. Another [quadruped] was calld [*sic*] by the natives Je-quoll; it is about the size of, and something like, a pole-cat, of a light brown, spotted with white on the back, and white under the belly.

tammar /ˈtæmə/
Also **tamar** and formerly **dama**, **damar**, and **tamma**.
[Nyungar, Perth–Albany region *damar*.]

The greyish-brown wallaby, *Macropus eugenii*, of southern South Australia and south-west Western Australia (including adjacent islands). Also called *tammar wallaby, scrub wallaby*. [1831]

> **1976** *Ecos*, VII, 10. The tammar, a small wallaby-like animal, likes a closed scrub canopy.

tillikin /ˈtɪləkɪn/
[Probably Yitha-yitha, south-west New South Wales (north of Mildura) *diligin*.]
The white-tailed rat, *Leporillus apicalis*, which built its nests of sticks, often in caves and overhangs. It is believed to be extinct. Also called *lesser stick-nest rat* and *white-tipped stick-nest rat*. [1866]

> **1862** G. KREFFT, *Transactions of the Philosophical Society of New South Wales*, 1866 5. Tillikin of the natives … They are gregarious in their habits. I have dislodged as many as 15 specimens from a single tree, and kept large numbers in captivity. They became quite tame; and many which had escaped would return to join my frugal supper at night, and help themselves, to damper especially. This is a very graceful animal, strictly nocturnal in its habits, and its flesh white, tender, and well-tasted.

toolache /tuˈleɪtʃi/
Also **toolach**, and formerly **toolatchee** and **dulachie**.
[Yaralde, mouth of Murray River, South Australia, probably *dulaj*.]
The large wallaby, *Macropus greyi*, formerly of south-eastern South Australia and adjacent Victoria, now extinct. [1879]

> **2001** *Advertiser* [Adelaide]. 22 September (Magazine Section), 6. Especially sad was the toolache wallaby, a fleet creature hunted for sport and skin. When they tried to herd up the last pocket from the South-East to place on a sanctuary on Kangaroo Island, they over-extended the creatures' stamina and most died from exhaustion or shock.

tuan /ˈtyuən/
Chiefly used in Victoria.
[Wathawurung, Geelong region (and neighbouring languages), Victoria *duwan*, probably originally the name for a small, gliding possum, extended by settlers to cover the brush-tail phascogale. See Luise Hercus' article on the tuan in *Victorian Naturalist*, Vol. 105, No. 2, pp. 4–8, 1988.]
The *brush-tail phascogale* or *common wambenger*, *Phascogale tapoatafa*. It is nocturnal, mostly solitary, and shy, thus being rarely seen. [1842]

> **1845** MRS THOMPSON, *Life in the Bush*, 20. We sometimes got some skins of the … flying squirrel, or tuan, from the natives.

tungoo /'tʌŋgu/, /'tʌŋgoʊ/
Also **tungo, tchungoo.**
[Western Desert language *juŋgu.*]
A central Australian name for the rat-kangaroo, *Bettongia lesueur*; also called *burrowing bettong* or *boodie*. [1924]

> **1924** F. WOOD JONES, *The Mammals of South Australia*, II, 211. When times are bad, and when the cattle and rabbits have eaten all the herbage of the sand hills, the Tungoos become extremely bold, and will enter a homestead in their search for anything to eat. They will come into a room and boldly face a cat in order to obtain some potato peelings; they will scramble over a paling fence four or five feet high in order to get at the vegetable garden. They are bold and enterprising little animals which have made, and are making, a brave struggle against what seems an almost inevitable extermination.

wallaby /'wɒləbi/
Formerly also with much variety, as **wallaba, wallabee, wallabi, wollaba,** and **wollabi.**
[Dharuk, Sydney region *walabi* or *waliba* (sources vary).]
Any of about two dozen smaller marsupials of the family *Macropodidae* (the larger marsupials are kangaroos) of the genera *Macropus, Wallabia, Lagorchestes, Lagostrophus, Onychogalea, Petrogale, Thylogale,* and *Setonix*. [1798]

> **1798** D. COLLINS, *An Account of the English Colony in New South Wales*, I, 614. *Wali-bah*, black [kangaroo].

> **1799** *Ibid.*, II (1802), 167. The grey kangaroo ... abounded in the open forest; the brushes were tenanted by the smaller black kind, or, as it is named by the natives of Port Jackson, the Wal-li-bah:

The word **wallaby** has been used in several other ways.

1. With a distinguishing word, for example:
agile wallaby, the large sandy-brown wallaby, *Macropus agilis*, of Western Australia, the Northern Territory, Queensland and New Guinea; **Bennett's wallaby**, the brownish-grey wallaby, *Macropus rufogriseus rufogriseus*, of Tasmania and Bass Strait islands (formerly also known as *Bennett's kangaroo*); **black-gloved wallaby**, the wallaby, *Macropus irma*, of south-west Australia, having black fore-feet; **brush wallaby**, any of several macropodids, usually larger wallabies, of coastal scrubs and more open inland forest; **hare wallaby** (also called *spinifex wallaby* and *grass wallaby*), any of several small wallabies of the genera *Lagorchestes* and *Lagostrophus* of mainland Australia; **nail-tailed wallaby**, any of three species of wallaby of the genus *Onychogalea*, members of which have a horny nail at the tip of the tail (the *bridled nail-tailed wallaby* is the wallaby *Onychogalea fraenata*, now

found only in mid-east Queensland, with bridle-like markings on the head and shoulder); **parma wallaby**, see *parma*; **red-necked wallaby**, the wallaby, *Macropus rufogriseus*, of east and south-east Australia, including Tasmania; **rock wallaby**, any small wallaby of the genus *Petrogale*, inhabiting rocky ranges and rock-strewn outcrops of mainland Australia (also known as *wirrang*); **scrub wallaby**, any of several macropodids of various sizes inhabiting rainforest, brigalow or other densely vegetated country, especially *Macropus dorsalis* of eastern Queensland and eastern New South Wales, having a brown back with a dark mid-dorsal stripe; **swamp wallaby**, the dark-coloured wallaby, *Wallabia bicolor*, of areas of dense, moist undergrowth in eastern mainland Australia; **tammar wallaby**, see *tammar*; and **whiptail wallaby**, the wallaby, *Macropus parryi*, of east Queensland and east New South Wales, light to brownish-grey in colour, having a long, slender dark-tipped tail (also called *Parry's wallaby* and *pretty face wallaby*).

2. In the combination **wallaby track**, the path worn by the wallaby, or the route followed by one who journeys through the country in search of seasonal work. This gives rise to the phrase **on the wallaby track** or **on the wallaby**.

> **1867** *Australian Monthly Magazine* [Melbourne], IV, 41. I have just had a row with my people and am off anywhere, on the *wallabee*, to try my luck.

> **1871** *Illustrated Sydney News*, 23 December, 210. Men 'on the wallaby' are those who continue to exist without a settled home and with little work or none at all.

> **1900** R. BRUCE, *Benbonuna* (1904), 70. The station hands, many of whom soon found themselves on what they called the 'wallaby track'—walking from station to station in search of employment, with their sole worldly effects rolled tightly as a 'swag' in a pair of red or blue blankets, and strapped to their shoulders.

On the wallaby can also mean 'on the move'.

> **1906** *Bulletin* [Sydney], 19 April, 14. In Central Australia the black ... is incessantly 'on the wallaby', so as to procure food.

Someone 'on the wallaby', usually an itinerant rural worker or swagman, is a **wallaby tracker** or, in shortened form, **wallaby**.

> **1904** *Bulletin* [Sydney], 14 April, 15. Of all the wallaby-trackers' substitutes and make-shifts for tobacco I find honeysuckle ... the best-flavoured.

> **1905** *Ibid.*, 12 October, 15. I have read ... about mystic signs Hindu hawkers, wallaby trackers, etc, leave behind them to signify the dispositions of residents along the tracks of trade, truck and cadge.

> **1956** H. FRAUCA, *In a New Country*, 59. We didn't know his kind existed in Australia any longer, but there he was, a real swagman walking down the road ... We waved at him but he didn't wave back at us. 'He's probably a "wallaby",' said Wally.

3. Figuratively, to mean a member of an Australian international Rugby Union team.

1908 *Referee* [Sydney], 4 November, 9. The discussion as to the name by which the team should be called was settled by the 'Daily Mail' wiring to the 'Wallabies', asking them to choose and nominate their sobriquet. They duly chose the name 'Wallabies' at a special meeting. 'Rabbit' has, therefore, been dropped by many papers.

4. In the following combinations:

wallaby drive, an operation in which wallabies are herded, trapped, and slaughtered, or otherwise hunted.

1897 *Western Champion* [Barcaldine], 31 August, 3. At a wallaby drive outside Gulgong recently 307 kangaroos and wallabys were shot.

wallaby hunt or **hunting**

1889 *Barrier Miner* [Broken Hill], 21 May, 2. All this … was gone through for the best part of two rounds, William puffing like an over-fed sheep dog in a wallaby hunt.

1885 D. E. MCCONNELL, *Australian Etiquette*, 467. It is impossible to devote space to a full description of the exciting and pleasurable features of kangaroo-hunting, or of that other native sport, wallaby-hunting, which latter is pursued in a similar way to kangarooing though the subject is a tempting one.

wallaby jack, a heavy-duty, lever-action jack used for lifting logs or stumps.

1949 B. O'REILLY, *Green Mountains*, 107. The great pine trees were felled and 'barked' … Finally with the aid of wallaby jacks they were set in motion and shot like meteors to the bottom of the gorge.

wallaby net, a net used by Aborigines to snare wallabies.

1923 T. HALL, *A Short History of the Downs Blacks*, 11. It was the duty of the old women and widows to teach the girls to cook the food and train the children, also to make … wallaby nets.

wallaby rug, a rug made from wallaby skin.

1892 'R. BOLDREWOOD', *Nevermore*, II, 159. Lance was invited to avail himself of a comfortable shake-down, where … wallaby rugs protected him from the searching night air.

wallaby scalp

1885 *Bulletin* [Sydney], 5 December, 10. Kangaroo scalps are paid for at the rate of 9d. each … Wallaby scalps are only worth 4d.

wallaby skin

1938 D. BATES, *The Passing of the Aborigines*, 50. Three pairs of laced wallaby-skin shoes.

wallaby stew, a stew of wallaby meat, often a symbol of poverty (see the song of this name).

> **1895** *Devil in Sydney*, 61. I consider a wallaby stew one of the greatest delicacies a person can sit down to.

wallaby tail, the tail of a wallaby as an article of food, particularly in **wallaby-tail soup**.

> **1979** D. LOCKWOOD, *My Old Mates and I*, 69. And wallaby tail soup! She has a recipe she could sell for a thousand dollars if enough people were hungry castaways with money to spend.

wallaby trap and **wallaby trapping**

> **1930** 'BRENT OF BIN BIN', *Ten Creeks Run* (1952), 246. Abracadabra, a mountain-bred horse, had fallen into old Billy Heffernan's wallaby-traps.

> **1906** *Bulletin* [Sydney], 18 October, 44. Dave goes to look after his private enterprise of wallaby trapping.

5. In the names of flora and fauna:

wallaby grass, any of many perennial grasses, usually of the genus *Australodanthonia*, of Australia and elsewhere, typically fine-leaved tussocky plants valued as winter fodder.

wallaby rat, a Tasmanian name for the long-nosed potoroo, *Potorous tridactylus apicalis*.

wallaby /wɒləˈruː/
[Inland dialect of Dharuk, Sydney region *walaru*.]
Used for several large, stocky kangaroos of rocky or hilly country. *Macropus robustus* is known as the *common wallaroo* or *eastern wallaroo* or *euro* or *biggada*; it occurs on rocky ranges and hills over almost all the continent. The *black wallaroo* (also called *Woodward's wallaroo* or *Bernard's wallaroo*), *Macropus bernardus*, is only in Arnhem Land. *Macropus antilopinus*, found across the far north, has been called the *antelope kangaroo* or the *antilopine wallaroo*. [1826]

> **1926** A. S. LE SOUEF et al., *The Wild Animals of Australasia*, 178. The wallaroo is a powerful, thickset animal, especially adapted for life in the mountains.

wambenger /ˈwɒmbɛndʒə/
[Possibly from Nyungar, Perth–Albany region *wambanaŋ*.]
Either of the two species of tree-living, carnivorous marsupials of the genus *Phascogale*. The *red-tailed wambenger* (or *red-tailed phascogale*), *Phascogale calura*, is mostly found in inland woodland habitats, while the *common wambenger* (also called *brush-tailed phascogale* or *tuan*) is found close to the coast in dry sclerophyll forest and monsoonal forest and woodland. [1928]

1955 *Bulletin* [Sydney], 28 December, 12. The brush-tailed phascogale (or wambenger), is disturbing poultry in the lower sou'-west.

warabi /ˈwɒrəbi/
[Wunambal, North Kimberley, Western Australia *warabi*, see below]
The smallest rock wallaby, which is restricted to rugged, inhospitable parts of the Kimberley region, Western Australia was only identified in 1978, being accorded the scientific name *Petrogale burbidgei* and common designation *warabi*, which was supposed at the time to be its name in Wunambal. However, later investigation revealed that *Warabi* is the name of a major mythological site on the coast of Montague Sound, not the name of an animal. In 1990, this rock wallaby was renamed *monjon*, which is its name in Wunambal. [1978]

> **1988** *Australian Encyclopaedia*, 1679. The diminutive warabi, described in 1978, is genetically a little rock-wallaby which lacks the continuous molar eruption found in its closest relatives.

warrigal /ˈwɒrəgəl/
Formerly also **warragal**, **warragul**, **warregal**, **warrigul**, and **worrogal**.
[Dharuk, Sydney region *warrigal*, 'wild dingo'.]
A dingo: see the entry for *dingo* (p. 54) for an explanation of the distinction between the two. [1790]

> **1867** A. K. COLLINS, *Waddy Mundoee*, 12. Them Warregals is most owdacious bad about us. They was howling and yelpin' around Crowther's Creek last night.

warrigal has several other uses in which the sense of 'wild' is preserved.
1. As a synonym for *myall* (see p. 171). Like *myall*, it can be used both as a noun and as an adjective.

> **1847** *Port Phillip Herald*, 21 January, 2. On his way to the scrub, one of the Warrigals yabbered to him, which seemed to frighten him.

> **1978** D. STUART, *Wedgetail View*, 229. Half a dozen real warrigal knock-about men, proper bloody tearaway types.

2. As the name of the plant, *Tetragonia tetragonoides*, occurring in Australia and elsewhere, having fleshy leaves used as a vegetable. Also called warrigal cabbage.

> **1996** J. ROBINS, *Wild Lime*, 144. Warrigal Greens. Also known as Botany Bay greens, New Zealand spinach, warrigal cabbage.

3. In a transferred sense, 'a wild or untamed horse'.

> **1935** G. MCIVER, *A Drover's Odyssey*, 204. When the white stockman could not … ride a wild horse or 'warrigal' from fear of being thrown, the black would be ordered to mount him.

wirrang /ˈwɪræŋ/
Also **wherang**, **wirring**, **worrang**, and **worrung**.
[Wiradhuri, south-west New South Wales *wiraŋ*.]
A name for *rock wallaby*. [1833]

> **1850** *Australasian Sporting Magazine*, 92. The Woorang or Wirring, as it is there called, is the Rock Wallaby. They average about twenty five pounds weight, and would bother a chamois with their pace over a country all but impracticable to human beings.

wogoit /ˈwɒgɔɪt/
[Waray, Adelaide River region, Northern Territory, probably *wogoj*.]
The *rock ringtail possum*, *Pseudocheirus dahli*, of north-east Western Australia and the north of the Northern Territory. [1897]

> **1926** K. DAHL, *In Savage Australia*, 203. Upon my questions as to the nature of the 'wogoit', he informed me that the wogoit was a large kind of opossum which spent the days in hollows and crevasses among the rocks, feeding in the trees at night.

wombat /ˈwɒmbæt/
Formerly also with much variety, as **wambat**, **whombat**, **whombatt**, **womat**, **wombach**, and **womback**.
[Dharuk, Sydney region *wambad*, *wambaj*, or *wambag* (possibly dialectal variants).]
Any of three thickset, burrowing, plant-eating marsupials of southern and eastern Australia, including Tasmania. The *common wombat*, *Vombatus ursinus*, is the most widespread. The *northern hairy-nosed wombat*, *Lasiorhinus krefftii*, and the *southern hairy-nosed wombat*, *Lasiorhinus latifrons*, are much more sparsely distributed. [1798]

> **1798** *Historical Records of New South Wales*, III (1895), 821. We saw several sorts of dung of different animals, one of which Wilson called a Whom-batt, which is an animal about 20 inches high, with short legs and a thick body forwards, with a large head, round ears, and very small eyes; is very fat, and has much the appearance of a badger.

> **1846** *Tasmanian Journal of Natural Science, Agriculture, Statistics, &c.*, II, 117. A young wombat, stuffed and roasted whole in the same manner as a sucking pig, makes a most delicious dish.

> **1986** *Cairns Post*, 4 January, 10. The hairy-nosed wombat has been voted the Endangered Animal of the Year. Its numbers have been reduced to a tiny colony in central Queensland.

The word **wombat** has several other meanings.

1. Figuratively, with reference to apparent characteristics of the wombat, it means either 'a slow or stupid person' or 'one who burrows'.

> **1917** *Byron Bay Record*, 7 July, 4. In addition to the important work of tunnelling, units under the supervision of officers and n.c.o.'s, thousands of infantrymen, the greater majority of whom were ignorant of underground work, have been transformed into excellent wombats.

2. As an adjective used of a tract of land: 'inhabited by wombats'.

> **1824** W. BLAND (ed.), *Journey of Discovery to Port Phillip, New South Wales, by Messrs W. H. Hovel, and Hamilton Hume in 1824 and 1825* (1831), 2. In the evening pass through wombat brush. [*Note*] This brush, like most other parts of the country frequented by the animal from which it takes it name, is an excellent light soil.

3. In combinations:

wombat berry, the climbing vine, *Eustrephus latifolius*, of eastern mainland Australia and elsewhere, bearing a globular orange berry and cultivated as an ornamental.

> **2001** M. HANKS, *Grower's Guide to Australian Natives*, 109. Wombat berry should be planted where it can scramble up through other shrubs.

wombat crossing, a pedestrian crossing with a raised speed hump.

> **2000** *Manly Daily*, 25 July, 5. Vigorous lobbying by Narrabeen Lakes Public School has paid off in terms of a new wombat crossing to enable children, parents and staff to cross the road behind the school more safely.

wombat hole, the burrow made by a wombat.

> **1845** E. J. EYRE, *Journal of Expeditions of Discovery into Central Australia and Overland from Adelaide to King George's Sound in the years 1840–1*, I, 190. There were in places a great many wombat holes.

> **2001** G. TIPPET, *Writing on Gravestones*, 23. I remember I jumped over a little river, dived through wild rose bushes, ran a bit and seen a wombat hole.

4. As a verb, **to wombat**, 'to dig or tunnel, like a wombat'.

> **1973** D. WOLFE, *The Brass Kangaroo*, 143. Above the road a bent figure scratched around in the last remnants of the morning mist. 'And that there's old Clarrie trying to wombat the spuds out.'

woylie /ˈwɔɪli/
Also **woilie**.
[Nyungar, Perth–Albany region *walʸu*.]

The small marsupial rat-kangaroo, *Bettongia penicillata*; also called *brush-tailed bettong*. [1839]

> **1842** G. F. MOORE, *Descriptive Vocabulary of the Language … of Western Australia*, 72. Wal-yo … the Kangaroo-rat. An animal nearly as large as a wild rabbit, tolerably abundant, and very good for eating. The natives take them by driving a spear in the nest, sometimes transfixing two at once, or by jumping upon the nest, which is formed of leaves and grass upon the ground.

wurrung /'wʌrʌŋ/
[Probably Nyungar, Perth–Albany region *waraŋ*.]
The *crescent nail-tailed wallaby*, *Onychogalea lunata*, having a white shoulder marking. Now extinct. [1875]

> **1962** B. W. LEAKE, *Eastern Wheatbelt Wildlife*, 46. To procure Wurrungs for food, the aborigines used to light a fire and smoke them out.

yallara /yə'larə/
[Wangganguru, north South Australia *yadluru*.]
The small bandicoot, *Macrotis leucura*, which lived in the deserts of central Australia and closed the entrance to its burrow so that this was not readily perceivable; believed to be extinct. Also called *lesser bilby*, *white-tailed bilby*, and *lesser rabbit-eared bandicoot*. [1935]

> **1978** D. OVINGTON, *Australian Endangered Species*, 62. The most recent report of the yallara was in January 1967 when skull and jaw fragments were recovered from the nest of an eagle on Andado Station in central Australia.

yalwa /'yælwə/
Also **yalva**.
[Karajarri, La Grange Bay, Western Australia, *yalwa*]
A name applied in north-west Western Australia to the *burrowing bettong*, *Bettongia lesueur*, and elsewhere used as a generic name for the hopping-mouse.

> **1926** K. DAHL, *In Savage Australia*, 280. A few green bushes were scattered between the yalva burrows and their reddish heaps of freshly excavated sand.
>
> **1989** *North West Telegraph* (Port Hedland), 18 October, 23. It has been variously called a boodie rat, a kangaroo rat, a burrowing rat, a burrowing rat kangaroo, a tchungoo or a yalwa.

yarraman /'yærəmən/
Chiefly used in Australian pidgin. Also **yanaman**. Plural **yarraman(s)** or **yarramen**.

This word, meaning a horse, was part of the early pidgin used by white settlers and Aborigines to communicate with each other; each believed that *yarraman* was the word for 'horse' in the other's language. In this way, the name *yarraman* was adopted into numerous Australian languages as the horse itself moved into their territory. There is no reliable information on where the word originated. W. Ridley in his book, *Kamilaroi and other Australian languages* (1875, p. 112), gives *yarāman* from Wodi-wodi, a dialect of Dharawal spoken from Wollongong to the Shoalhaven River, but by this date the word was in dozens of languages. In the same book, Ridley gives three quite different etymologies, two on page 21: 'All the Australians use this name—probably from the neighing of the horse, or, as some think, from "yira" or "yera" (teeth) and "man" (with)'; and one on page 104 (concerning an inland dialect of the Sydney language): 'from "yara" "throw fast"'. The word 'throw' was probably *yiri* in the Sydney language; 'tooth' is *yira* at Sydney, on the New South Wales south coast, and in the southern highlands. There is no record of *man* meaning 'with'. Peter Austin points out that in Kamilaroi, from eastern New South Wales, 'tooth' is *yira* and 'horse' *yarraman*, involving different types of 'r' sounds; this sheds further doubt on an etymology involving 'tooth'. Ridley's etymologies, which have often been quoted, cannot therefore be confirmed. [1833]

> **1882** A. J. BOYD, *Old Colonials*, 69. So, you see, I just had to pay for my team. Now, you seems to be a bit of a scholar. You reckon it all up. There's a waggon as costs eighty pounds—say a hundred, tarpaulin and all; that's one hundred … Well, then there's seventeen yarramen—call 'em thirty pounds a head. How much is that? What d'ye say—five hundred and ten? Put that down.

Birds

A wide range of birds were traditionally eaten by Aborigines. Birds' eggs were part of the staple diet in many areas. Birds were usually caught with throwing sticks, boomerangs, or spears, but there were other more ingenious ways to catch them, such as putting sticky glue on a perch. Ducks were sometimes netted from canoes, and other game birds were trapped or snared.

boobook /'bubʊk/
[Dharuk, Sydney region *bug-bug* or *bubug*, an imitative name.]
The owl, *Ninox novaeseelandiae*, of Australia and elsewhere, having a characteristic two-note call. Also called **boobook owl**, the bird became well known to early settlers for its night-cries in bushland areas. Another name for the *boobook*, and for some other nocturnal birds, is *mopoke*. **Mopoke** may possibly be derived from *boobook*, but may also be an independent representation of the bird's call. It is sometimes spelt **mopehawk** or **morepork**. [1790]

1827 *Transactions of the Linnean Society of London*, XV, 188. Boobook Owl ... 'The native name of this bird', as Mr Caley informs us, 'is *Buck'buck*. It may be heard nearly every night during winter uttering a cry corresponding with that word ... The note of the bird is somewhat similar to that of the European *cuckoo*, and the colonists have hence given it that name.'

brolga /'brɒlgə/

[Kamilaroi, eastern New South Wales (and other languages across to Lake Eyre) *burralga*.]

A large bird, the crane *Grus rubicundus*, with silver-grey plumage and a red patch on the head, living near water in eastern and northern Australia and in New Guinea. Brolgas, which are fairly common in eastern Australia, can sometimes be seen in flocks of from half a dozen to several hundreds. They perform a courtship dance in which they strut and prance about with considerable grace. Aborigines occasionally mimicked the actions of the brolga in ceremonial dancing. The brolga is also called *native companion* as it was frequently seen in the vicinity of Aboriginal communities. [1896]

> **1986** *Courier-Mail* [Brisbane], 15 January, 1. The brolga ... was adopted by State Cabinet yesterday as the official bird emblem of Queensland. The native bird, which has earned the admiration of naturalists and the scorn of crop growers, will join the Cooktown orchid (floral emblem) and the koala (faunal emblem) in representing the State.

budgerigar /'bʌdʒəriga/

Formerly also **betcherrygah**, **betshiregah**, and **budgerygah**.

[Possibly mispronunciation of Kamilaroi, eastern New South Wales *gijirrigaa*. It has been suggested that the name is based on the adjective *budgeree*, from the Sydney language, but this seems unlikely.]

The small green and yellow parrot *Melopsittacus undulatus*, occurring in drier mainland areas, often in large flocks. The budgerigar has become extremely popular throughout the world as a cage-bird. It is also called *love-bird*, *shell parrot*, *warbling grass parakeet*, and *zebra parrot*. The shortened form **budgie** is very common. [1840]

> **1949** H. C. JAMES, *Gold is Where you Find it*, 27. I knew then the water was permanent because there was thousands and thousands of budgerigars and blood-finches there.

bullan-bullan /'bʊlən-bʊlən/

Also **bullen-bullen** and **buln-buln**.

[Wuywurung, Melbourne region *bulen-bulen*, probably imitative.]

The *superb lyrebird, Menura novaehollandiae*, a ground-dwelling bird of the coastal region of south-east Australia, and introduced into Tasmania. It is noted for its resounding call and remarkable power of mimicry. This name is used in the title of Joseph Furphy's novel *The Buln-Buln and the Brolga*. [1838]

1858 *Illustrated Journal of Australasia*, IV, 120. The native name of the bird is Bullan Bullan, and it is said to be derived from a sort of gurgling sound which it makes when alarmed.

bullan-bullan /ˈbʊlən-bʊlən/

Also **buln-buln**.

[Yuwaalaraay, north New South Wales *bulun-bulun*.]

The parrot *Barnardius zonarius barnardi* from the mallee and other inland regions, which blends into its surroundings when feeding on the outer branches of eucalypts, and on the ground. Also known as *Mallee ringneck*. [1905]

> **1949** C. BARRETT, *Parrots of Australasia*, 51. The common Ring-neck, or Mallee Parrot (*Barnardius barnardi*), known also as Barnard's Parrakeet, and 'Buln Buln', is an inland species, widely distributed in southern Queensland, New South Wales, Victoria and South Australia. This handsome green-plumaged bird, with a yellow band on the hind-neck, a red forehead, and an orange-yellow band across the abdomen, though still plentiful in parts of its range, has become scarce in many districts where formerly it flourished.

chowchilla /tʃaʊˈtʃɪlə/

[Dyirbal and Yidiny, Cardwell to Cairns, North Queensland *jawujala* for *Orthonyx spaldingii*.]

The dark-coloured perching bird, *Orthonyx spaldingii*, whose distinctive call is heard at dusk and dawn in the rainforest of north-east Queensland, is called *northern chowchilla*. The similar bird, *Orthonyx temminckii*, of the New South Wales coast, is called *spine-tailed chowchilla*. Both species are also known as *logrunner* (although officially the northern species is called just *chowchilla* and the southern one *logrunner*). [1889]

> **1934** A. H. CHISHOLM, *Bird Wonders of Australia*, 206. Settlers in northern Queensland know the Black-headed Logrunner … as the 'Chow-chilla', since they say, a company of birds freely shouts, 'Chow-chilla-chow-chow, Chowy-chook-chook, Chowy-chook-chook'.

corella /kəˈrɛlə/

[Wiradhuri, south-west New South Wales, probably *garila*.]

Either of three predominantly white cockatoos of the genus *Cacatua*: **little corella** (*C. sanguinea*), **western corella** (*C. pastinator*), and **long-billed corella** (*C. tenuirostris*). The name is occasionally given to *Major Mitchell's cockatoo*, the predominantly pink and white cockatoo *Cacatua leadbeateri*, occurring in arid and semi-arid Australia. [1859]

> **1999** *Advertiser* [Adelaide], 26 May, 39. The Mid Murray Council, based in Mannum, is using firecrackers and light aircraft to scatter corellas which have been damaging parks and gardens and the town's bowling green.

The **corella pear** is a variety of pear grown in South Australia. The pear has a red blush and is probably named after the long-billed corella, which has crimson feathers about its face.

> **1975** *Bulletin* [Sydney], 26 July, 50. The Corella pear is grown only in South Australia, and is almost manufactured. Cross-pollination is done by hand and the beautiful red blush is created by a cold-storage technique. The pear is named after a red-coloured parrot found in South Australia.

currawong /'kʌrəwɒŋ/

[Probably Yagara, Brisbane region (and neighbouring languages) *garrawaŋ*, or possibly Dharuk, Sydney region *gurawaruŋ*.]
Any of the three species of the genus *Strepera*, having predominantly black or grey plumage and a ringing call. The species are distinguished by colour, as **black currawong**, the predominantly black bird *Strepera fuliginosa* of Tasmania; **grey currawong**, the predominantly black or grey bird *Strepera versicolor* of southern Australia, including Tasmania; and **pied currawong**, the bird *Strepera graculina* of eastern Australia, excluding Tasmania. The currawong is also known as the *bell magpie*. [1905]

> **1988** *Australian Encyclopaedia*, 887. In Queensland the pied currawong (known there as the scrub-magpie) was for many years outlawed under suspicion of being a spreader of prickly pear; in eight years one Board alone (that of the Brisbane district) paid for the killing of 55 204 scrub-magpies, and another Board (that of Toowoomba) paid for the heads of 1756 of the birds; yet even then the currawongs remained, as they are at the present day, moderately abundant.

galah /gə'la/

Formerly also **galar** and **gillar**.
[Yuwaalaraay, north New South Wales (and neighbouring languages), *gilaa*.]
The grey-backed, pink-breasted cockatoo *Eolophus roseicapillus* (or *Cacatua roseicapilla*), occurring in all parts of Australia except the extreme north-east and south-west. Also known as *red-breasted cockatoo* and *rose-breasted cockatoo*, the galah is very popular as a cage-bird. [1862]

> **1976** *Reader's Digest Complete Book of Australian Birds*, 256. Galahs ... are such a common sight in Australia that their beauty is often taken for granted. They are usually seen in flocks of 30 to 1000 birds, foraging together or flying over the plains—now pink, now grey as they change direction.

The word **galah** is used in a number of other ways.

1. To refer to a fool, or a nincompoop.

> **1951** E. LAMBERT, *The Twenty Thousand Thieves*, 160. Yair, and I got better ideas than some of the galahs that give us our orders.

2. In combination with other words:

galah pie

> **1962** J. MARSHALL & R. DRYSDALE, *Journey among Men*, 169. One old country dish, and a very good one too, was galah pie.

galah session, a period allocated for private conversation, especially between women on isolated stations, over an outback radio network. It can also refer to 'a long chat'.

> **1976** B. NORMAN, *Bush Pilot*, 81. Storm clouds built up during the day and wandered around the country pouring rain on the parched land and giving the 'Galah Session' on the radio plenty to talk about.

gang-gang /ˈgæŋ-gæŋ/

Also **gangan**.

[Wiradhuri, south-west New South Wales *gaŋ-gaŋ* (imitative).]

The predominantly grey cockatoo *Callocephalon fimbriatum* of south-eastern Australia, the mature male having an orangish red head and crest. Also known as **gang-gang cockatoo**. [1833]

> **1890** G. J. BROINOWSKI, *Birds of Australia*, III, Pl. 20. The discordant grating cry of the Gang-gang ... is an experience in ugly sounds not easily forgotten.

gnow /naʊ/

Formerly also **ngowa** and **ngow-oo**.

[Nyungar, Perth–Albany region, Western Australia *ŋow* and *ŋowu* (dialectal variants).]

A Western Australian name for the bird usually known as the *mallee fowl*. In Victoria, it is sometimes called *lowan*. See *lowan* for a description. [1840]

> **1842** G. F. MOORE, *Descriptive Vocabulary of the Language ... of Western Australia*, 67. Ngow-o ... Colonial pheasant, nondescript? It scrapes together a large heap of earth or sand, perhaps two to three feet high, and five to six feet in diameter, in which it deposits its eggs about a foot deep, which are left to be hatched by the sun. It is the only bird of this habit in the colony. The eggs are very large in proportion to the size of the bird, and of a delicate flavour. It would be very valuable if domesticated. The mother is said to come and uncover the eggs at the time of maturity.

jerryang /ˈdʒɛriæŋ/

[Probably Dharuk, Sydney region *jirraŋ*.]

The 'little lorikeet', the small lorikeet, *Glossopsitta pusilla*, of eastern and south-eastern Australia, a predominantly green bird with a red face. [1843]

1945 C. BARRETT, *Australian Bird Life*, 76. The musk lorikeet … and the little keet or 'jerryang' are familiar birds from Queensland to Victoria.

kookaburra /'kʊkəbʌrə/

Formerly also with much variety, especially **kukuburra**.

[Wiradhuri, south-west New South Wales (and nearby languages) *gugubarra* (imitative) for *Dacelo novaeguineae*.]

Either of two Australian kingfishers, the large, predominantly brown and white laughing kookaburra, *Dacelo novaeguineae*, of southern and eastern Australia (introduced into Tasmania and south-west Western Australia), having a distinctive raucous call, and the *blue-winged kookaburra*, the large *Dacelo leachii* of woodlands in northern Australia and New Guinea, having conspicuous blue areas on the wing. The former was commonly known as the *laughing jackass*, and both were formerly sometimes known as **goburra** (possibly an abbreviated form of *kookaburra*). *Laughing jackass* was abbreviated to *Jack* or *Jacky*, kookaburra to **kooka** or **kooky**. Also called **laughing kookaburra** (which is the official name). [1834]

> **1834** G. BENNETT, *Wanderings in New South Wales … during the years 1832, 1833 and 1834*, I, 222. The natives at Yass call the bird 'Gogera', or 'gogobera', probably from its peculiar note, which has some resemblance to the sound of the word.

> **1847** *Moreton Bay Courier*, 29 May, 4. They are most absurdly named laughing-jackasses, though some designate them the colonist's clock, and the natives, *cucuburra*.

lowan /'loʊən/

[Wemba-wemba, western Victoria (and neighbouring languages) *lawan*.]

A predominantly Victorian name for the *mallee fowl*, the mound-building *Leipoa ocellata*, a mottled grey, brown, and white bird of dry, inland, southern Australia. In Western Australia, it is also known as the *gnow*. [1847]

> **1886** W. J. WOODS, *A Visit to Victoria*, 24. The lowan, or native hen, has a curious practice of heaping up its eggs in the form of a pyramid, and leaving them to get hatched in the sand.

mook-mook owl /'mʊk-mʊk aʊl/

Also **mook-mook** and **muk-muk**.

[*Mug-mug* occurs in many languages in the central northern part of the Northern Territory, variously meaning 'barking owl', 'all owls', or 'call of an owl'.]

An owl, perhaps the 'barking owl', *Ninox connivens*, of all except the arid regions of Australia. [1946]

> **1962** D. LOCKWOOD, *I, Aboriginal*, 25. A mook mook owl hooted solemnly from its perch in a paperbark overhanging the Alawa camp.

There is a second meaning of the word **mook-mook**:

1978 R. D. EAGLESON, *Urban Aboriginal English*, 61. *Muk-Muk*, spirit, ghost.

mopoke /ˈmoʊpoʊk/
Also **mopehawk** and **morepork**.
See *boobook*.

1872 'A RESIDENT' (J.H. Kerr), *Glimpses of Life in Victoria*, 246. The 'mopoke', a kind of owl, is so called from its note, which is said to be in approximation of these two syllables.

1934 'S. RUDD' *Green Grey Homestead*, 72. Murphy'll whisper in a way that will make the night seem more haunted than the mopokes behind the sheds.

punkari /ˈpʌŋkəri/
Also **punkary**.
[Yaralde, mouth of the Murray River, South Australia, probably *baŋgari*.]
The 'white-eyed duck', the duck *Aythya australis* of all states, the mature male having predominantly brown plumage and a white eye. [1879]

1955 S. OSBORNE, *Duck Shooting in Australia*, 11. Punkary are generally fat and well rounded in the body; the flesh is very dark, and they are good eating.

quarrion /ˈkwɒriən/
Also **quarien**, **quarrian**, **quarrien**, and **quarry hen**.
[Wiradhuri south-west New South Wales *guwarrayiŋ*.]
A name for the 'cockatiel', the crested, predominantly grey parrot *Leptolophus hollandicus*, widespread in mainland Australia and popular as a cage-bird in Australia and elsewhere. [1900]

1945 C. BARRETT, *Australian Bird Life*, 75. Graceful as a crested pigeon and charmingly coloured—the quarrion (*Leptolophus hollandicus*), has long been familiar as an aviary bird, overseas as well as in Australia.

wahkun /ˈwʌkʊn/
Also **wahgoon** and **wagoon**.
[Dharuk, Sydney region *waagan*.]
Used of the two species of crow and three of raven indigenous to Australia. In most Australian languages, the crow or raven is given an imitative name, often something like *waagan* or *waga*. Wagga Wagga, the town in New South Wales, derives its name from the fact that many ravens (*waga*) were said to gather there. [1790]

1917 *Bulletin* [Sydney], 23 August, 22. Amongst several N.S. Wales clans bur-al-ga is the native companion; hence our word brolga, Bel-bundalooie is the bellbird, and wah-gon is the crow.

wee juggler /wi ˈdʒʌɡlə/
Also **weejugla**.
[Wiradhuri, south-west New South Wales *wijagala*.]
Major Mitchell's cockatoo, the predominantly pink and white cockatoo *Cacatua leadbeateri*, having a scarlet crest with a central yellow band, and occurring in arid and semi-arid Australia. [1886]

> **1943** C. BARRETT, *An Australian Animal Book*, 183. 'Wee juggler' is another popular name for this cockatoo, but nearly always it is called 'Major Mitchell'.

weelo /ˈwiloʊ/
Also **weeloo** and **weelow**.
[Nhanta, Geraldton region (and other Western Australian and South Australian languages) *wirlu*.]
Either of two ground-nesting birds of the genus *Burhinus*, especially *Burhinus grallarius*, formerly widespread in Australia but no longer found in closely settled areas. Also known as *curlew*, *stone curlew*, *bush stone-curlew*, and *stone plover*. [1845]

> **1917** *Bulletin* [Sydney], 5 July, 22. The keenness of the aborigine's ear for bird notes is evidenced in the names resembling their call which he gave to familiar species … The stone curlew was called weelo, or weeloo.

weero /ˈwiroʊ/
[Several languages of north-west Western Australia, including Yindjibarndi, Panyjima, Martuthunira, and Jiwarli, *wiru*.]
A Western Australian name for the cockatiel. See *quarrion*. [1948]

> **1948** D. L. SERVENTY, *A Handbook of the Birds of Western Australia*, 3. Some aboriginal names … have passed into use as vernacular names, either locally or generally. Such include … 'Weero' for the Cockatoo Parrot.

wompoo pigeon /ˈwɒmpu ˈpɪdʒən/
Also **wampoo** and **whampoo pigeon**.
[An imitative call, which could be a borrowing from an Australian language.]
The fruit-pigeon *Ptilinopus magnificus* of near-coastal rainforest in north-eastern Australia, also occurring in New Guinea. Also known as *king pigeon*, *magnificent fruit pigeon*, and *painted pigeon*. [1870]

> **1992** S. BREEDEN, *Visions of a Rainforest*, 7. Flying low along the path a wompoo pigeon comes straight towards me, seemingly aiming for my waist. At the last minute it veers to one side and shows off the bright yellow under its wings and its purple chest.

wonga-wonga /ˈwɒŋɡə-wɒŋɡə/
Also **wonga pigeon**, **wonga wonga pigeon**, and **wanga-wanga**.
[Probably Dharuk, Sydney region *waŋa-waŋa*.]

The ground-feeding grey and white pigeon *Leucosarcia melanoleuca* of eastern mainland Australia. [1821]

> **1821** L. MACQUARIE, *Journals of his tours in New South Wales and Van Diemen's Land 1810–1822*, 20 November (1956), 223. Major Morisett has most kindly sent his young friend Lachlan the following very handsome present of pets; viz. Four black swans … and one wanga-wanga pigeon.

> **1860** G. BENNETT, *Gatherings of a Naturalist in Australia*, 4. The Wonga-Wonga among the pigeon tribe is not less esteemed, its flesh being white, delicate, and of surpassing flavour.

The **wonga-wonga vine** is the climbing plant *Pandorea pandorana* of eastern Australia including Tasmania, bearing clusters of showy, pale-coloured flowers and cultivated as an ornamental. Also called **wonga vine**. The name of the vine is possibly associated with that of the pigeon.

> **1936** F. CLUNE, *Roaming Round the Darling*, 162. Another shrub was the wonga-wonga vine. It has white flowers, and the blacks used to hollow out the stems and make whistles from them.

yahoo /ya'hu/, /'yahu/
[An imitative name, possibly from a New South Wales language.]
The 'grey-crowned babbler', *Pomatostomus temporalis*, of northern and eastern Australia and southern New Guinea, having a grey crown with two broad, white stripes. Note that *yahoo* is also the name of an evil spirit (p. 161). [1835]

> **1948** R. RAVEN-HART, *Canoe in Australia*, 99. And a band of street-urchin birds, quarrelling … and chasing each other … black and white tail-tips and white 'eye-brows', and Bevan called them 'Cat-birds'—a more official name is Grey-crowned Babbler but another popular name fits them even better, 'Yahoo', both imitating their call and suggesting their behaviour.

Fish and other water animals

There was an extensive range of seafood available for Aborigines to eat, and in many areas the rich supplies of fish, shellfish, crustaceans, and turtles comprised a major part of their diet. Both women and men traditionally procured fish, and they used a variety of techniques. Frequently hooks and lines or nets were used, and sometimes elaborate stone weirs were built to catch fish and other seafood. Traditionally, most of the small fish and shellfish were collected by women and the larger fish were caught by men.

The huge coastline with its great abundance of unusual water life meant that the colonists had to create many new words, some of which were certainly borrowed from Australian languages. Mystery surrounds a number of fish names. Some (but not all) authorities suggest that *cunjevoi, mado, morwong, tallegalane, teraglin, tilliwurti, turrum, wirrah,* and *wobbegong* (all listed below) are borrowings from local languages, but do not specify which language. A thorough study of the data on likely languages has failed to uncover any of these names. It is possible that some of them may have a quite different source.

barramundi /bærəˈmʌndi/, /ˈbærəmʌndi/
Also **barramunda** and **burramundi**.
[Said to be from a language spoken around the Dawson and Fitzroy Rivers, central Queensland; however, it has not been possible to confirm this from data available on languages of the region. It has also been suggested (by Morris, *Austral English*, 1898, p. 67) that the original form was *burramundi*, and that this was altered to *barramundi* by analogy with *barracouta*. Note though that the earliest reference in print does give *barramundi*.]

Any of several northern Australian fish found in rivers, now chiefly *Lates calcarifer* of warm rivers and coastal waters from Japan to the Persian Gulf and south to Western Australia, the Northern Territory, and Queensland. It is highly valued as food both by Aborigines and Europeans. The name can also refer to the 'lungfish', *Neoceratodus forsteri*, or either of two other fish, *Scleropages leichhardti*, of the north of the Northern Territory and Queensland, and *Scleropages jardini*. Also abbreviated as **barra**. [1864]

> **1864** E. S. H. [Edward S. Hill], *Narrative of a Trip from Sydney to Peak Downs, Queensland and Back*, 28. At Princhester … there is also a fine large fish in the river, called by the aborigines 'Barramundi', which attains a weight of more than 20 lbs., and is excellent eating.

callop /ˈkæləp/
[Possibly Ngayawang, lower Murray River, *galaba*.]
A South Australian name for the 'golden perch' or 'yellowbelly', the yellowish or white freshwater fish *Macquaria ambigua* of south-east Australia, and probably introduced into Western Australia and the Northern Territory. This fish is one of the most important eating fish in the Murray-Darling river system, but the building of dams and reservoirs has reduced the available habitats. [1845]

> **1951** T. C. ROUGHLEY, *Fish and Fisheries of Australia*, 147. The name 'callop' has been customarily used for this fish in South Australia over a long period of years, whereas in New South Wales it was until recently referred to as golden perch or yellowbelly, in Victoria frequently as freshwater bream, and in Queensland and Western Australia as Murray perch.

cherabin /ˈtʃɛrəbɪn/
Also **cher(r)abun, cherubin**.
[Walmatjarri, Great Sandy Desert, *jarramba* 'freshwater prawn'; Gooniyandi, south Kimberley, *jarramba*.]

The freshwater crustacean *Macrobrachium rosenbergii* of the Kimberley region of Western Australia. [1986]

> **1986** *Bushdriver*, May, 78. The magic of the Kimberleys is in the gorges … they are a refuge for the wildlife of the region, home of waterbirds … and cherrabuns, a large freshwater prawn.

cobra /ˈkɒbrə/
Also **cobbera**.
[Dharuk, Sydney region, probably *gabara*.]
A shipworm, a mollusc native to mangroves, boring into wood in brackish or sea water, and traditionally eaten by Aborigines. Note that *cobra* is also 'head or skull' (p. 196). [1836]

> **1845** c. hodgkinson, *Australia from Port Macquarie to Moreton Bay, with Descriptions of the Natives*, 225. The trees which fall into the brackish water in the lower part of the rivers soon become riddled by the Cobberra worm, which is of considerable length, and half an inch thick. It exhibits but faint indications of being a living animal when extracted from the wood, as it appears almost devoid of motion, and the natives let it slide down their throats with great gusto, in much the same way that the Italian lazzaroni swallow macaroni, to which cobbera has a great resemblance.

condolly /ˈkɒndəli/
[Gaurna, Adelaide region, *gandali*, 'whale'.]
Whale blubber. [1839]

> **1894** *Proceedings of the Royal Geographical Society of Australasia, South Australian Branch* (1899), 42. There was a strong smell of 'condolly' pervading the atmosphere, accompanied by a subtler odor that appeared strongest near the suspended figure, and not devoid of that fragrance so frequently found where soap is absent.

congolli /kənˈɡoʊli/
[Yaralde, mouth of the Murray River, South Australia, *gun-gali*.]
The small, chiefly marine fish *Pseudaphritis urvillii* of south-eastern Australia, including Tasmania; also called *tupong*. [1879]

> **1995** *Advertiser* [Adelaide], 25 August, 12. As lads, we always caught more little callop, catfish and congolli (three–six inches) at willows than along open riverbank. Today, of course, these are too rare for a comparison.

cunjevoi /ˈkʌndʒəvɔɪ/
Chiefly used in New South Wales. Also **cungeboy**.
[Probably from a New South Wales language.]

The ascidian or sea-squirt *Pyura praeputialis*, occurring on inter-tidal rocks in southern Australia, the flesh of which is used as bait. Also abbreviated as **cunji** or **cunjy**. *Cunjevoi* is also the name of a plant (p. 119). [1821]

> **2001** S. WILBY, *Surviving Australia*, viii. We all take the seaside for granted, so even though eighty-five per cent of us cling like cunjevoi (sea squirts) to the seaboard, the sea itself is substantially uncharted and untamed territory.

gilgie /'dʒɪlgi/
A Western Australian word. Also **jilgie**.
[Nyungar, Perth–Albany region, *jilgi*.]
Either of two very small freshwater crayfish, *Cherax quinquecarinatus* and *C. crassimanus*, which live in small semi-permanent streams and swamps; they burrow to escape drought. Gilgies are dark brownish-black with a blue-brown, mottled pattern on the claws and body. [1840]

> **1987** S. MORGAN, *My Place*, 59. I caught gilgies by hanging over an old stormwater drain and wriggling my fingers in the water. As soon as the gilgies latched on, it required only a flick of the wrist to land them, gasping, on the bank.

koonac /'kunæk/
A Western Australian word.
[Nyungar, Perth–Albany region, *gunag*.]
Either of two small freshwater crayfish, *Cherax plebejus* and *C. glaber*, which live in inland rivers and swamps which dry up seasonally; like gilgies, they burrow to escape drought. Koonacs are dark blue-black to mottled brown-black in colour, and have a broader claw than gilgies. Like *marron*, koonacs are farmed. [1839]

> **1983** *Western Australian Naturalist*, XV, 113. Twenty-eight koonacs (14 males and 14 females, carapace length 15.2–16.1 mm) were recovered during the exercise. A single specimen was found in 16 burrows, the remaining 6 occupied burrows harboured 1 female and 1 male specimen in each case. Each koonac was located in the bottom chamber of the burrow and, where male and female were found together, the female was situated vertically above the male; the significance of this is not known.

luderick /'ludərɪk/
Formerly also **ludrick**.
[Ganay (Kurnai), Gippsland, Victoria, *ludarag*.]
The large plant-eating *Girella tricuspidata*, a brown or silvery-green marine and estuarine fish with dark, vertical bands, of commercial importance in eastern Australia. Also called *darkie*, *nigger*, and *blackfish*. [1886]

> **1987** E. GRANT, *Fishes of Australia*, 229–30. Anglers float-fish for Luderick with baits of the threadlike 'Blackfish Weed', or 'Sea Cabbage' … They know that

a hooked Luderick can and does put up a fight that is totally out of proportion to the size of the fish—a fight that can go on minute after minute, while the fish is held and played on the immensely flexible and sensitive 12-foot (3.6 m) rod. It is truly said that no Luderick is ever in the bag until it is safely held in the landing-net.

mado /ˈmeɪdoʊ/
[Possibly from a New South Wales language.]
Either of two small marine fish, *Atypichthys mado* and *Atypichthys strigatus*, commonly found near wharves and inlets of eastern Australia. [1906]

> **1978** N. COLEMAN, *Australian Fisherman's Fish Guide*, 139. The mado seems to prefer a somewhat sheltered habitat and is more likely to be found in bays, inlets and estuaries than open water.

maramie /ˈmærəmi/
Also **moramy**.
[Wiradhuri, south-west New South Wales, probably *marramin*.]
A freshwater crayfish. [1844]

> **1845** J. O. BALFOUR, *A Sketch of New South Wales*, 35. A small crayfish called by the aborigines '*morramma*', is better eating than any shellfish I ever tasted.

marron /ˈmærən/
A predominantly Western Australian word. In the plural, frequently **marron**.
[Nyungar, Perth–Albany region, probably *marran*.]
The large freshwater crayfish *Cherax tenuimanus*, which lives on the sandy bottoms of permanent rivers and streams. Unlike gilgies and koonacs, marron do not burrow to escape drought. They are usually brown when young and jet black when full grown although the colour can vary. They are farmed in Western Australia, as are *koonacs*. [1886]

> **2000** *Australian*, 21 October (Magazine Supplement), 48. Marron may originate from Western Australia, but Kangaroo Island in South Australia has become their second home. There are now so many marron naturalised in its streams farming them is becoming big business.

Also in the combinations: **marron farm/farming/grower/licence/poaching/ pond/ season**.

The word **marron** is used in two other ways:

1. As an agentive nominalisation **marroner**

> **1970** *Collie Mail*, 23 Dec, 20/4. Honorary fisheries inspectors were very active in the Collie region and a number of marroners found their catches being emptied back by the benevolent inspectors.

2. As a verb, **marron** 'catch marrons'

> **1990** *West Australian* [Perth], 5 January (Supplement), 5. Marroning is on the boil again.

morwong /ˈmoʊwɒŋ/, /ˈmɔwɒŋ/
[Possibly from an Australian language.]
Any of several edible marine fish, especially *Nemadactylus douglasii* (**blue morwong**) of southern Australia and New Zealand, which has a distinctive elongated ray of the pectoral fin, *Nemadactylus macropterus* (**jackass morwong**), and *Cheilodactylus fuscus* (**red morwong**). Frequently abbreviated to **mowie**. [1871]

> **2002** *Wollongong Advertiser*, 9 January, 39. An Angler's charter over the weekend on the trap reef turned up a swag of pinkies and blue morwong on pilchard baits.

mulloway /ˈmʌləweɪ/
Formerly also **mullaway**.
[Yaralde, mouth of the Murray River, South Australia, probably *malowe*.]
The large, edible fish, *Argyrosomus hololepidotus*, occurring in marine and estuarine waters of Australia. Also called *butterfish*, *jewfish*, or *kingfish*. [1843]

> **2002** *Border Watch* [Mount Gambier], 28 March, 42. The fishing is fabulous at the moment with good numbers of mulloway to 10 pound up around the caves.

nannygai /ˈnænigaɪ/
Also **nannagai** and **nannygy**.
[From the 1871 and 1882 quotes, we would infer an original name something like *muraɲinagay* in an Australian language, probably one in the vicinity of Sydney. Dawes, in his 1790 notebook on the Sydney language, gives *murraynangul* as 'the flat head', which may possibly relate to the same fish.]
The marine fish of southern Australia, *Centroberyx affinis*, a short-bodied, reddish fish valued as food. Also called *red fish*. This name has also been applied to two fish found in northern waters; the sea perch, *Lutjanus malabaricus*, is known as **large-mouth nannygai**, while the crimson sea perch, *Lutjanus erythropterus*, is known as **small-mouth nannygai**. [1871]

> **1871** *Industrial Progress in NSW*, 791. The … king-fish, 'moorra nennigai' … and a variety of other less familiar forms, may be taken by the line in almost unlimited quantities.

> **1882** J. E. TENNISON-WOODS, *Fish and Fisheries of New South Wales*, 52. The name of Nannygai is said by Mr. Edward Hill to be derived from the aboriginal name of *Mura ngin a gai*, whatever that may mean. Amongst the early colonists it used also to be called 'Mother nan a di' probably a corruption of the native name.

pombah /ˈpɒmba/
[Yagara, Brisbane region *bon-ba*.]
A Queensland name for the *tailor fish*, *Pomatomus saltatrix*, of temperate Australian waters.

> **1906** D. G. STEAD, *Fishes of Australia* 154–6. The tailor (*Pomatomus salatrix*) … is very common along the coasts of Queensland, New South Wales, Victoria, South Australia and Western Australia … In Victoria and Western Australia this fish is known as 'Skipjack', while in Queensland the native name of 'Pombah' is sometimes used.

pondi /ˈpɒndi/
[Yaralde, mouth of Murray River, *ponde*.]
Australia's largest freshwater fish, the Murray cod (*Maccullochella peeli*) of the Murray-Darling system and elsewhere. [1843]

> **1948** F. D. MARSHALL, *Let's Go Fishing*, 96. Fishing for Murray Cod. (In South Australia they are known as pondi.)

> **2002** *Advertiser* [Adelaide], 21 January, 77. The exhibition weaves together four themes: the origins of the river for Aboriginal people; the river as a community of connected interests; the impact of European colonisation; and the ecological damage the river has suffered over the past century. There is a marvellous representation of Pondi, the giant cod which created the river, a story common to Aboriginal communities along the river.

pudding-ball /ˈpʊdɪŋ-bɔl/
Also **puddenba** and **puddinba**.
[Probably Yagara, Brisbane region *budinba*.]
An edible marine fish resembling the mullet, perhaps the 'sea mullet' *Mugil cephalus*. The name **poddy mullet**, which may derive from this word, is also used, particularly of the young of *Mugil cephalus*. [1847]

> **1847** J. D. LANG, *Cooksland in North-eastern Australia*, 96. The species of fish that are commonest in the Bay are mullet, bream, puddinba (a native name, corrupted by the colonists into pudding-ball) … the puddinba is like a mullet in shape, but larger, and very fat; it is esteemed a great delicacy.

tallegalane /təˈlɛgəleɪn/
Also **tallagallan**, **tallegallan**, **talleygallan**, **tallygalann**, **tallygalone**, and **tellegalene**.
[Possibly from an Australian language.]
The small marine and estuarine fish *Myxus elongatus* of southern Australia. Also called *sand mullet*. [1879]

1896 F. G. AFLALO, *A Sketch of the Natural History of Australia*, 232. The Sand Mullet or Talleygallan (*Myxus*) … frequents the rivers, but goes down to the sea each winter.

1965 *Australian Encyclopaedia*, VI, 195. The sand mullet or tallegalane … of New South Wales is less valuable as a food fish although it is at times plentiful in the markets.

tarwhine /ˈtawaɪn/
[Probably Dharuk, Sydney region *darrawayin*.]
The silvery marine fish *Rhabdosargus sarba* of Australia and elsewhere. [1790]

> **2000** *Northern Beaches Weekender* [Sydney], 25 February, 34. All this activity has created a constant berley trail that also brought some solid bream and tarwhine foraging under the schools.

teraglin /təˈræɡlən/
Also **traglin**.
[Possibly from an Australian language.]
The marine fish *Atractoscion aequidens* of New South Wales, southern Queensland and South Africa. The name is also abbreviated to **trag**, used as both the singular and the plural. [1871]

> **1999** *Manly Daily*, 11 June, 39. As an avid fish eater, it was warming to hear reports of teraglin coming from Boultons, Trawleys and East Reef last weekend … Teraglin (commonly called trag) are usually caught in numbers once a patch is located, but reports to date are only showing single fish.

tillywurti /tɪliˈwɜti/
Also **tilliwurty**.
[Possibly from a South Australian language.]
A chiefly South Australian name for the 'strongfish', the grey marine fish *Dactylophora nigricans* of southern Australia. [1924]

> **1974** T. D. SCOTT et al., *Marine and Freshwater Fishes of South Australia*, 233. This species … which is also known as 'Tilliwurti' and 'Nuncla' is most abundant in shallow rocky areas off our coasts.

tupong /ˈtupɒŋ/
Also **toopong**.
[Kuurn Kopan Noot (Gunditjmara), around Portland and Warrnambool, Victoria *dubŋ*.]
The small, chiefly marine fish *Pseudaphritis urvilli* of south-eastern Australia, including Tasmania. Also known as *congolli*. [1897]

1897 *Proceedings of the Linnean Society of New South Wales*, XXII, 57. Some months ago I received … three fine specimens of a *Pseudaphritis* from the fresh waters of Victoria, where it is known to anglers as the 'Tupong'.

1974 L. WEDLICK, *Sporting Fish of Inland Lakes and Streams*, 17. The tupong is dark blue to purple on the back, and silver on the belly. The dark blotches on the back, and the stripes below the lateral line give the fish a marbled effect.

turrum /ˈtʌrəm/
[Possibly from an Australian language.]
Any of several large marine fish of northern Australia valued as game fish, including *Carangoides fulvoguttatus*, *Carangoides emburyi*, and *Caranx sexfasciatus*. [1936]

> **1981** G. ELLIS, *Hey Doc, Let's Go Fishing!*, 14. The turrum belongs to the trevally family, but it is a very deep chunky fish with shoulders (if such a description can be used of fish) like a working bullock.

ugari /ˈyugəri/
[Yagara, Brisbane region *yugari*.]
A Queensland name for the 'pipi', the edible marine bivalve *Plebidonax deltoides*, found in coastal waters from southern Queensland to southern Western Australia, including Tasmania. [1904]

> **1904** C. C. PETRIE, *Tom Petrie's Reminiscences of Early Queensland*, 72. Fish were scaled by the blacks with the 'donax' shell, or 'yugari' (the native name) and then put whole on a nice fire of mostly red-hot coals.

wirrah /ˈwɪrə/
[Possibly from an Australian language.]
Either of two marine fish of rocky reefs of the genus *Acanthistius*, *A. ocellatus* of south-east Australia and *A. serratus* of south-west Australia. [1880]

> **1978** N. COLEMAN, *Australian Fisherman's Fish Guide*, 16. Most commonly found in shallow water around rocky reefs, the wirrah is often termed as a 'boot'. This is due to the fishes' poor eating qualities which in no uncertain terms resemble a 'boot', both in texture and lack of flavour.

wobbegong /ˈwɒbigɒŋ/
Also **wahbegong**, **wobbygong**, and **wobegong**.
[Possibly from a New South Wales coastal language.]
Any of several slow-moving, bottom-dwelling sharks, especially of the genus *Orectolobus*, commonly found among seaweed-encrusted rocks. Also called *carpet shark*, the wobbegong has a flattened head and longitudinal ridges along the body.

It is remarkable for its beautiful colour-markings; these form complex patterns of brown, violet, and lilac, and sometimes resemble the ornate design of a handsome carpet (providing an effective camouflage). The wobbegong may attack humans and can inflict a painful wound with its long, pointed teeth. [1852]

> **1988** *Albany Advertiser*, 14 July, 24. To obtain the best eating quality of a wobbegong, as with most other sharks, it is necessary to freeze the flesh for at least two weeks.

wollamai /'wɒləmaɪ/
Also **wollomai**.
[Dharuk, Sydney region *walamay*.]
The marine fish *Chrysophrys auratus*, a 'snapper' (or 'schnapper'). [1790]

> **1793** J. HUNTER, *An Historical Journal*, 410. *Woolamie*, a fish called a light-horseman.

yabby /'yæbi/
Also **yabbie**.
[Wemba-wemba, western Victoria *yabij*.]
Any of several freshwater crayfish (usually of the genus *Cherax*) valued as food, especially the common *Cherax destructor*, native to south-east Australia. Also called *lobby* and *crawbob*. In Queensland, *yabby* may also refer to any of several small, burrowing, shrimp-like marine crustaceans known as *nippers*. [1878]

> **1970** *Sunraysia*, 28 October, 5. Over two years ago the department began a campaign to protect the yabby by limiting fishermen to five drop nets.

The word **yabby** is used in two other ways.

1. As a verb, meaning 'fish for yabbies'.

> **1992** *Advertiser* [Adelaide], 27 July, 14. With this knowledge I swam, fished and yabbied in all the pools from the foot of the Road Transport Building in Walkerville to past the old Gilberton swimming pool.

> **1962** E. LANE, *Mad as Rabbits*, 161. The glorious summer-time sport of yabbying.

2. Figuratively, to mean 'wicket-keeper' in cricket.

> **1983** J. HIBBERD and G. HUTCHINSON, *The Barracker's Bible*, 235. *Yabbie* … wicket keeper: from the curious stance and gauntlets of the pudgy breed.

yungan /'yʌŋgən/
Also **yangan**, **youngon**, **youngun**, and **yungun**.
[Yagara, Brisbane region (and neighbouring languages) *yaŋan*.]
A name for the 'dugong', the large plant-eating marine mammal *Dugong dugon*, occurring in coastal waters of northern Australia and elsewhere. Also known as the *manatee*, the yungan was highly valued as food by the Aborigines, and said to taste like pork when cooked. The oil of the yungan was believed to have medicinal

value. To catch the animal after it had been sighted, a group of men in canoes would herd it into a net or harpoon it. A successful hunter of yungan attained great status in his community. The yungan is now protected in Australia except for subsistence hunting by Aborigines in the north. [1836]

> **1841** C. EIPPER, *Statement ... of the German Mission ... at Moreton Bay*, 6. Should any of the tribes on the sea coast have been so fortunate as to catch a sea-hog—called *youngun*—which sometimes is the size of a young bullock, intelligence of the event is immediately sent along the coast to invite the neighbouring tribes to the banquet; this lasts, between incessant eating and sleeping when quite gorged, two or three days until the whole animal is consumed; their gluttony then obliges them to change their place of encampment, and sometimes oftener than once, as their olfactory nerves seem to be very sensitive, not withstanding their voracious appetites.

> **1904** C. C. PETRIE, *Tom Petrie's Reminiscences of Early Queensland*, 68. When a dugong or 'yangon' (yung-un) was pulled ashore it would be rolled up on to dry ground. The aborigines had a peculiar superstition that should the gins see a dugong before it was cut up it would not be fat—would not, in fact, be in good condition.

Reptiles

bandy-bandy /'bændi-bændi/
[Probably Kattang, Taree region, New South Wales *bandi-bandi*.]
Either of two small snakes patterned with black and white bands around the body, *Vermicella annulata* of eastern and central Australia, and *Vermicella multifasciata* of northern Western Australia and the Northern Territory. Also called *ring snake*. [1898]

> **1993** D. BURKE, *Burke's Backyard*, 177. One of our more unusual creatures is the Bandy-bandy Snake (*Vermicella annulata*), which is ringed with black and white (or yellow) stripes.

boggi /'bɒgaɪ/
Also **bog-eye**, **bogghi**, and **bogi**.
[Wiradhuri, south-west New South Wales, probably *bugay*.]
Any of several lizards including the 'bobtail', the slow-moving 'shingleback lizard', *Tiliqua rugosus*, of southern mainland Australia, having large, ridged scales on the back and a short rounded tail, and some other species of the genus *Tiliqua*. [1911]

> **1965** R. OTTLEY, *By sandhills*, 29. A bog-eye ain't much. They seldom bite you.

The word is also used as the name of the handpiece of a shearing machine.

> **1915** *Bulletin* [Sydney], 14 October, 24. The jumbuck barber has a vocabulary of his own ... In a shed where the barbering is done by machinery he always alludes to his handpiece as 'a bog-eye'. This is from the likeness to the lizard of that name.

bungarra /ˈbʌŋərə/
Also **bung-arrer** and **bungarrow**.
[Nhanta, Geraldton region, Western Australia, probably *baŋarra*.]
The widespread sand monitor, *Varanus gouldii*, usually having a dark horizontal stripe through the eye, bordered by pale lines. Also called *sand goanna* and *Gould's goanna*. [1897]

> **1993** T. PRIOR, *Sinners' Club*, 268. Also known as 'racehorse goannas', the bungarras can run, for short distances, standing on their hind legs, at 70 kilometres an hour.

carney /ˈkani/
Also **cadney**, **carni**, and **carnie**.
[Baagandji, Darling River, New South Wales, and languages across to Lake Eyre *gaani*.]
Any of several lizards in the traditional diet of Aborigines, especially the 'bearded dragon', *Amphibolurus barbatus* (formerly *Pogona barbata*), of eastern Australia, having large, spiny scales on the throat pouch and other parts of the body. Also known as *bearded lizard*, *eastern bearded dragon*, or *Jew lizard*. [1873]

> **1881** J. C. F. JOHNSON, *To Mount Browne and Back*, 13. The carnie or Jew Lizard is esteemed a luxury by many of the central Australian men.

dugite /ˈdʒugaɪt/, /ˈdugaɪt/
Also **dukite**.
[Nyungar, Perth–Albany region, probably *dugaj*.]
A predominantly grey, olive, or brown venomous snake, *Pseudonaja affinis*, of south-west Australia. Also called *dugite snake*. [1831]

> **1950** *Bulletin* [Sydney], 8 November, 12. The only poisonous snake around Perth that I know of that will attempt to enter a house is the dugite … This snake is the western counterpart of the Eastralian brown snake, and it's deadly.

gwarda /ˈgwadə/
Also **gwardar** and **gwarder**.
[Nyungar, Perth–Albany region, *gwanda*, *gunda* (dialectal variants).]
The highly venomous brown snake, *Pseudonaja nuchalis*, of all mainland states. It grows up to a metre and a half in length. Also called *western brown snake*. [1842]

> **1988** *Wheatbelt Mercury*, 7 September, 1. The gwardar snake resembles the dugite, but is the most dangerous snake in the wheatbelt.

norne /nɔːn/
Chiefly used in Western Australia.
[Southern dialect of Nyungar, Perth–Albany region, probably *nurn*.]

The black tiger snake, *Notechis ater*, which feeds largely on frogs and small animals. [1831]

> **1990** *West Australian* [Perth], 31 December, 39. The tiger snake was known as 'the norne' to the Aborigines and so the name Nornalup really means 'the place of the tiger snake'.

perentie /pəˈrɛnti/, /ˈprɛnti/

Also with much variety, as **parentie**, **parinti**, **perenty**, **prenti**, **printhy**, and **printy**.

[Diyari, around Lake Eyre, South Australia, and neighbouring languages *pirrinthi*.]

The large monitor lizard, *Varanus giganteus*, of rocky country in arid central and western Australia. [1905]

> **1962** D. LOCKWOOD, *I, the Aboriginal*, 12. Fat dripped from the cooking perentie, its tail alone more than a yard long.

taipan /ˈtaɪpæn/

[Wik-Mungkan, Cape York Peninsula, North Queensland *dhay-ban*.]

The brownish snake *Oxyuranus scutellatus* of northern and north-eastern Australia and southern New Guinea, at three to three-and-a-half metres, the longest Australian venomous snake. [1933]

> **1933** *Proceedings of the Zoological Society of London*, 858. The name 'taipan', by which *O*[*xyuranus*] *scutellatus* is known to the aborigines of Cape York Peninsula, is an excellent vernacular name for the species. The natives hold the taipan in great dread, and it appears to have been responsible for many deaths among them.

womma /ˈwɒmə/

Also **woma**.

[Diyari, around Lake Eyre, and neighbouring languages *wama*.]

The python *Aspidites ramsayi* of arid Australia; also called *sand python* and *Ramsay's python*. *Womma* is also the name of a honey ant (see p. 104). [1873]

> **1935** H. BASEDOW, *Knights of the Boomerang*, 75. Rock-pythons attain a length of from fifteen to seventeen feet. In Central Australia the recognised delicacy ... is a large brown variety of the carpet-snake ... By nature it is sluggish and voracious, and therefore usually well-nourished and fat ... It is known as 'womma'.

Insects

bardi /ˈbadi/

Chiefly used in Western Australia and South Australia. Also **barde**, **bardee**, **bardie**, and **bardy**.

[Nyungar, Perth–Albany region (and many other languages in Western Australia and South Australia) *bardi*.]

The edible larva or pupa of the beetle *Bardistus cibarius*, or of any of several species of moth, especially *Trictena atripalpis* (formerly *Trictena argentata*). The beetle larva bores into the stems of grass-trees, eucalypts and acacias, and the moth larva is found underground, feeding on roots of eucalypts and acacias. The name is also applied to *Abantiades marcidus*. Also called **bardi grub**. [1839]

> **1840** T. J. BUCKTON, *Western Australia, comprising a Description of the Vicinity of Australind and Port Lieschenault*, 97. The Bar-de (the native name for the white grub alluded to), has a fragrant, aromatic flavour; and is eaten either raw or roasted.

There is an idiom, '**starve the bardies!**' which, like 'stone the crows' or 'starve the lizards', is an exclamation of surprise or disgust.

bogong /ˈboʊɡɒŋ/

Formerly **bugong**. Now usually called **bogong moth**.

[Ngarigo, which was spoken from Queanbeyan in New South Wales to Omeo in Victoria, *buguŋ*.]

The brown moth *Agrotis infusa*, which breeds on plains in southern Australia. The adults, which migrate to hills where they collect in rock crevices during early summer, were eaten by Aborigines. People travelled from afar for the bogong moth season in the Snowy Mountains. It was a time of great festivity and collective ceremonies. Smouldering fires were used to suffocate the moths so that they could be collected from under rocks. The Aborigines removed the wings and down by placing the moths on hot stones and burning off the appendages. The scales were removed by fanning the moths in the breeze. The moths were eaten directly, or pounded into cakes, or smoked to enable them to be kept. The bodies of the moths contain an oil which tastes like a sweet nut and is extremely nutritious. For a full account, see J. Flood, *The Moth Hunters*, 1980. This insect has given its name to the **Bogong Mountains** in New South Wales; and to **Mount Bogong**, the **Bogong High Plain**, and the town of **Bogong**, all in Victoria. [1834]

> **2001** *Open Road*, March, 27. Bogongs taste a little like soft Macadamia nuts—a pleasant, surprisingly nutty taste. However, KFC has nothing to fear—Bogongs don't look any more appetising when cooked, so a Brindabella Fried Moths franchise is unlikely to appear in your neighbourhood any time soon.

karbi /ˈkabi/

[Probably Yagara, Brisbane region *gabay*.]

The small, dark-coloured, stingless bee, *Trigona carbonaria*; and its honey. [1838]

1904 C. C. PETRIE, *Tom Petrie's Reminiscences of Early Queensland*, 77. There were two kinds of native honey. One called 'kabbai' was pure white and very sweet, and was found always in small, dead, hollow trees.

kootchar /'kʊtʃə/
[Bandjalang, north-east New South Wales *guja*.]
Any of several small, stingless honeybees of the genus *Trigona*. [1884]

> **1884** *Transactions of the Entomological Society of London*, 149. The second species [of stingless bee] ('Kootchar') is also black in colour but has a fine yellow streak across the upper part of the thorax.

lerp /lɜːp/
Also (especially formerly) **laap**, **leurp**, and **loap**.
[Wemba-wemba, western Victoria *lerəb*.]
The whitish, sweet, waxy secretion produced as a shelter by immature insects of the family Psyllidae, on the leaves of mallee trees such as *Eucalyptus dumosa* and *E. incrassata*; the insects secreting this. They form a major component of the diet of numerous small forest birds, particularly pardalotes and honeyeaters. At certain times, the small sap-sucking insects congregated in huge numbers and made their deposits on the young shoots of mallee shrub. During the lerp season, a six-week period beginning in January each year, the Wemba-wemba people collected and consumed an enormous quantity of lerp. As large numbers of Wemba-wemba people gathered for this purpose, the season was also a period of collective religious ceremonies and marriage arrangements. The tree *Eucalyptus incrassata* is known as **lerp mallee** since lerp is often found on its leaves. [1845]

> **1845** *Papers and Proceedings of the Royal Society of Tasmania*, 25 March (1851), 242. I had no dinner, but I got plenty of lerp. Lerp is very sweet, and is formed by an insect on the leaves of gum trees; in size and appearance like a flake of snow, it feels like matted wool, and tastes like the ice on a wedding cake.

margoo /'magu/
[Western Desert language *magu*.]
Another name for *witchetty* (see below). [1916]

> **1973** V. SERVENTY, *Desert Walkabout*, 13. He had dragged out a four-inch long white grub and swallowed it with much satisfaction. 'Margo', he exclaimed, eyes gleaming with epicurean delight.

witchetty /'wɪtʃəti/
Also with much variety as **witchetty grub**, **widgery**, **witchety**, and **witjuti**.
[Probably Adnyamathanha, Flinders Ranges, South Australia from *wityu*, 'hooked stick used to extract grubs' + *varti*, 'grub', 'insect'.]

Witchetty was originally the name of an implement used to obtain a grub valued as food. It came to mean the grub itself and is now applied to the large edible, wood-eating larva or pupa of any of several moths of the family Cossidae (especially of the genus *Xyleutes*), and beetles of the family *Cerambycidae*. The witchetty grub is a very important food in the diet of both desert and forest Aborigines. The grubs can either be eaten raw or roasted in the ashes of a fire. They have a flavour often likened to that of almonds. Another name for the witchetty is *margoo* (see above). [1862]

> **1862** W. R. H. JESSOP, *Travels and Adventures in Australia*, II, 214. Besides the yam-stick, which is made of the hardest wood, there is the grub stick, called witchertie, a small hooked twig, which the women carry in the nose, and the men in a fillet round the head: this last is used for extracting the grub from crevices and holes.

> **1897** J. J. MURIF, *From Ocean to Ocean*, 176. The best bait one can use is a section of widgery (or 'witchery', a grub three or four inches in length, found at the roots of gum trees, and tasting, when slightly roasted, not unlike a hen's egg).

Witchetty is also used in the name **witchetty bush**, applied to any of several Acacia plants of drier Australia, especially the shrub or tree *Acacia kempeana* of all mainland states except Victoria, so named from the edible grub commonly found at its roots.

womma /ˈwɒmə/

[Yankunytjatjara dialect of Western Desert language *wama* 'any sweet substance or delicacy'.]

The 'honey ant', an ant of any of several genera, including *Melophorus*, *Leptomyrmex*, and *Camponotus*, able to store a honey-like liquid in its distended, pouch-like abdomen, which can swell to the size of a grape. The honey ant is a much sought-after food of Aborigines. In some Aboriginal communities of Central Australia, the term *womma* has been extended to refer to beer or other kinds of alcohol. *Womma* is also the name for a python (p. 101). [1916]

> **1932** *Bulletin* [Sydney], 13 January, 21. The sugar-ant provides a choice dainty. Binghi digs down into the nests, being very careful not to damage the 'womma' he is after.

Mythical creatures

bunyip /ˈbʌnjəp/, /ˈbʌnjɪp/

[Wathawurung, Geelong region, Victoria *ban-yib*.]

A fabulous, large, black amphibious monster supposed to inhabit waterways. It was thought to be the cause of loud noises in the night, and said to devour women and children. [1845]

> **1847** *Port Phillip Herald*, 11 February (supplement). Naturalists of every grade have, since the plantation of the Australian colonies, been racking their brains with

fruitless researches as to the existence or non-existence of the supposed amphibious monster y'clept, amongst many other designations, the Bunyip.

1847 *Bell's Life in Sydney*, 19 June, 3. That apocryphal animal of many names, commonly designated 'The Bunyip' has, according to a correspondent of the *Sydney Morning Herald*, been seen on the Murrumbidgee. It is described as being about as big as a six months old calf, of a dark brown colour, a long neck, a long pointed head, large ears, a thick mane of hair from the head down the neck, and two large tusks. It is said to be an amphibious animal, as it has been observed floundering in the rivers, as well as grazing on their banks.

1852 J. MORGAN, *Life and Adventures of William Buckley, thirty-two years a Wanderer amongst the Aborigines of the then unexplored country round Port Phillip, now the province of Victoria*, chap. III. 'In this lake [Moodewarre], as well as in most of the others inland, and in the deep water rivers, is a very extraordinary amphibious animal, which the natives call Bunyip, of which I could never see any part, except the back, which appeared to be covered with feathers of a dusky grey colour. It seemed to be about the size of a full-grown calf, and sometimes larger; the creatures only appear when the weather is very calm and the water smooth. I could never learn from any of the natives that they had seen either the head or tail, so that I could not form a correct idea of their size; or what they were like.

1857 *Moreton Bay Free Press*, 15 April, 3. Mr Stocqueler informs us that the bunyip is a large freshwater seal, having two small paddles or fins attached to the shoulders, a long swan-like neck, a head like a dog, and a curious bag hanging under the jaw, resembling the pouch of a pelican.

The word **bunyip** has been used in several other ways.

1. Figuratively, to mean 'an imposter'. Also in the compound **bunyip aristocracy**.

1852 G. C. MUNDY, *Our Antipodes: or, Residence and Rambles in the Australasian Colonies with a Glimpse of the Goldfields*, II, 19. A new and strong word was adopted into the Australian vocabulary: Bunyip became, and remains, a Sydney synonym for *imposter*, *pretender*, *humbug*, and the like.

1999 *Courier-Mail* [Brisbane], 5 June, 19. One mob was known as the bunyip aristocracy, twill-trousered adventurers who arrived with cattle, sheep and convict labour to squat.

2. In a transferred sense.

1952 A. C. C. LOCK, *Travels Across Australia*, 271. 'Now and again we have a combined muster … Sometimes we strike a few bunyips'. A bunyip … was a beast that had grown to full size without being branded.

3. As a name for the 'boomer' or bittern *Botaurus poiciloptilus*, a swamp bird with a booming call. In full **bunyip bird**.

> **1954** C. BARRETT, *Wild Life of Australia and New Guinea*, 112. Bitterns are sometimes called 'Bunyipbirds' ... When a booming call breaks the silence of the lonely swamp, it is the voice of the 'Bunyip-bird', largest of the five kinds of bitterns found in Australia.

mindi /'mɪndi/
Obsolete.
[Wemba-wemba, western Victoria *mirnday.*]
A fabulous hairy snake. [1844]

> **1844** H. MCCRAE, *Georgina's Journal: Melbourne a hundred years ago* (1934), 21 August, 129. The natives north of the Grampians talk about a species of Boa called Mindi, which lies in wait by waterholes, and, if an emu comes to drink, makes a meal of the complete bird!

> **1880** *Papers and Proceedings of the Royal Society of Tasmania* (1881), 8. With reference to the 'Mindi', or Mallee Snake, it has often been described to me as a formidable creature, of at least 30 ft in length, which confined itself to the mallee scrub. No one, however, has ever seen one for the simple reason that to see it is to die, so fierce it is, and so great its powers of destruction. Like the 'Bunyip', I believe the 'Mindi' to be a myth.

yowie /'yaʊi/
[Yuwaalaraay, north New South Wales *yuwi* 'dream spirit'.]
An ape-like monster supposed to inhabit parts of eastern Australia. [1975]

> **1999** *Australian* [Sydney], 26 August, 11. We bring to our credulous readers a description of a yowie, courtesy of Dean Harrison, a yowie expert from Beenleigh, south of Brisbane. They are about 2 m tall, muscular, with large heads and little or no neck. They have reddish, matted hair, and hairless, flattish faces. Sounds like a footballer.

FLORA

Aborigines practised hunting and gathering for tens of thousands of years before the arrival of Europeans. Some still continue the traditional techniques of food collection and preparation, which supply them with a rich and varied diet. Aborigines never fully domesticated plants because of the great variety of food resources that were available, and the absence of pressure to change to another subsistence technique. The importance of their religious life helped to sustain a balance between the people and their environment, any surplus energy being directed into religious and artistic expression rather than increased food production.

Aboriginal people had a deep knowledge of the environment. From an early age, children were taught in detail about the animals and plants that they would need to hunt and collect in later life. By their teens, girls were proficient in the basic skills of gathering and cooking, and boys had some experience in hunting.

Their knowledge of the life cycle of plants, insects, and animals was gradually growing, as was their experience of the seasonal availability of supplies.

The first white settlers in Australia tended to give local plants names based on those of old-world species to which they perceived a similarity. For example, the name *red cedar* was applied to the tree *Toona ciliata* (formerly *Toona australis*), botanically very different from old-world cedars, which belong to the genus *Cedrus*; the name may have been used because of a similar soft wood and colour. Many names were made up of two elements, one indicating a resemblance to a European plant and one making a distinction. *Native pomegranate*, *native poplar*, and *native potato* are examples. Some had both an English name and an Aboriginal name, such as the *bangalay*, sometimes called *southern mahogany*, and the *bumble tree*, which is also known as *wild orange*. For others, the only name is one adopted from an Australian language.

Edible flora

Fruits, nuts, and seeds

alunqua /əˈlʌŋkwə/
[Aranda, Alice Springs region *alangwe*, the name for the fruit (the vine itself is called *aljeye*).]
The twining plant *Leichhardtia australis* of drier Australia, the young fruit of which is edible. The fruit itself is also called *bush cucumber* or *desert banana*. If mature, it is baked, but it can be eaten raw when young. Both the outer skin and the pulp are edible. The leaves may also be steamed and eaten. [1935]

> **1974** M. TERRY, *War of the Warramullas*, 151–2. The alunqua, or bush cucumber, is an important source of food ... The fruit looks rather like a large banana passion-fruit ... The fruit is deep green in colour and tastes like fresh green peas.

amulla /əˈmʌlə/
[Dharumbal, Rockhampton region. Recorded by Thozet (1866) as 'amulla', and by Roth (1898 ms.) as 'nâ-moo-lă'; it is likely that the original form was *ŋamula*.]
The shrub *Eremophila debilis* (formerly *Myoporum debile*) of New South Wales and Queensland, with pink or white edible fruit. [1866]

> **1889** J. H. MAIDEN, *Useful Plants of Australia*, 46. 'Amulla,' of the Aborigines. The fruit, which is a quarter of an inch in diameter, is slightly bitter to the taste. It is eaten by the aboriginals.

> **1981** G. M. CUNNINGHAM et al., *Plants of Western N.S.W.*, 614. Amulla is not a common species and appears to be restricted to small colonies of plants in widely scattered sites.

ballart /'bælat/

[Kuurn Kopan Noot (Gunditjmara) around Portland and Warrnambool, and other Victorian languages *balad* for *Exocarpos cupressiformis.*]

Any of several shrubs or small trees of the genus *Exocarpos* having a cherry-like fruit which is often edible. **Cherry ballart** refers specifically to the *native cherry*, *Exocarpos cupressiformis*, common on the eastern coast of Australia. This bears a fruit which is sweet when it becomes red. [1870]

> **1988** *Australian Encyclopaedia*, 677. The most conspicuous species throughout the coast and range country of the south-eastern States is *E. cupressiformis*, a shapely small tree of conical to domed shape with dense, fine, deep green foliage. The Aboriginal name *ballart* (or *balot*) was reported for it by early European settlers and persists as a common name, mostly as cherry ballart. In books its use has been generalised to all species of the genus.

boggabri /'bɒɡəbraɪ/

[F. M. Bailey, *Comprehensive Catalogue of Queensland Plants* (1909, p. 272) said this was from the Flinders River, Queensland, but this cannot be confirmed from materials available on languages from this region.]

Any of several low herbs, especially *Amaranthus mitchellii, Chenopodium pumilio, C. carinatum*, and *Commelina cyanea*. The last of these is also known as *scurvy grass*. The seeds of these herbs can be ground and made into a damper. *Boggabri* is also the name of a town in New South Wales. [1893]

> **1985** *Longreach Leader*, 29 March, 5. Plants which contain nitrates include pigweed ... boggabri ... mintweed, goat head burr, variegated thistle, small flowered marshmallow and annual saltbush.

boobialla /bubi'ælə/

Also **boobyalla**.

[The language of south-eastern Tasmania *bubiala*.]

Either the small tree of coastal sand dunes, *Acacia longifolia* var. *sophorae*, or any of several small shrubs of the genus *Myoporum*, having pale flowers and globular, often purplish, fruits. *Boobialla* is also the name of a river in Tasmania. [1832]

> **1835** *Hobart Town Almanack*, 63. *Acacia sophora*. Sophora podded acacia or Boobyaloe ... a large shrub on the sand hills of the coast ... [The seeds are] roasted in pods among the ashes by the Aborigines.

bumble tree /'bʌmbəl tri/

[Kamilaroi, Yuwaalaraay, east New South Wales and nearby languages *bambul.*]

Any of several trees or shrubs of the genus *Capparis*, especially the shrub *Capparis mitchellii*. Also known simply as **bumble** and as *wild orange*. The fruit is a delicacy and is found only in summer. The seeds, which are a rich source of vitamin C, are ground and made into a damper. [1846]

> **1932** *Victorian Naturalist: the Journal and Magazine of the Field Naturalists' Club of Victoria*, XLIX, 189. C[*apparis*] *Mitchellii* is the Bumble, which develops from an untidy struggling shrub into a shapely little tree … The fruit … is edible … The taste suggested an over-mellow papaw with turpentine sauce.

bunya /'bʌnyə/
Also **bunya-bunya** and **bunya-bunya pine**.
[Yagara, Brisbane region *buña-buña*, Gabi-gabi and Waga-waga, south-east Queensland *buñi*.]
The very tall Queensland pine tree, *Araucaria bidwillii*, the cones of which contain seeds which are eaten raw, roasted, or pounded to a flour. The seeds of the tree are known by the same name. The pine occurs primarily in the south-east of Queensland, between Gympie and the Bunya Mountains near Dalby. Although the trees fruit each year, they are particularly plentiful about every third year. Traditionally, Aborigines gathered in large numbers in the bunya region when the fruit ripened in the early January of a plentiful year. The large ceremonies that occurred with the bunya nut feasts were important as social, religious, and musical events. [1841]

> **1886** J. MATHEW, in E. M. CURR, *The Australian Race*, III, 161–2. But by far the most important and most valued vegetable product was the bunya. The bunya-tree, or Araucaria Bidwillii, is a very conspicuous ornament of the scrubs in the Kabi country, and, by its dome-shaped crown, can be distinguished from the surrounding trees at a great distance. The cones, when full-grown, are fourteen to sixteen inches in length, and at the thickest part about nine inches through. The edible portions, the seeds, or ovules rather, are an inch or an inch and a half long, and about half an inch thick. Their tissues much resembles that of a potato. They are of conical shape, covered with a tough envelope, and are found one on each scale. When the cone is young, the edible portions are juicy and sweet, and are eaten entire and raw. As the seed matures, and the embryo assumes a definite form, the surrounding tissue becomes drier and less palatable; the embryo is then rejected. When matured, the natives prefer to roast the nut-like seed. Before being roasted, each seed is partially bruised with a stone, and when it has been in the fire for a minute or two it gives a crack, the signal that it is cooked. These kernels are also pounded into a kind of meal, called maɲu, and eaten in that form. In laying up a store of bunyas the Blacks exhibited an unusual foresight. While the fruit was in season, they filled netted bags with the seeds, and buried them generally about the beds of creeks, to be ready for use when the season was long past. Bunyas that had lain for months underground had, when taken up, a most offensive smell, which they imparted to all that came in contact with them. Nevertheless, the

Blacks ate them with great relish. In some seasons, the yield was very scant. At the prospect of an abundant yield, tribes would come the distance of a hundred miles to feast upon the bunya, and to finish up the feast with fighting.

burrawang /ˈbʌrəwæŋ/, /ˈbʌrəwɒŋ/
Also **buddawong**, **burrawong**, and **burwan**.
[Dharuk, Sydney region *buruwan*.]
Any of several plants of the genera *Macrozamia* and *Cycas*, especially *Macrozamia communis*, which have palm-like fronds and pineapple-like cones yielding nuts. The nuts are poisonous and can only be eaten after treatment. The name of *Mount Budawang*, New South Wales, relates to this plant. [1790]

> **1826** J. ATKINSON, *Account of Agriculture and Grazing*, 19. The burwan is a plant with leaves very much like the cocoa nut, growing out from a stem about a foot high; at certain seasons it produces a flower, which is succeeded by a cluster of nuts, enclosed in a hard woody shell; this nut in its raw state is a poison; the natives, however, convert it into a very pleasant and nutritive article of food. They first roast the nuts in the ashes of their fire for a short time; then crack them between two stones, separating the kernels and breaking them also; they then roll up a piece of bark in the form of a tube, and placing some grass or other substance to prevent their escape, immerse them in a running stream for twelve hours; they are then good and wholesome food, tasting much like roasted chesnuts [sic]. The burwan is found in great plenty in the scrubs and poor forest lands near the sea coast.

by-yu /ˈbaɪ-yu/
[Nyungar, Perth–Albany region, probably *bayu*.]
The seed of the cycad of south-west Western Australia *Macrozamia riedlei*, once a popular Aboriginal plant food. Also called **by-yu nut**. It was a much sought after food and was very nourishing. The Nyungar people often buried a store of the nuts to be kept for up to several months, so as to maintain an almost continuous supply of the foodstuff throughout the year. [1833]

> **1839** G. GREY, *Vocabulary of the Dialects of South Western Australia*, 22. By-yu—The nut of the Zamia tree, when enveloped with pulp. In the natural state the pulp of this nut is poisonous, but the natives who are very fond of it, deprive it of its poisonous qualities by first soaking it in water for a few days, and then burying it in the sand, where they leave it until the pulp is nearly dry; it is then fit to eat. They generally roast it; after which process it has a mealy flavour, not unlike a chesnut [sic]. It is in full season in the month of May.

canagong /ˈkænədʒɒŋ/
Also **canajong**.
[A Tasmanian language, probably *ganajaŋ*.]

Any of several succulent, perennial plants of the genera *Disphyma* and *Carpobrotus* of coastal and dry inland Australia, especially *Disphyma crassifolium*, which also occurs in New Zealand and South Africa. Commonly called *pigface*. [1834]

> **1889** J. H. MAIDEN, *Useful Native Plants of Australia*, 44. The 'canajong', of the Tasmanian aboriginal. The fleshy fruit is eaten raw by the aborigines. The leaves are eaten baked [This refers to *Carpobrotus*].

colane /kə'leɪn, /'kɒleɪn/

[Wiradhuri, south-west New South Wales, probably *galayin*.]
One of several names for the 'emu apple'. See *gooya*, *gruie*, and *mooley apple*. [1903]

> **1981** G. M. CUNNINGHAM et al., *Plants of Western NSW*, 451. Colane usually occurs as scattered single trees or in small clumps.

coohoy nut /'kuhɔɪ nʌt/
Obsolete.
[Dyirbal, Herberton region, North Queensland *guway*.]
The Queensland walnut, *Endiandra palmerstonii*, of the North Queensland rain-forests; the nut itself. [1886]

> **1886** C. PALMERSTON, in *Transactions and Proceedings of the Royal Geographical Society of Australasia NSW Branch* (1888), 242. Our dinner consisted of a few coohoy nuts, so named by the aborigines. The nut is perfectly round, and about 6 inches in circumference, with a thin shell … The nut needs no preparation, only roasting till nicely browned.

coolah grass /'kulə ɡras/
Also called **cooly** and **coolly**.
[Wiradhuri and Kamilaroi, New South Wales, probably *gulu*.]
Any of several grasses, especially the introduced *Panicum coloratum*, a summer-growing tufted perennial of New South Wales, Queensland and Victoria, and the widespread native *Panicum prolutum* and *P. decompositum*. The name applies also to the edible seed of the grasses. [1847]

> **1848** T. L. MITCHELL, *Journal of an Expedition into the Interior of Tropical Australia*, 90. The *Panicum laevinode* [= *P. decompositum*] of Dr Lindley seemed to predominate, a grass whereof the seed ('Cooly') is made by the natives into a kind of paste or bread. Dry heaps of this grass, that had been pulled expressly for the purpose of gathering the seed, lay along our path for many miles.

dillon bush /'dɪlən bʊʃ/
[Wemba-wemba, western Victoria *dilañ*.]

The salt-tolerant plant of all mainland states, but not the Northern Territory, *Nitraria billardieri*, a rigid, spreading shrub, bearing edible fruits. [1885]

> **1885** P. R. MEGGY, *From Sydney to Silverton*, 21. Among the plants we noticed on the way were … the porcupine grass, so named from the porcupine like bristles springing from a mound resembling a porcupine's back, and another succulent shrub known as the 'dillon' bush, the last being the only … which sheep will eat.

dugulla /'dʒugələ/
[Dyirbal, Herberton region, North Queensland *jarrgala*.]
The tree *Pouteria chartacea* (formerly *Planchonella chartacea*), which has small, black, fleshy, edible fruit and a timber which was used for spears and boomerangs. [1909]

geebung /'dʒibʌŋ/
Also formerly **geebong** and **jibbong**.
[Dharuk, Sydney region, probably *jibuŋ*.]
The fruit of any of several shrubs or small trees of the genus *Persoonia*, of southern and eastern regions of Australia, which have an edible (but rather tasteless) fleshy layer around the stone. The plant itself is known by the same name as the small green fruit, which is eaten raw. In Arnhem Land, the shavings from the inner bark of a young tree are soaked in liquid to be used in the treatment of irritated eyes. [1790]

> **1978** E. SIMON, *Through My Eyes*, 127. The nut of the Geebung was chewed, as was charcoal, for teeth and for indigestion.

The word **geebung** has a further sense, see quotation:

> **1859**. *Southern Cross* [Sydney] 12 November, 12. Born and bred—(the geebung is always a native)—where pecuniary success is with the majority, the only test of worth, intelligence and respectability—the object of all honour and the aim of life, the Geebung's first business is to make money.

gooya /'guyə/
[Yuwaalaraay, north New South Wales, *guuya*.]
One of several names for the 'emu apple'. See *colane*, *gruie*, and *mooley apple*. [1849]

> **1955** H. G. LAMOND, *Towser, The Sheep Dog*, 82. A clump of gooya, or emu apple, stood out on a small plain.

gruie /'grui/
Formerly also **gruie-colane**, a compound formed from words borrowed from two Australian languages (see *colane*).

[Kamilaroi, east New South Wales, *garuy*.]

The small tree *Owenia acidula*, which has an edible, apple-like fruit with bitter, red flesh. Commonly called the *emu apple*, it is also known as *colane*, *gooya*, and *mooley apple*. [1888]

> **1889** J. H. MAIDEN, *Useful Native Plants of Australia*, 49. 'Gruie-Colaine.' The sub-acid fruit of this tree relieves thirst. It is eaten by colonists and aboriginals, and is of the size of a small nectarine.

gunyang /ˈgʌnyæŋ/

[Ganay (Kurnai), Gippsland, Victoria, *guñaŋ*.]

Any of several plants, especially the shrub *Solanum vescum* of south-east Australia and Tasmania, bearing a green to ivory-coloured globular berry which is edible. Also called *kangaroo apple*. [1855]

> **1855** J. BONWICK, *Geography of Australia and New Zealand*, 204. The Gunyang fruit of the Gipps Land sand ridges is of the taste and size of a Cape gooseberry, on a sort of night-shade shrub 6 feet high.

joonda /ˈdʒundə/

[Kuku-Yalanji, Bloomfield River, North Queensland *junda*.]

The 'wild almond tree' *Prunus turneriana*. Its plum-like fruit is poisonous, but the kernel can be made edible by leaching. [1909]

karkalla /kaˈkælə/

[Gaurna, Adelaide region and other South Australian languages *garrgala*.]

Any of several species of 'pigface', including *Carpobrotus rossii* of coastal Tasmania, Victoria, South Australia, and Western Australia, the fruit of which is edible. [1840]

> **1862** C. WILHELMI, *Manners and Customs of the Australian Natives*, 12. The most important and abundant fruit is that of a mesembrianthemum, to which the Europeans have given the somewhat vulgar name of pigfaces, but the natives the more euphonical one of karkalla.

karpe /ˈkapi/

[Dyirbal, Herberton region, North Queensland *gabi* for *Ficus pleurocarpa* and *Ficus platypoda*.]

The parasitic fig tree, *Ficus pleurocarpa*, which bears edible fruit (which is yellow, turning pink when fully ripe) and has a bark once used by Aborigines to make blankets. Timber-getters refer to the wood as *karpe*. [1909]

> **1909** F. M. BAILEY, *Comprehensive Catalogue of Queensland Plants*, 504. Ficus pleurocarpa, F. v. M.—'Kar-pe' of Atherton natives. The fruit is prominently ribbed in a dry but not in a fresh state.

kurrajong /ˈkʌrədʒɒŋ/
Also **currajong** and **currijong**.
[Dharuk, Sydney region *garrajuŋ* referring to 'fishing line'; the English loan was extended to the tree (probably the *black kurrajong*) from whose bark fishing lines were generally made.]
A name given to any of several plants yielding a useful fibre; specifically, any of several such trees of the genera *Brachychiton*, *Commersonia*, and *Sterculia*, especially the fodder tree *Brachychiton populneum* of New South Wales, Queensland, Victoria, and the Northern Territory, and *Asterotrichion discolor* of Tasmania. The fibre of the kurrajong was used by the Dharuk for making fishing lines, fishing nets, and carrying bags. The roots are said to have been cooked for food.

Three species are particularly useful:
The **red kurrajong**, *Brachychiton paradoxum*, of the Northern Territory, Queensland, and Western Australia, bears single red flowers. The nuts which follow are still eaten by Aborigines in northern Australia, but must be carefully processed before eating as the packing around the seeds is poisonous. The pods are baked in ashes and then the seeds are carefully removed from the film of poisonous material that surrounds them.

The **black kurrajong**, *Brachychiton populneum*, grows on rocky slopes of New South Wales and Victoria, and is planted by farmers for fodder in times of drought.

The **desert kurrajong**, the tree *Brachychiton gregorii* of Western Australia, the Northern Territory, and South Australia, occurs in dry, sandy country. The seeds of this tree can be ground into flour to be baked into dampers, but need the same treatment as the seeds of the red kurrajong, as they, too, are dangerous. [1793]

1895 *Proceedings of the Linnean Society of New South Wales*, X, 396 (*note*). Among the white people of Australia the name kurrajong is applied to a tree (*Brachychiton*), but the natives in most parts give it a different name and say that kurrajong is white fellow name. It seems to me that the tree obtained its name through a misunderstanding because it yields a fibre that is frequently used by aborigines for making nets. This fibre is called kurrajong by some natives, which seems to have led to the name being applied to the tree. On the other hand, as the Omeo blacks called their bush as well as the fibre kurrajong, such may possibly be the case with the Brachychiton tree in some tribal districts.

2001 *North Shore Times* [Sydney], 23 February 135. The comfortable homestead … is surrounded by mature peppercorn and kurrajong trees.

midyim /ˈmɪdʒəm/
Also **midgem**, **midjum**.
[Yagara, Brisbane region, probably *mijan*.]

The shrub *Austromyrtus dulcis*, growing along the coast from Grafton to Fraser Island, with edible berries. [1904]

> **1922** T. WELSBY, *Memories of Amity*, 237–8. The midjum berry is perhaps the most prolific of the fruit-bearing tree or shrub … Children will collect it by the tin full, and even the elders will join with gusto in its eating. The shrub grows no higher than one's knees and becomes laden with fruit, easily gathered. Its taste is of a sweetish nature, and not altogether unpalatable.

millaa /ˈmila/
Also **millaa-millaa**.
[Ngajan dialect of Dyirbal, North Queensland *malaymalay, malaamalaa*.]
The sprawling vine *Elaeagnus triflora* of rainforests north from the central Queensland coast. It bears an edible red fruit, rather like a wild mulberry. It is eaten raw and tends to leave the throat with a burning taste (especially if eaten when immature). [1909]

> **1994** N. & H. NICHOLSON, *Australian Rainforest Plants* IV, 29. *Elaeagnus triflora* Millaa Millaa, the aboriginal name for this plant, has been used for a town on the Atherton Tableland, presumably because it was a significant plant there … It is seen in rainforests at various altitudes north from the central Qld coast.

mooley apple /ˈmuli æpəl/
[Malyangaba, west of Lake Frome, South Australia and New South Wales *muli*.]
One of several names for the 'emu apple'. See *gooya*, *gruie*, and *colane*. [1888]

> **1966** A. MORRIS, *Plantlife of the Western Darling*, 70. 'Mooley Apple'. Handsome tree, fruit a drupe, dark red.

muntry /ˈmʌntri/
Now usually in the form of **muntries**, as either a singular or plural. Formerly also **monterry**, **montry**, **muntree**, and **muntri**.
[Gaurna, Adelaide area, probably *mandirri*, and Yaralde, mouth of the Murray River, South Australia, probably *mandharri*.]
The edible fruit of the low shrub *Kunzea pomifera* of dry, sandy soils and near-coastal western Victoria and eastern South Australia. It is also known as *native apple*. [1840]

> **1847** G. F. ANGAS, *Savage Life and Scenes in Australia and New Zealand*, I, 65. Monterries, or native apples. This fruit is a little berry, the production of a running plant that grows in profusion upon the sand-hills. These berries are precisely like miniature apples, and have an aromatic flavour, which is not unpleasant. When the monterry is ripe, the natives disperse themselves over the sand-hills in search of them.
>
> **1955** M. BUNDEY, *My Land*, 34. There is a berry called the muntri and with this you can make a lovely pie and tasty jam.

nardoo /naˈduː/

Formerly also **ardo** and **nardu**.

[The name *ŋardu* occurs in Australian languages over a wide area of south Australia, south-west Queensland, and western New South Wales. The first written mention is in an account of the Burke and Wills expedition, and the location given indicates contact with the Yandruwandha language, Cooper's Creek, South Australia. In Kamilaroi, east New South Wales, and neighbouring languages, the name of the plant is *nhaadu*.]

The perennial fern *Marsilea drummondii* of mainland Australia, having clover-like fronds and occurring chiefly in arid areas along stream-beds and near lakes. It occurs in swamps and waterways, with the leaves floating on the surface of the water. The name is also used of several other ferns of the same genus, the spores of which are smaller than a pea and can be ground into flour and used as food.

Nardoo damper, or **nardoo cake**, is made by grinding the spores into a flour between two stones (**nardoo stones**), making it into a paste with water, kneading it, and then baking it in an earth oven. This was a food of last resort, only used in 'hard times' when no other food was available. [1860]

> **1867** S. MCTAVISH, *Chowla*, 16. There are a devoted band of Moravian missionaries bound for Cooper's Creek … exchanging the sausages and sauer-kraut of the Vaterland for opossum and nardoo.

> **1977** J. O'GRADY, *There was a Kid*, 39. Nardoo is a species of clover fern—*Marsilea drummondii*—and its spores were collected and pounded by Aboriginal women, and made into a sort of bread, or porridge. Although often short of food on the farm, our father said that he hoped we would never have to 'come at nardoo bread', or porridge.

nonda /ˈnɒndə/

[The Leichhardt quotation suggests that a similar tree may have been called *nonda* in the Moreton Bay language, Yagara (*Parinari nonda* itself is only found in the far north), but sources on Yagara do not refer to any tree name of this form.]

The tree *Parinari nonda* of the northern parts of Queensland and the Northern Territory, often found growing in groves on sand ridges. It bears an astringent, edible, yellow fruit. [1845]

> **1845** L. LEICHHARDT, *Journal of an Overland Expedition in Australia, from Moreton Bay to Port Essington … during the Years 1844–1845* (1847), 315. A middle sized shady wide spreading tree … attracted our attention, and excited much interest. Its younger branches were rather drooping, its fruit was an oblong yellow plum, an inch long and half an inch in diameter, with a rather rough kernel. When ripe, the pericarp is very mealy and agreeable to eat, and would be wholesome, if it were not so extraordinarily astringent. We called this tree the 'Nonda' from its resemblance to a tree so called by the natives in the Moreton Bay district.

quandong /ˈkwɒndɒŋ/

Also known as **quondong**, and formerly **quandang** and **quantong**.

[Wiradhuri, south-west New South Wales *guwandhaaŋ*.]

The shrub or small tree *Santalum acuminatum* of dry country in southern Australia, which bears a globular, usually bright red fruit with a deeply wrinkled stone that contains an edible seed. It is sometimes known as *native peach*. The ripe red quandong fruit is mostly eaten fresh, but can be dried for later consumption. The distinctive rough seeds are often worn as body decoration, particularly made into necklaces. The quandong continues to be a very popular fruit among Aborigines of the drier areas of Australia. [1836]

The name is also applied to a number of other species:

The **bitter quandong**, *Santalum murrayanum*, as its name suggests, has bitter and inedible fruit.

The **silver quandong** (or simply **quandong**) is a rainforest tree, *Elaeocarpus angustifolius*, of east Queensland and eastern New South Wales, which bears a globular, blue, edible fruit with a deeply wrinkled stone, and yields a useful timber.

The name is also applied to any of several other plants, usually of the genera *Santalum*, *Elaeocarpus*, or *Peripentadenia*—for example, **Kuranda quandong** (*Elaeocarpus bancroftii*) and **northern quandong** (*Elaeocarpus foveolatus*).

> **2000** *Nature Australia*, Autumn, 25. Aborigines ate the fruits of the Desert Quandong, and country people still gather them today to bake in pies.

Apart from its use in the naming of plants, **quandong** occurs in the phrase **to have (the) quandongs**, meaning 'to be stupid', and as a term for 'one who exploits or imposes on another', or for 'a country bumpkin'.

> **1899** *Bulletin* [Sydney], 4 March, 15. F'instance, in N.-W. N.S.W., the man with wheels in his head has 'Darling Peas' or 'rats', whereas, in the Cobar and Lachlan country, he has 'quandongs' or 'rabbits'. ('Rabbits' means very severe quandongness).

> **1985** P. CAREY, *Illywhacker*, 246. 'What's an illywhacker?' … 'A spieler … a trickster. A quandong. A ripperty man. A con-man.'

> **1978** T. DAVIES, *More Australian Nicknames*, 84. *Quandong*, was born and bred in the bush.

ulcardo melon /ʌlˈkadoʊ mɛlən/

[Aranda, Alice Springs region, *ulkarte*]

The fruit-bearing plant *Cucumis melo* subsp. *agrestis*, also called native gooseberry, native melon, and native cucumber. [1994]

> **1995** P. LATZ *Bushfires and Bushtucker, Aboriginal Plant Use in Central Australia*, 155. Ulcardo melon … An annual twining creeper, rough to the touch, with small yellow flowers and green fruits which mature to a yellowish colour. Because of their colour the immature fruits are well concealed amongst the leaves until they reach

maturity … The keeping qualities of the fruit are important because it means that this fruit source is available for several months of the year.

waratah /wɒrə'ta/, /'wɒrətə/
Formerly also **warata**, **warratah**, **warrataw**, and **warrettah**.
[Dharuk, Sydney region *warrada*.]
Any shrub or small tree of the genus *Telopea* of south-east Australia, especially *Telopea speciosissima* (the floral emblem of New South Wales) and the Tasmanian *Telopea truncata*. Both plants have a striking, bright red flower-head, for which they are often cultivated. Aborigines once sucked the flowers, which contain a sweet nectar. The waratah has also been called the *tulip tree*, *native tulip*, or *telopea*. In Queensland, *Alloxylon pinnata* (formerly *Oreocallis pinnata*) is called **Queensland waratah**, **waratah silky oak**, or *Dorrigo oak*. [1788]

> **1790** J. E. SMITH, *A Specimen of the Botany of New Holland*, 19. The most magnificent plant which the prolific soil of New Holland affords is, by common consent both of Europeans and Natives, the Waratah.

wongai /'wɒŋgaɪ/
Also **wongi** and **wongai plum**.
[Kala Lagaw Ya (the western language of the Torres Strait) *woŋay*.]
The seashore tree *Manilkara kauki*, which occurs in the north-east part of the Cape York Peninsula, Queensland, and on offshore islands. It bears a fruit, which is maroon red when ripe and matures three to seven days after being picked, with a taste something like a date. [1898]

> **1898** E. ROWAN, *Flower-hunter in Queensland and NZ.*, 169. We sat under the shade of two magnificent wongi trees, whose thick branches, laden with date-like plums in every stage of ripeness, formed an impenetrable shade.

Roots and tubers

adjigo /'ædʒɪgoʊ/, /'ædʒɪkoʊ/
Also **adjiko** and **ijjecka**.
[Probably Nhanta, Geraldton region, Western Australia *ajuga*, 'vegetable food'.]
The native yam *Dioscorea hastifolia* of near-coastal, south-western Western Australia, also known as *warran*. The edible underground part of the plant is known by the same name. This plant was once so prolific that it could, in one small area, play a part in supporting a large population of Aborigines, who rarely exhausted its supply. [1863]

> **1903** H. TAUNTON, *Australind*, 28. She it was that showed me the 'ajigo' plant, and taught me how to dig up its succulent root, which when cooked resembles a cooked yam in size, shape, and flavour.

bulkuru /bʌlkə'ru/

[Dyirbal, Herberton–Tully region, North Queensland *bulguru*]

Eleocharis sphaceleta and *Eleocharis dulcis*, sedges which grow in swamps. They have a nut-like tuber underneath, which can be eaten raw or roasted or baked. [1900].

> **1982** U. ROWLETT, *Water Plants of the Townsville Town Common*. Possibly the most abundant water plant on the Townsville town common is the bulkuru or soft spikerush. This species of sedge is found elsewhere in Queensland, in the Northern Territory, and in Malaysia and South-east Asia.

bungwall /'bʌŋwɔl/

[Yagara, Brisbane region *baŋwal*.]

The fern of swampy land, *Blechnum indicum*, occurring in Queensland, New South Wales, the Northern Territory, and elsewhere, the root of the plant being an important traditional food. The roots are pounded to make them less fibrous, and then roasted. This food is available all year around, and is still collected and eaten in Arnhem Land and North Queensland. [1824]

> **1841** C. EIPPER, *Statement … of the German Mission … at Moreton Bay*, 6. From the vegetable kingdom they derive, amongst other edibles, two roots, which constitute their chief food, and which it is the daily occupation of the women to dig out of the swamps; the one is called *Bangwall*, the other *Imboon*; the plants somewhat resemble the fern tree, but the imboon is more farinaceous than the bangwall. They are found in pieces the size of a man's thumb. When the root is roasted on the fire and the black skin pulled off, it is not unpalatable; but, to increase its relish, the good housewife has a smooth stone with which she pounds it into small cakes and then hands them to different members of her family.

cunjevoi /'kʌndʒəvɔɪ/

Also **cunjiboy**.

[Probably from Bandjalang, north-east New South Wales.]

The plant *Alocasia brisbanensis* (formerly *Alocasia macrorrhiza*), occurring in moist forests of New South Wales and Queensland. The leaves were said to be a remedy for the sting caused by the stinging-tree. Pounded roots were also used to relieve insect bites. *Cunjevoi* is also the name of a sea-squirt (pp. 91–2). [1845]

> **1845** C. HODGKINSON, *Australia, from Port Macquarie to Moreton Bay, with Descriptions of the Natives*, 225–6. The root of the Conjeboi, a large-leaved plant, which grows on very moist alluvial land, often flooded, is also eaten. The leaves and stalk of the conjeboi are full of a burning acrid juice, which blisters the lips if applied to the mouth. The root also contains this sap, but by pounding it between flat stones, and thereby expressing all the juice by continued beatings … it at last becomes an insipid farinaceous mass, which is then cooked and eaten.

maloga /məˈloʊɡə/
[Mayi-Thakurti, around Cloncurry, North Queensland *malaka.*]
The vine *Vigna lanceolata* of northern Australia. [1909]

> **1988** T. LOW, *Bush Tucker: Australia's Wild Food Harvest*, 99. In northern Australia there is a bean vine that produces 'peanuts'. This is maloga bean (*Vigna lanceolata*), a creeper of woodlands and desert watercourses, the white taproot of which was important Aboriginal tucker.

murnong /ˈmɜnɒŋ/
Also with much variety, as **mernong**, **mirr'n-yong**, **murnung**, **murrnong**, and **myrnong**.
[Wathawurung and Wuywurung, southern Victoria, probably *mirnaŋ*.]
The edible tuber of the perennial herb *Microseris lanceolata* of temperate Australia. The plant itself is known by the same name, and bears a yellow, dandelion-like flower-head. The tubers are washed, then eaten raw or roasted; they are sweet and milky, and taste like coconut. This was a staple food for Aborigines in many parts of Victoria (see the article by Beth Gott in *Australian Aboriginal Studies*, 1983, No. 2, pp. 2–17). Myrniong, a town west of Bacchus Marsh in Victoria, is named after this plant, which today cannot be found in its vicinity. [1835]

> **1922** C. DALEY, *Early Squatting Days: from the Papers of the Late A.F. Mollison*, 5. Murnong ... is about the size of the upper half of a small carrot, a milky juice exudes through the skin, and when roasted in the ashes it is palatable, and no doubt wholesome and nutritious. The Port Phillip tribes bake these roots in a hole in the ground when they half melt down into a sweet, dark-coloured juice.

warran /ˈwɒrən/
[Nyungar, Perth–Albany region *warran.*]
The native yam *Dioscorea hastifolia*; also called *adjigo*. [1839]

> **1842** G. F. MOORE, *Descriptive Vocabulary of the Language ... of Western Australia*, 74. Warran ... One of the Dioscoreae. A species of yam, the root of which grows generally to about the thickness of a man's thumb; and to the depth of sometimes four to six feet in loamy soils. It is sought chiefly at the commencement of the rains, when it is ripe, and when the earth is most easily dug; and it forms the principal article of food for the natives at that season. It grows in light rich soil on the low lands, and also among the fragments of basaltic and granitic rocks on the hills. The country in which it abounds is very difficult and unsafe to pass over on horseback, on account of the frequency and depth of the holes. The digging of the root is a very laborious operation.

yelka /ˈyɛlkə/
Also **yalka** and **yulka**.
[Aranda, Alice Springs region *yalge* (a similar name is found in neighbouring languages).]

Any of several sedges of the genus *Cyperus* yielding a small, edible tuber. This tuber is also known from its appearance as a *wild onion*. After gathering, it is peeled and then eaten raw or lightly roasted. [1896]

> **1957** M. GARTRELL, *Dear Primitive: a Nurse Among the Aborigines*, 10. Along the creek-bank collected a few handfuls of yelka (a bulb-like grass-root that looks like an onion but tastes like a potato).

Other edible flora

bangalow /ˈbæŋgəloʊ/
Formerly also **bungalow**.
[Dharawal, Illawarra region, New South Wales, probably *baŋgala*.]
The tall palm *Archontophoenix cunninghamiana* of New South Wales and Queensland, having arching, feather-like fronds. Also called *piccabeen*. (The palm *Archontophoenix alexandrae*, of North Queensland, is sometimes erroneously called *bangalow*.) [1818]

> **1818** I. LEE, *Early Explorers in Australia* (1925), 415. (Allan Cunningham's Journal, 26 October 1818) Amongst a group of fourteen natives from Shoalhaven who were encamped near the Merrimorra River Farm, I observed they had their fresh water in baskets made of the leaf-sheaths of some palm, which they called Bangla, and which they informed us grew under the mountain range.

> **1851** J. HENDERSON, *Excursions and Adventures in New South Wales*, II, 229. The Bangalo, which is a palm, and a native of the brushes ... The germ, or roll of young leaves in the centre, and near to the top, is eaten by the natives ... either raw or boiled.

conkerberry /ˈkɒŋkəbɛri/
Also **coongaberry**, **konkleberry**, **koonkerberry**, and **kunkerberry**.
[Mayi-Yapi and Mayi-Kulan, spoken around the Cloncurry River and the Norman River, North Queensland *gaŋgabarri*. The final two syllables of the name have been interpreted as English *berry*.]
Either of two species of small shrubs of the genus *Carissa*, especially *Carissa lanceolata*, the spiny shrub or small tree of Western Australia, the Northern Territory, and Queensland, having edible fruits. In the Northern Territory, different parts of the shrubs are used for herbal remedies. When the root is boiled and the bark removed, the liquid can be used as an all-purpose medicine, and is particularly useful for toothache. The oily sap of the tree was used to treat rheumatism. [1883]

> **1888** J. H. MAIDEN, *Proceedings of the Linnean Society of New South Wales*, III, 495. *Carissa ovata* ... 'Kunkerberry' of the aboriginals of the Cloncurry River ... This little bush produces a very pleasant fruit which is both agreeable and wholesome. It

is like a sloe, egg-shaped, and about half-an-inch long. It exudes a viscid milky juice and contains a few woody seeds.

cumbungi /kʌmˈbʌŋgi/
Also **combungie** and **kumpun**.
[Wemba-wemba, western Victoria *gambaŋ*.]
A tall, reed-like plant growing in or near water, either *Typha domingensis* or *Typha orientalis*, of all states, New Zealand, and Asia. Also known, with other similar plants, as *bulrush*. The explorer Major Thomas Mitchell noted that this plant was the principal food of the people who lived along the Lachlan River (and noted its name there as 'Balyan'). The new shoots were gathered and eaten raw or cooked; the roots were roasted. Also called *wonga*. [1878]

> **1878** R. BROUGH SMYTH, *The Aborigines of Victoria*, I, xxxiii. The kumpung, a bulrush almost identical with one found in Switzerland … is eaten during the summer either raw or roasted, and the fibres are used for making twine.

junga /ˈdʒʊŋə/, /ˈdʒʌŋə/
[Panyjima, around Tom Price, Western Australia *jaŋa*.]
Another name for *parakeelia*, herbs of the genus *Calandrinia*. [1932]

> **1984** W. W. AMMON et al., *Working Lives*, 151. There was a plant there called junga or parakeelya. It is very sappy and keeps the sheep from needing water till late in the summer.

mingil /ˈmɪŋgəl/
[Western Desert language *miŋgurl* 'native tobacco (which is chewed rather than being smoked)' (synonym of *ugiri*, see *okiri*).]
Another name for either *okiri* or *pituri*. [1935]

> **1935** H. BASEDOW, *Knights of the Boomerang: episodes from a life spent among the native tribes of Australia*, 67. These men of the bush had used to 'dope' the emus. … They had employed only the leaves of a plant they called 'mingul' (*Duboisia hopwoodii*), the same as they themselves use for chewing.

mungite /ˈmʌŋgaɪt/
[Nyungar, Perth–Albany region, probably *maŋgayit*, 'the flower of the banksia'.]
A Western Australian name for the nectar-rich, flowering spike, which becomes the woody cone, of a plant of the genus *Banksia*. [1831]

> **1842** G. F. MOORE, *Descriptive Vocabulary of the Language … of Western Australia*, 50. Man-gyt … The large yellow cone-shaped flower of the Banksia, containing a quantity of honey, which the natives are fond of sucking. Hence the tree has obtained the name

of the honeysuckle tree. One flower contains at the proper season more than a table-spoonful of honey. Birds, ants, and flies consume it.

munyeroo /mʌnyə'ru/
Also **munyeru**.
[Diyari, Lake Eyre region, South Australia (and related languages) *muñurra*.]
Either of two succulent plants, both the seeds and leaves of which are used as food. Originally, the name referred to *Calandrinia balonensis*, and now it usually refers to the 'pigweed', *Portulaca oleracea*. The leaves, which taste rather bitter, are ground, rolled into little balls and eaten immediately. The seeds may be collected and stored to be used in times of drought, as they can keep for indefinite periods. Also useful as a forage plant for cattle. [1874]

> **1886** *Transactions and Proceedings of the Royal Society of South Australia*, VIII, 27. *Claytonia Balonnensis*—This showy plant, called 'Munyeroo' by the aboriginals … has a cluster of thick fleshy leaves, with a flower stem some six or more inches high, crowned with bright deep pink flowers as large as a shilling.

nelia /'niliə/
Formerly also **neelya**, and **nealie**.
[Ngiyambaa, central New South Wales *nhiilʸi* for *Acacia loderi*.]
Any of several small trees or shrubs of inland Australia of the *Acacia* genus, especially *Acacia rigens*, having needle-like foliage, and *Acacia loderi*. The gum of the tree was once eaten by Aborigines. [1867]

> **1885** *Once a Month: an illustrated Australian magazine* [Melbourne], June, 448. There is a small tree very common along the seventy-mile track. It is an acacia; its leaves are long and very narrow, but are in great masses. The wood … is what is used by the blacks for making their spears. They call it Neelya.

okiri /'ɒkəri/
[Western Desert language *ugiri*.]
Either of the soft-leaved plants of the genus *Nicotiana*, also known as *native tobacco*. The leaves and stems are chewed rather than smoked. They are usually ground fresh, but can also be dried and made into balls to be used later. [1891]

> **1891** *Transactions and Proceedings of the Royal Society of South Australia*, XVI, 293. The blacks had gathered some native tobacco plants which they call 'okiri'.

parakeelia /pærə'kilyə/
Also with much variety, as **parakeelya**, **parakelia**, **parakylia**, and **parrakeelya**.
[Guyani, Lake Torrens region, South Australia, probably *barrgilʸa* (also occurs in languages to the north and west of Guyani).]

Any of several herbs usually of the genus *Calandrinia*, especially *Calandrinia balonensis* and *Calandrinia polyandra*, which have thick, succulent leaves, and occur in arid, inland Australia. The leaves of the parakeelia can be eaten and are frequently used to quench thirst. The seeds may be ground into a paste to be eaten raw or cooked. Also called *junga* and *munyeroo*. [1885]

> **2003** *The Land*, 3 January, 20. The best feed is parakeelya. It's got nearly as many nutrients as lucerne and cattle go onto it and not need a drink of water for up to three months. It comes in September after rain.

piccabeen /ˈpɪkəbin/

[Yagara, Brisbane region (and neighbouring languages), Queensland, originally *bigi* for the palm and a water carrier made from it; the *been* may have been added from English.]
A name used mainly in Queensland for the palm *Archontophoenix cunninghamiana*. Also called **piccabeen palm** or *bangalow*. The green heart of the piccabeen palm was eaten, and the expanded leaf base could be used as a water carrier. [1887]

> **1904** C. C. PETRIE, *Tom Petrie's Reminiscences of Early Queensland*, 93. The common palm (*Archontophoenix cunninghamii*). Young shoots coming out at the top were just pulled and eaten raw as a vegetable … called 'pikki'. Of late years, the name has grown to 'pikkibean'.

pituri /ˈpɪtʃəri/

Also with much variety, especially as **pitcheri**, **pitcherie**, **pitchery**, and **pitury**.
[This word came into English from Yandruwandha, around Cooper's Creek, see quotation. The Yandruwandha would have borrowed the name *bijirri* from their northerly neighbours Pitta-pitta and Wangka-Yutjuru, from whom (or from whose territory) they obtained the plant.]
The shrub *Duboisia hopwoodii*, whose leaves were traditionally used as an animal poison and narcotic. Also known as *mingil* and *native tobacco*. It contains an alkaloid which is four times more powerful than nicotine. The leaves are ground and then mixed with ashes before being chewed. The crushed leaves of pituri were also placed in waterholes to catch animals, especially emus, which were stunned by the substance. The shrub grows sparsely in many parts of arid Australia, but more profusely around the Mulligan River in south-west Queensland. Aborigines would travel a considerable distance to the Mulligan for the plant, and it was traded to tribes hundreds of kilometres away (see Pamela Watson, *This Precious Foliage*, Oceania Monographs, 1983). The meaning of *pituri* has been extended, and in central Australia it can now refer to any chewable species of *Nicotiana*. [1861]

1861 *The Burke and Wills Exploring Expedition: reprinted from 'The Argus',* 28. They gave us some stuff they call bedgery, or pedgery. It has a highly intoxicating effect when chewed even in small quantities. It appears to be the dried stems and leaves of some shrub.

weir mallee /wɪə 'mæli/
Obsolete.
[The first part of the name is based on the first part of Wergaia dialect of Wemba-wemba (Wimmera district, Victoria) *wiyar-gajin*, which was used for any of the species of mallee-gum from whose roots water could be obtained, especially *Eucalyptus incrassata* and *Eucalyptus dumosa*. The second element is simply *mallee*.]
The mallee or small tree, *Eucalyptus dumosa*, of drier south-east mainland Australia. [1858]

1878 R. BROUGH SMYTH, *The Aborigines of Victoria*, I, 220. Stanbridge says that the hunter, in places far removed from permanent water, has to draw his supply of that element from the roots of the swamp-box and the weir-mallee, which run a few inches below the surface of the earth.

wonga /'wɒŋgə/
[Wemba-wemba, western Victoria *waŋgal*.]
Another name for *cumbungi*, especially its root, when old. *Wonga* is also the name for a corroboree (p. 160). [1865]

1888 *Proceedings of the Linnean Society of New South Wales*, III, 550. *Typha angustifolia* … is the 'Wonga' of the Lower Murray aboriginals, the young shoots are edible, and resemble asparagus.

General flora

balga /'bælgə/
[Nyungar, Perth–Albany region, *balga*.]
A Western Australian name for a grass tree, especially *Xanthorrhoea preissii*. [1840]

1842 G. F. MOORE, *A descriptive vocabulary of the language in common use among the Aborigines of Western Australia* …, 3. Balga, s,—Xanthorea arborea, grass-tree or blackboy. This is a useful tree to the natives where it abounds. The frame of their huts is constructed from the tall, flowering stems and the leaves serve for a thatch and for a bed. The resinous trunk forms a cheerful blazing fire. The flower-stem yields a gum used for food. The trunk gives a resin used for cement and also, when beginning to decay, furnishes large quantities of marrow-like grubs, which are considered a delicacy. Fire is readily kindled by friction of the dry flower-stems, and the withered leaves furnish a torch.

bangalay /ˈbæŋɡəleɪ/, /bæŋˈɡæli/
[Probably from Dharawal of the Illawarra region, New South Wales.]
The tree *Eucalyptus botryoides* of New South Wales and Victoria, commonly found on saline coastal soils; also known as *southern mahogany*. [1810]

> **1861** *Catalogue of Natural and Industrial Products of New South Wales*, 28. Bangalay … a crooked growing tree, the timber much valued for knees and crooked timbers of coasting vessels.

belah /bəˈla/
Also **belar**, **billar**, and **beal**.
[Wiradhuri, south-west New South Wales, and neighbouring languages *bilaarr*.]
Any of several trees or large shrubs of the family Casuarinaceae, with slender, jointed branchlets and woody cones, especially *Casuarina cristata* of drier regions of Australia. In the Boulia area of Queensland, *Acacia peuce* is called **belah**. [1862]

> **1887** W. H. SUTTOR, *Australian Stories Retold and Sketches of Country Life*, 117. On the low-lying, black, flooded land, the belar, a species of native oak or casuarina, is found, casting so dense a shade as to prevent all other vegetation from showing.

bendee /ˈbɛndi/
Also **bendi**.
[Possibly from an Australian language.]
The tree of Queensland and the Northern Territory *Acacia catenulata*, found on shallow stony soils and usually having a deeply-fluted trunk. The wood of the tree is known by the same name. [1881]

> **1911** ST. C. GRONDONA, *Collar and Cuffs: the adventures of a jackeroo*, 69. Bendi, as a very thick scrub is called, is almost impenetrable, certainly so for a horseman. I have never seen any of it alive. … I have encountered a good deal of dead stuff, however, and it is most awkward if the stock you are after take it into their heads to investigate the interior of a patch of bendi.

bimble box /ˈbɪmbəl bɒks/
Also **bibbil**, **bimble**.
[Wiradhuri, south-west New South Wales *bimbil*.]
The tree *Eucalyptus populnea* of New South Wales and Queensland, having a fibrous, brownish-grey bark and glossy, green leaves. Also known as *poplar box*. [1839]

> **1901** K. L. PARKER, in M. MUIR, *My Bush Book* (1982), 102. A few bibbil, wide-leaved box trees … whose leaves after rain or in sunlight look as if they had been dipped in liquefied silver.

bindi-eye /'bɪndi-aɪ/

Also **bindy-eye** and formerly with much variety, as **bindei**, **bindeah**, **bindii**, **bindiyi**, and **blindy-eye**.

[Kamilaroi and Yuwaalaraay, east New South Wales *bindayaa*.]

Any of several plants bearing barbed fruits, especially herbs of the widespread genus *Calotis*. The fruit of these plants is known by the same name. [1896]

> **1896** K. L. PARKER, *Australian Legendary Tales*, 7. In the country of the Galah are lizards coloured reddish brown, and covered with spikes like bindeah prickles. *Ibid.*, 129. Bindeah, a prickle or small thorn.

> **1930** K. G. TAYLOR, *Pick and the Duffers*, 254. If you'd've been pelted off in the bindy-eyes and got your pants full o' them you wouldn't think it so extremely amusing.

bolly gum /'bɒli gʌm/

[*Bolly* may possibly be from an Australian language. If so, probably one from south Queensland or north New South Wales.]

Any of several trees especially of the genera *Beilschmiedia*, *Litsea*, *Neolitsea*, *Cinnamomum*, and *Blepharocarya*. Also called **bolly wood**. [1904]

> **1956** N. K. WALLIS, *Australian Timber Handbook*, 4. Other timbers have special uses, such as … bollywood (aircraft construction), and brush box (bridge decking and flooring).

boonaree /'bunəri/

Also **boonery**.

[Probably Kamilaroi, east New South Wales *bunari*.]

The plant *Heterodendrum oleifolium*. Also known as *cattle bush*, *inland rosewood*, and *western rosewood*. [1912]

> **1974** S. L. EVERIST, *Poisonous Plants of Australia*, 438. Boonaree is one of the most useful fodder trees in inland Australia and sheep and cattle often live on it during drought periods.

booyong /'buyɒŋ/

Also **boyung**, **byong**, and **boing**.

[Bandjalang, north-east New South Wales *buyaŋ*.]

Any of several ornamental and timber trees of the genus *Argyrodendron*, of New South Wales and Queensland. Also called *black jack*, *crowsfoot elm*, and *tulip oak*. [1908]

> **1923** T. HALL, *A Short History of the Downs Blacks known as 'the Blucher Tribe'*, 25. The boomerangs were made from the booyong (or Black Jack) tree, which was considered the finest timber to be had for that purpose.

boree /'bɔri/, /bɔ'ri/
Also known as **boree shrub**.
[Wiradhuri and Kamilaroi, New South Wales *burrii*.]
Any of several *Acacia* species. In New South Wales and parts of Queensland, the name is used specifically of *Acacia pendula*, also known as *myall, weeping myall*, and **weeping boree**. The leaves of this tree are eaten by cattle and its timber is an excellent firewood. [1845]

> **1878** 'IRONBARK' (G. H. GIBSON), *Southerly Busters*, 144.
>
> Where the tangled 'boree' blossoms,
> Where the 'gidya' thickets wave,
> And the tall yapunyah's shadow
> Rests upon the stockman's grave.

brigalow /'brɪgəloʊ/
Formerly also **bricklow**.
[Possibly Kamilaroi, east New South Wales *burrii* (see *boree*) plus plural suffix *-gal*.]
Any of several trees of the genus *Acacia*, especially the New South Wales and Queensland tree *Acacia harpophylla*, having a dark, furrowed bark and silver foliage. Also called **brigalow spearwood**. [1844]

> **1844** L. LEICHHARDT, *Journal of an Overland Expedition in Australia, from Moreton Bay to Port Essington … during the Years 1844–1845* (1847), 8 October, 9. The Bricklow shrub compelled us frequently to travel along the flood-bed of the river.

> **1889** J. H. MAIDEN, *Useful Native Plants of Australia*, 356. 'Brigalow' … Wood brown, hard, heavy, and elastic; used by the natives for spears, boomerangs, and clubs. The wood splits freely, and is used for fancy turnery. Saplings used as stakes in vineyards have lasted twenty years or more. It is used for building purposes, and has a strong odour of violets.

budda /'bʌdə/
Also **buddha** and **budtha**.
[Yuwaalaraay, north New South Wales and nearby languages *badha*.]
Any of several shrubs or small trees of inland Australia, especially *Eremophila mitchellii*, the leaves and timber of which have a strong aroma resembling that of sandalwood. Also called *sandalwood, false sandalwood*, and *sandalbox*. [1890]

> **1930** *Bulletin* [Sydney], 17 December, 21. Up till quite recently N.S. Wales farmers (and bushmen generally) have remained blind to the many virtues of the budda-tree. … Budda is now beginning to come into its own. … The proper spelling … is 'budtha', an aboriginal word meaning strong-smelling.

bullich /ˈbʊlɪtʃ/
[Nyungar, Perth–Albany region, probably *bulij*.]
The medium-sized tree *Eucalyptus megacarpa* of south-western Western Australia; also called *swamp karri*. [c. 1891]

> **1996** J. WHEELER, *Common Trees of the South West Forests*, 36. Bullich, like karri, is a smooth-barked eucalypt which sheds its old grey bark to reveal mottled tonings of yellow, pink, orange, pale grey and white.

bulwaddy /bʊlˈwɒdi/
Also **bullwaddi**, **bullwaddie**, and **bullwaddy**.
[The origin of this word is obscure. It may come from a Northern Territory language or it may be a compound of English *bull* (as in *bull oak*) and *waddy*, q.v.]
The tree of northern Australia *Macropteranthes kekwickii*, which forms dense thickets. [1925]

> **1925** M. TERRY, *Across Unknown Australia*, 194. Bull-waddi grows in ... thickets ... It ... gives off greater heat than any other Australian wood ... Gidgee is supposed to be one of the hottest, but it is cool compared with bull-waddi.

bundy /ˈbʌndi/
[Probably Dharuk, Sydney region *bunda*.]
The rough-barked *Eucalyptus goniocalyx* and *E. nortonii* of south-east Australia. Also called *long-leaved box* and *olive-barked box*. [1899]

> **1981** A. B. CRIBB & J. W. CRIBB, *Useful Wild Plants in Australia*, 28. Several other species of *Eucalyptus* are exploited for their high cineole content. These include the bundy or long-leaved box, *E. goniocalyx*, of the Dividing Range areas of New South Wales and Victoria, extending into some of the South Australian Ranges.

burgan /ˈbɜɡən/
[Wuywurung, Melbourne region, probably *burgan*.]
The shrub *Kunzea ericoides* of Victoria, New South Wales, and Queensland. (What were earlier thought to be three distinct species are now regarded as variants of a single species. They were *Kunzea peduncularis*, *Leptospermum ericoides* and *Leptospermum phylicoides*.) [1866]

> **1988** G. ELLIOT, *New Australian Plants*, 188. *Kunzea ericoides* Burgan 3–6 m x 2–4 m Qld, NSW, Vic. A shrubby plant with crowded, narrow green leaves. Showy cluster of white, or pale pink, tea-tree-like flowers are produced near the ends of the branchlets during spring to summer.

carabeen, red /ˈkærəbin/
[Bandjalang, north-east New South Wales *garrabin* for *Geissois benthamii*.]

The 'brush mahogany tree', *Geissois benthamii*, of south Queensland and New South Wales, and the related 'northern brush mahogany', *Geissois biagiana*, of North Queensland. [1946]

> **1965** *Australian Encyclopaedia*, IV, 250. Of the two Australian species, *G. benthamii* (red carabeen) is a medium to tall tree of brush forests and extends from the Manning River, N.S.W., northward into south-eastern Queensland (McPherson Range). ... The timber is close-grained, easily worked and reddish when first cut, but it dries pale; hard flinty pockets detract from its value for indoor work and careful seasoning is necessary.

carbeen /ˈkabin/

Also **carbean** and **karbeen**.

[Kamilaroi and Yuwaalaraay, east New South Wales *gaabiin*.]

The eucalypt *Eucalyptus tessellaris*, also known as *Moreton Bay ash* (and, in Queensland, **carbeen bloodwood**) that occurs from the far north of New South Wales through the eastern part of Queensland. The related *Eucalyptus confertiflora* is known as the **broad-leaved carbeen**. In far west Queensland, the ghost gum *Eucalyptus papuana* is called **carbeen**. [1888]

> **1935** F. D. DAVISON & B. NICHOLLS, *Blue Coast Caravan*, 156. ... The Moreton Bay ash—called by some the Carbeen—distinguished among the eucalypts. The bark, for six or eight feet above the ground, is grey in colour and rough and tessellated like crocodile skin. Above that it is light buff, smooth and of fine texture. The branches are slender and the leaves, much smaller and more numerous than is usual among gums, are of a light shade of green.

chittick /ˈtʃɪtɪk/

Also **chittock**.

[Nyungar, Perth–Albany region, probably *jidiyug*.]

The medium-sized shrub *Lambertia inermis* of Western Australia, having yellow or red flowers. [1891]

> **1960** *Countryman* [Perth], 14 July, 36. Blocks with bigger acreages are chiefly plain country clothed with scrub, mallee, black boys and chittock, the soil being mainly sandy with a gravel or clay sub-soil.

cooba /ˈkubə/

Also **couba**, **coobah**, and **cuba**.

[Wiradhuri, south-west New South Wales *gubaa*.]

Any of several Acacia plants, especially *Acacia salicina* of drier mainland Australia, the leaves of which are eaten by cattle. Also called *native willow*, *willow wattle*, and *wirra*. [1878]

1889 J. H. MAIDEN, *Useful Native Plants of Australia*, 115. *Acacia salicina* ... called 'Cooba' or 'Koobah' by the aboriginals of western New South Wales ... This is another tree which is rapidly becoming scarce, owing to the partiality of stock to it.

coojong /ˈkudʒɒŋ/
Also **cujong** and **kudjong**.
[Nyungar, Perth–Albany region, probably *galʸaŋ*.]
The small wattle *Acacia saligna* of south-western Western Australia; also known as *black wattle* and *golden-wreath wattle*. [1842]

1842 G. F. MOORE, *A descriptive vocabulary of the language in common use among the Aborigines of Western Australia*, 27. Gal-yăng, s.—Species of acacia. Colonially, the wattle-tree, from its partial resemblance to the wattle or osier-tree of England.

coolibah /ˈkuləba/
Also **coolabah**, **coolobar**, and **coolybah**.
[Yuwaaliyaay, north New South Wales and nearby languages *gulabaa*.]
Any of several Eucalyptus trees, especially the bluish-leaved *Eucalyptus microtheca* found across central and northern Australia, a fibrous-barked tree yielding a heavy durable timber and occurring in seasonally flooded areas. [1883]

The name has been made universally familiar by its use in 'Banjo' Paterson's 'Waltzing Matilda' (1903):

> Once a jolly swagman camped by a billabong,
> Under the shade of a coolibah tree.

1995 C. MCADAM, *Boundary Lines*, 63. That country used to be riddled with kangaroos before the cattle took over. It's all black soil country with red Flinders grass up to your waist, coolibah and bloodwood country.

cooloolah /kəˈlulə/
Also **caloola** and **caloolah**.
[Gabi-gabi, south-east Queensland *gululay*.]
A cypress pine, *Callitris columellaris*, often used for telegraph poles. Used in many street names and place names (for example, Cooloola National Park on the south Queensland coast). [1910]

The **Cooloola monster** is a cricket-like insect, *Cooloola propator*, discovered in the late 1970s in Cooloola National Park.

2001 *Geo Australasia*, March, 32. One cricket-like invertebrate, popularly known as the 'Cooloola monster', has a voracious appetite for larvae. This bright orange creature lives only in the Great Sandy Region of Fraser Island and Cooloola.

cudgerie /'kʌdʒəri/
[Probably Bandjalang, north-east New South Wales *gajari*.]
Any of several rainforest trees, especially *Flindersia schottiana* (also called *bumpy ash* and *southern silver ash*) of New South Wales, Queensland, and New Guinea, *Canarium australasicum* (**brown cudgerie**, also called *mango, mangobark,* and *carrotwood*), and *Euroschinus falcata* var. *falcata* (**blush cudgerie**, also called *pink poplar, maiden's blush,* and *ribbon wood*). The common factor of these trees is that they all have a strong turpentine-type smell. The timber, known by the same name, is pale and durable. [1884]

> **1925** *Bulletin* [Sydney], 24 September, 22. Cudgerie is a tall, smooth-barked Queensland tree.

ghittoe
See *jitta*.

gidgee /'gɪdʒi/
Also **gidga**, **gidgea**, and **gidyea**.
[Yuwaalaraay, north New South Wales *gijirr*.]
Any of several *Acacia* trees of drier inland Australia, especially *Acacia cambagei*, the foliage of which at times emits an odour often considered disagreeable. The **Georgina gidgee** is the small tree *Acacia georgina* of eastern Northern Territory and the Georgina River basin in north-west Queensland, sometimes poisonous to stock. Used in the name of the **Gidgee skink**, *Egernia stokesii*. *Gidgee* is also a name for a spear (p. 177). [1862]

> **1987** *New Idea*, 2 December, 81. MM had some friends around for tea and got talking about a local character who was described as being 'as tough as a gidgee fence post'. When I asked MM what that expression meant, he said: 'Even white ants don't find gidgee appetising'.

gilja /'gɪldʒə/
[Wirangu, Port Lincoln to Head of Bight, South Australia *jilʸa*.]
The tree *Eucalyptus brachycalyx* var. *brachycalyx* of South Australia. [c. 1900]

> **1969** S. KELLY, *Eucalypts*, 27. This is a little-known species which does not appear to have been cultivated anywhere. It occurs on the Eyre Peninsula, and in the Flinders Ranges, and eastward in South Australia … Shining, narrow leaves, hemispherical, striated budcaps, and fruiting capsules with the valves hardly, if at all, exserted, help to distinguish gilja, which is known by this aboriginal name mainly on the Eyre Peninsula.

> **1994** I. G. READ, *The Bush: A Guide to the Vegetated Landscapes of Australia*, 99. May also be found in the understorey of some mallee scrubs (dominated by red mallee/ gilja), black box woodlands and, rarely, belah low woodlands.

gungurru /gʌŋgəˈruː/
Also **gungunnu**.
[Probably from Kalaaku, the language spoken at Fraser Range, Western Australia, see quotation.]
A small eucalypt of south-west Western Australia, usually *Eucalyptus caesia*, cultivated as an ornamental. [1949]

> **1954** *Journal of Agriculture, Western Australia*, 105. Gungunnu (*Eucalyptus caesia* …). For the want of a good descriptive common name for this handsome mallee I have used the name which Richard Helms stated was used by the aborigines of the Fraser Range district.

gympie /ˈgɪmpi/
Also **gympie-gympie**.
[Gabi-gabi (and other south-east Queensland languages) *gimbi*.]
The shrub *Dendrocnide moroides* of northern New South Wales and Queensland. The huge leaves of this shrub have hairs which inflict an extremely painful recurring sting. Also called *stinging tree*. *Gympie* is the name of a town in south-eastern Queensland. [1886]

> **1949** B. O'REILLY, *Green Mountains and Cullenbenbong*, 103. The Gympie stinging tree, or Gympie Gympie, as it is called by the blacks, is readily identified by its huge dinner plate leaves a foot across. The leaves and young stems are hairy with transparent, stinging spines and contact with them is as painful as a scald.

illyarrie /ɪlˈyæri/
[Nhanta, Geraldton region, Western Australia, probably *iliyari*.]
The small tree *Eucalyptus erythrocorys* of Western Australia, with large and striking budcaps, being bright scarlet, square, and topped with a cross, followed by large bright yellow flowers with an emerald centre. It is a popular ornamental tree. [1865]

> **1945** C. A. GARDNER, *West Australian Wild Flowers*, 79. Illyarrie (*Eucalyptus erythrocorys*). This is a shrub or slender tree of 10 to 30 feet in height, which has a comparatively restricted range on the coastal country between the Murchison River and Dandarragan.

jarrah /ˈdʒærə/
[Nyungar, Perth–Albany region, probably *jarril^y*.]
The usually tall tree of south-west Western Australia *Eucalyptus marginata*, valued for its hard, durable, reddish-brown wood. Also known as *native mahogany*. [1831]

1842 G. F. MOORE, *Descriptive Vocabulary of the Language … of Western Australia*, 21. Djarryl … Eucalyptus robusta; mahogany tree. This tree has its bark disposed in longitudinal slips, running with the grain of the wood, straight, waved, or spiral as the grain runs. It is an excellent timber for building, as the white ants do not attack it, and it works well for leaves of tables and other articles of furniture. It grows in sandy districts, and on poor soil in the hills.

The word is also used in the following combinations:

jarrah-jerker

> **1980** E. TRAUTMAN & J. TRAUTMAN, *Jinkers and Jarrah Jerkers*, 1. The descriptive term 'jarrah-jerker' was one term coined to cover all men who 'worked the bush'.

Jarrahland, the state of Western Australia.

> **1928** *Bulletin* [Sydney], 25 April, 25. One of the strangest things about the abo. is his absence from the sou'-west portion of Jarrahland.

jitta /ˈdʒɪtə/

Also called **ghittoe**, **jhito**, **jidu**, **jitter**, and **jitto**.
[Dyirbal and Warrgamay, Herbert and Tully Rivers, North Queensland *jidu* for *Halfordia scleroxyla*.]
Either of two rainforest trees of the genus *Halfordia* of New South Wales, Queensland, New Guinea and New Caledonia, yielding a tough, flexible timber which is easily burnt when green. Sometimes known as *saffron heart*, it is also called *kerosene wood* because the wood can be used for a torch which will burn for a long time. It is also used by the Dyirbal people to make a long stick, called *gugulu*, which is carefully shaped and polished. When hit with a piece of cane, the gugulu is used as the musical accompaniment for a special style of love song. The Dyirbal also use this wood for spears, carved fishhooks, and wooden knives, which are hardened in a fire; they say that the fruit is eaten by the cassowary. [1899]

> **1945** J. DEVANNY, *Bird of Paradise*, 24. The wood was that remarkable product known variously among bushmen as jitter, jitto and ghito. So saturated with resin is it that when splinters were laid upon the wet mud and a match put to them they flamed up instantly.

kanji /ˈkændʒi/, /ˈkandʒi/

[Yindjibarndi, Hamersley Range, Western Australia (and neighbouring languages) *gañji*.]
The wattle *Acacia pyrifolia* of north-western Western Australia. [1960]

> **1987** I. G. READ, *The Bush*, 107. Other species include Kanji, occasionally in alliance with dead finish and Pindan wattle, on the plains and low rises of the Pilbara region.

karara /kəˈrarə/
Also **karrara** and **kurara**.
[Panyjima, around Tom Price, Western Australia, and other languages to the south *kurarra*.]
The shrub or small tree *Acacia tetragonophylla*, also known as *dead finish*, which forms prickly thickets. [1929]

> **1942** *Bulletin* [Sydney], 22 July, 13. Every blackfellow in my mustering team carried on his saddle a koondy—a heavy stick, usually of karara wood, sharpened at each end by charring and scraping.

> **1984** W. W. AMMON et al., *Working Lives*, 150. The kurara grows mostly in watercourses and, like spinifex further north, give it a few millimetres of rain and it throws out thousands of new, green leaves.

karri /ˈkærɪ/
Also **kari**.
[Probably Nyungar, Perth–Albany region *karri*.]
The tall timber tree of south-west Western Australia *Eucalyptus diversicolor*, which has a straight, smooth-barked trunk and reaches a height of 70 metres. The wood of the karri is a hard, heavy, red wood. See also *bullich*. [1866]

> **1934** T. WOOD, *Cobbers*, 81. Karri is the king of the bush … A giant two hundred feet high, slim and straight and graceful, whose bark is watered silk.

koie-yan /ˈkɔɪ-yæn/
Obsolete.
[The dialect of Warrgamay spoken on Dunk Island, North Queensland, probably *guriyan*.]
The vigorous climbing plant *Faradaya splendida* of the rainforest in north-east Queensland, which has large leaves and clusters of fragrant white flowers and snowy white fruit. The fruit is said to be eaten by cassowaries. Traditionally, the inner bark of the koie-yan was used by Aborigines to poison fish left in rock pools by the receding ocean tide. [1908]

> **1914** *Bulletin* [Sydney], 26 February, 22. Of these [fish poisons] the best is 'koie-yan', a Queensland vine, from which the outer bark is scraped, while the inside is macerated and thrown into the water.

lapunyah
See *yapunyah*.

mallalie /məˈlæli/
[Nhanta, Geraldton region, Western Australia, probably *mayali*.]

The tree *Eucalyptus eudesmioides*, a mallee of non-arid areas of southern Western Australia, as far north as Shark Bay. [1865]

> **1969** S. KELLY, *Eucalypts*, 9. Mallalie … A mallee which grows from six to ten feet high, mostly in sandy soils north of Perth … The name mallalie is an aboriginal name recorded in the Murchison area.

mallee /ˈmæli/

[Probably Wemba-wemba, western Victoria *mali*.]

Any of many eucalypts characteristically small and having several stems arising from a common base, including *Eucalyptus dumosa*, *E. socialis*, and *E. oleosa*. The name **mallee**, or **mallee scrub**, also refers to a vegetation community in drier Australia, characterised by the presence of mallee eucalypts. The semi-arid areas of New South Wales, South Australia, Western Australia and especially Victoria, in which the principal vegetation is mallee scrub, are called **mallee**, or referred to as **mallee country**, **mallee desert**, **mallee district**, or **mallee land**. *Mallee scrub* was considered by early explorers to be difficult to penetrate and generally miserable and uninviting. *Mallee* is the official name for a district of north-west Victoria. [1845]

> **1920** R. T. BAKER & H. G. SMITH, *A Research on the Eucalypts especially in regard to their Essential Oils* (2nd edition), 185. The term 'Mallee' is applied in Australia to those Eucalypts which differ in their mode of growth from other species, by sending out a number of small stems from an expanded root-stock.

The word **mallee** has been used in a number of other ways.

1. In the phrase **fit as a mallee bull**, which means 'fighting fit'.

> **1968** D. O'GRADY, *Bottle of Sandwiches*, 11. Three raw eggs for breakfast, then a quick jog around the park with a coupla jerseys on, and by the time the footy season gets under way, you'll be fit as a mallee bull.

2. In the names of birds:

mallee fowl, hen, and formerly **bird**, the mound-building *Leipoa ocellata*; also known as *gnow*, *leipoa*, *lowan*, or *native hen* (see *lowan* for description).

mallee ringneck (parakeet, parrot), the parrot *Barnardius barnardi* of eastern Australia, a predominantly green bird with a green head, blue back, and yellow collar (also known as *bullan-bullan*).

3. In combination with other words:

mallee cocky (or **farmer**), a small farmer in mallee country.

> **1962** *Meanjin*, 357. He would never ask the Mallee cockies to help.

mallee gate, a makeshift gate; also called *Queensland gate* and *panel gate*.

> **1964** *Overland*, XXX, 21. 'D'you know what a mallee gate is, Bob?' 'Yes, it's a short loose panel, just droppers and wires.'

mallee roller, a heavy roller used to crush and flatten mallee shrub.

> **1926** A. A. B. APSLEY, *Why and How I Went to Australia as a Settler*, 14. The invention of the mallee roller … It was found that by hitching a large iron roller, generally an old boiler with a heavy timber framework, to a team of from ten to twelve horses, the mallee could be crushed and rolled flat on the ground.

mallee root, the large, woody rootstock of any of several species of mallee eucalypt, valued as firewood.

> **1982** K. WILLEY *The Drovers*, 17. Drovers came in all shapes and sizes. Some, like Scotty Watson, were deceptively lean but tough as mallee roots.

In rhyming slang, **mallee root** is used for 'prostitute'.

mallee soil, a brownish, alkaline, soil.

> **1948** G. W. LEEPER, *Introduction to Soil Science*, 26. Mallee soils and mallee vegetation are not always associated even in Victoria.

mallee stump, **mallee root**.

> **1980** *Sunraysia*, 24 April, 4. Loads and loads of Mallee stumps will also be put up for auction during the day.

mallee town, a town in mallee country.

> **1981** B. GREEN, *Small Town Rising*, 139. The festival was unusual for a Mallee town.

mallett /ˈmælət/

[Nyungar, Perth–Albany region, probably *malard*.]
Any of several eucalypts (notably the **brown mallett**, *Eucalyptus astringens*) of south-west Western Australia, typically having bark that is rich in tannin. [1837]

> **1908** W. G. FREEMAN & S. E. CHANDLER, *The World's Commercial Products*, 355. Mallet bark … contains as a rule from thirty-five to forty-five and occasionally up to fifty per cent. of a readily soluble, yellow-brown tannin, which yields a firm, tough, light-brown leather.

marara /məˈrarə/

Also **marrara**.
[Bailey, *Comprehensive Catalogue of Queensland Plants* (1909), p. 169 says that *marara* comes from an Aboriginal language at Nerang, which should be Bandjalang; however, this cannot be confirmed from the extensive materials available on Bandjalang.]
A large rainforest tree belonging to the family Cunoniaceae, i.e. *Pseudoweinmannia lachnocarpa* (also called **rose marara** or *scrub rosewood*), *Geissois benthamii*, *Geissois*

biagiana (both called **brush marara** or *red carabeen*), and the **rose-leaf marara**, *Caldcluvia paniculosa*, of eastern Queensland and New South Wales. [1884]

> **1981** H. HANNAH, *Together in This Jungle Scrub*, 19. To start with they lived in a big marara tree. They've got big spurs on the hips. They felled that and they used it until they got a hut built.

marlock /ˈmalɒk/
[Probably Nyungar, Perth–Albany region *malag* or *malug*.]
Any of several, small, mallee-like trees of the genus *Eucalyptus*, typically *Eucalyptus platypus*, occurring in south-west Western Australia; also called *moort*. *E. redunca* is known as **black marlock**. [1863]

> **1908** *Emu*, III, 11. A dwarf eucalyptus called 'marlock' which much resembles mallee scrub.

marri /ˈmæri/
[Nyungar, Perth–Albany region *marri* for *Eucalyptus calophylla* and its bark.]
The tree *Eucalyptus calophylla* of south-west Western Australia, having rough, grey-brown bark and ornamental flowers. The wood of the marri is hard and durable. The early settlers are believed to have used the secretions from the tree for tanning. Also called **marri tree** and *red gum*. [1831]

> **1972** B. FULLER, *West of the Bight*, 123. Marri, the most widely distributed eucalypt in the south-west, is the old red-gum of the early settlers, who used the secretions for tanning. The native name was adopted some fifty years ago to avoid confusion with the River Red Gum.

minnerichi /mɪnəˈrɪtʃi/
Also with much variety, as **minni ritchi** and **minnaritchi**.
[Probably *miniriji* from a language of the regions in which the plant is found; it has not been possible to ascertain which language.]
Any of a number of small acacia trees which have thin, peeling curls of reddish bark; typically *Acacia cyperophylla*, which is also called *red mulga*. [1929]

> **1973** C. AUSTIN, *I Left My Hat in Andamooka*, 148. The presence of the red-trunked minaritchi trees would have told the old prospectors to start digging here because there is a saying that 'where the minaritchi grows, there you will find opal'.

mooja /ˈmudʒə/
[Nyungar, Perth–Albany region *mujarr*.]
The arborescent mistletoe *Nuytsia floribunda* of south-western Western Australia. It is parasitic, attaching itself to the roots of other trees and drawing nutrients and moisture from them. Commonly called (*Western Australian*) *Christmas tree*. [1833]

1990 R. POWELL, *Leaf and Branch, Trees and Tall Scrubs of Perth*. 184. Christmas tree, mooja ... dense masses of brilliant orange flowers contrast strongly with the bluish-green foliage ... Flowering in Perth from late spring to early summer, it marks the approach of Christmas.

moort /mɔt/

[Nyungar, Perth–Albany region *murd*.]
Any of three varieties of *Eucalyptus platypus*, mallees of coastal areas of south-western Western Australia; also called *marlock*. [1891]

1990 J. TAYLOR, *Australia's South West*, 10. Claypan areas often have groves of moort gums, which are dense little bushes with dark rounded leaves, quite unlike any other gum tree.

morrel /'mɒrəl/, /mə'rɛl/

[Nyungar, Perth–Albany region, probably *murril*.]
Any of several eucalypts of south-western Australia, especially the rough-barked trees *Eucalyptus longicornis* (which yields a strong, durable, reddish wood) and *Eucalyptus melanoxylon* (which yields a very hard, strong, blackish wood). [1837]

1893 A. F. CALVERT, *Western Australia and its Gold Fields*, 8. The dark wood of the Morrel (*Eucalyptus longicornis*), which in the vicinity of the Swan River mounts to 150 feet, is remarkable for its hardness, and is much used by wheelwrights.

mugga /'mʌgə/

[Wiradhuri, south-west New South Wales *maga*.]
The tree *Eucalyptus sideroxylon*, which has a deeply furrowed, dark bark, red under the surface, and which yields a tough, durable, red timber. Also called *red ironbark*. [1834]

1900 *Proceedings of the Linnean Society of New South Wales*, 715. E. sideroxylon ... By some it is called Black and by others Red Ironbark owing to the colour of the bark and wood respectively. The aboriginal name is Mugga.

mulga /'mʌlgə/

Formerly also **malga**, **mulgah**, and **mulgar**.
[Kamilaroi, Yuwaalaraay, and other languages in New South Wales and South Australia *malga*.]
Any of several *Acacia* plants of dry inland Australia, especially the widespread shrub or tree *Acacia aneura*, which has grey-green foliage regarded as useful fodder for stock in times of drought. It yields a distinctive brown and yellowish timber, and is also called **mulga bush**, **mulga tree**, and **mulga wood**. **Scrub mulga** is a name for *thorny yellowwood* (*Zanthoxylum brachyacanthum*). [1846]

1878 R. BROUGH SMYTH, *Aborigines of Victoria*, I, 127 (*note*). Giles … supposed that the natives get water in this arid tract from the roots of the Mulga-tree.

The word **mulga** is also used in several other ways.

1. In the phrase **the mulga**, to refer to the outback, to remote, sparsely populated country, as distinct from that which is more closely settled. Also as **Mulgaland**.

1978 D. BALL, *Great Australian Snake Exchange*, 114. Stranded in the bloody mulga with no transport.

2. By transference, to refer to an inhabitant of the mulga:

1904 *Bulletin* [Sydney], 15 September, 18. The back-o'-beyond Jay Pee is often a tricky bit of mulga.

3. In compounds to mean 'characterised by the presence of mulga', as in **mulga country**, **flats**, **paddocks**, or **scrub**.

1991 *North West Telegraph* [Port Hedland], 3 April, 25. After the rains the mulga country becomes alive with the colour of up to 20 species of flowers in any one area.

1889 W. H. TIETKENS, *Journal of the Central Australian Exploring Expedition* (1891), 15. These mulga flats are intersected by small gum creeks.

1896 *Bulletin* [Sydney], 15 February, 3.

> Where the mulga paddocks are wild and wide,
> That's where the pick of the stockmen ride.

2000 K. MAHOOD, *Craft for a Dry Lake*, 58. Most days she rides out bare-back on the piebald horse … and explores the surrounding mulga scrub and the claypan country.

4. As an adjective, to mean 'rustic', or 'countrified':

1937 M. TERRY, *Sand and Sun*, 211. With a stick of tobacco and some tucker the mulga mailman set off for the home of the cattleman.

5. In the names of flora and fauna:

mulga ant, the ant *Polyrhachis macropus* of inland Australia, which builds a mud nest to which mulga leaves are applied.

2001 *Landscope*, Autumn, 27. In the Pilbara, native mice often shelter from predators in the nests of large ants, such as those of the mulga ant (*Polyrhachis macropus*).

mulga apple, a large edible swelling on the branches of mulga trees.

1888 *Proceedings of the Linnean Society of New South Wales*, III, 483. *Acacia aneura* … In western New South Wales two kinds of galls are commonly found on these trees; one kind is very plentiful … but the other is less abundant, larger, succulent and edible. These latter galls are called 'Mulga apples', and are said to be very welcome to the thirsty traveller.

mulga grass, any of several grasses of mulga country and elsewhere, especially the common *Thyridolepis mitchelliana*, a tufted perennial regarded as good fodder, and *Aristida contorta*, having tufts which whiten on drying.

> **1935** H. H. FINLAYSON, *Red Centre*, 33. The mulga grass … one of the best fodder grasses is conspicuous in summer owing to the curious spirally twisted habit assumed by the tussocks during desiccation.

mulga parrot (or **parakeet**), the parrot of drier mainland Australia, *Psephotus varius*, a predominantly green bird with yellow, blue, and red markings, which is also called the *many-coloured parakeet*.

> **2000** J. BENNETT et al., *Watching Wildlife Australia*, 221. At first light in the Loop and other gorges, red-tailed black-cockatoos, brilliant-green mulga parrots and other chorusing birds approach the river to drink.

> **1951** *Bulletin* [Sydney], 3 January, 12. We rise as mulga-parakeets for whirring through the dawn.

mulga snake, the *king brown snake*, the large venomous snake *Pseudechis australis*, occurring throughout northern and drier, southern mainland Australia.

> **1990** *West Australian* [Perth], 31 December, 39. The mulga snake may reach two metres but is often bigger in the Kimberley, where it is known as the king brown.

6. In the following combinations:

Mulga Bill

> **1972** A. CHIPPER, *The Aussie Swearer's Guide*, 66. *Mulga Bill*, a simpleton, specifically from the Bush.

mulga black, an Aborigine from a remote place.

> **1910** C. E. W. BEAN, *On the Wool Track*, 7. The Mulga blacks from out-back had to come down to the Darling for water.

mulga-bred, reared in the country.

> **1930** A. E. YARRA, *Vanishing Horsemen*, 56. Mr Somerville … was mulga-bred and had never lived in Sydney.

mulga madness, eccentricity attributed to living in the outback.

> **1980** S. THORNE, *I've Met Some Bloody Wags*, 115. He was a prime example of 'mulga madness'. Given a good drench and put on a small lush block in the 'inside country' he would be a new man.

mulga mafia, a name for the National Country Party.

1998 *Courier-Mail* [Brisbane], 30 May, 23. Sir Robert Sparkes ... has long been regarded by opponents as the don of the mulga mafia.

mulga message, a message conveyed by *mulga wire*.

1943 L. MCLENNAN, *Spirit of the West*, 2

> They sent a mulga message through all of the cattle-land
> For Dingo Joe, the trapper, to come and try his hand.

mulga rum, crude or illicitly made alcoholic liquor.

1910 *Bulletin* [Sydney], 21 April, 39. You ... poured gallons of Mulga rum down your throat!

mulga scrubber

1945 S. J. BAKER, *The Australian Language*, 67. Mulga Scrubbers ... stock that have run wild and deteriorated in condition.

mulga wire, or *bush telegraph*, an informal network by means of which information or rumour is conveyed in remote areas; **mulga wire** refers also to a means of long-distance communication used by Aborigines, usually that of employing smoke signals.

1935 F. BIRTLES, *Battle Fronts of Outback*, 174. Long columns of smoke were rising ... The 'Stone Men of the Hills' were replying ... They, too, were coming down to the coastal plains ... 'Mulga wires' had told them of the arrival of 'Motor car Frank' and plenty of tobacco.

mulga wireless (radio, telegram, telegraph), *mulga wire*

1960 *Northern Territory News* [Darwin], 5 February, 10. According to 'mulga wireless' Hank will put in a period studying Jim's method of chasing and mustering wild scrub cattle.

1950 G. M. FARWELL, *Land of Mirage*, 98. 'We heard the Inspector was on his way up.' For once the mulga radio had proved unreliable.

1934 W. HATFIELD, *River Crossing*, 102. You've heard about 'mulga-telegrams'—say something away in the mulga scrub, an' the trees theirselves seems to pass it along.

1948 F. CLUNE, *Wild Colonial Boys*, 171. The 'mulga telegraph' was the word-of-mouth link of communication.

7. **Mulga** has also been used to mean 'a (false) rumour or tall story'.

1936 J. DEVANNY, *Sugar Heaven*, 216. 'D'ye hear the rumour that they've signed on a few boys in the mill today, Royle?' 'Yes. Might be "mulga". We'll have to be sharp about the rumours.'

mulla mulla /ˈmʌlə-mʌlə/

[Probably Panyjima, Tom Price region, Western Australia *mulu-mulu*.]

Any of several herbs or shrubs of the large genus *Ptilotus*, chiefly of arid Australia, bearing a soft, fluffy flower-head and usually known as *pussy tail*. [1954]

> **1984** *Age Weekender* [Melbourne] 7 December, 7. Pussy tails or Mulla Mulla (*Ptilotus exaltatus*) carpet the rocky slopes with pink and grey hairy flowers.

myall /ˈmaɪəl/, /ˈmaɪɒl/
Also **mial**, **miall**, and **myal**.
[May possibly relate—in some way that is not understood—to *myall* meaning 'stranger' (see pp. 171–2).]
Any of several *Acacia* trees, especially *Acacia pendula* (**weeping myall**) of inland areas and the Eyre Peninsula, having silvery foliage sometimes used as fodder, and the similar *Acacia melvillei*. See *boree*. [1840]

> **1845** J. O. BALFOUR, *Sketch of New South Wales*, 38. The myall-tree (*Acacia pendula*) is the most picturesque tree of New South Wales. The leaves have the appearance of being frosted, and the branches droop like the weeping willow … Its perfume is as delightful, and nearly as strong, as sandal-wood. *Ibid.*, 10. They poison the fish by means of a sheet of bark stripped from the Myall-tree.

napunyah
See *yapunyah*.

paddymelon /ˈpædimɛlən/
[The use of this word as a plant name probably developed from an association (possibly erroneous) with *pademelon* or *paddymelon* (see p. 69), which refers to a type of wallaby.]
Any of several plants of the Cucurbitaceae family, especially the trailing or climbing annual plant *Cucumis myriocarpus* of Africa, naturalised in inland Australia. It bears a bristly, melon-like fruit, and is widely regarded as a weed. [1891]

> **1891** *Bulletin* [Sydney], 19 December, 19.
>
> > They stole my pears—my native pears—
> > Those thrice convicted felons,
> > And ravished from me unawares
> > My crop of paddy-melons.

penda /ˈpɛndə/
[Said by F. M. BAILEY (*Comprehensive Catalogue of Queensland Plants*, 1909, p. 113) to come from the Noosa language, presumably Gabi-Gabi, but this cannot be confirmed by existing materials on this language.]

Any of several trees of the genera *Xanthostemon* and *Tristania*, originally the large *Xanthostemon oppositifolius* (now called **southern penda**) of south-east Queensland, having very hard, brown wood. [1890]

> **1996** *Australian Country Style*, December, 31. The massive structured timbers of the house are of black penda, the last bridging material from local sawmills before the World Heritage listing ended harvesting from the rainforest. The timber was seasoned for seven years before use.

punty /ˈpʌnti/
[Western Desert language *bundi*.]
Any of several shrubs of the genus *Cassia*, including *Cassia nemophila*, of all mainland states. Also known as **punty bush** and *kangaroo bush*. [1892]

> **1987** *Daily Sun* [Brisbane], 28 March (Weekend Magazine), 11. CSIRO studies have recently shown that the absence of fire, combined with overstocking, has led to a massive invasion of noxious inedible shrubs—'woody weeds' such as turpentine, punty and hopbush.

sallee /ˈsæli/
Also **sally**.
[This has often been quoted as a loan word from an Australian language (e.g. E. E. Morris, *Austral English*, 1898, p. 399), but in fact it comes from the British dialectal form *sally*, variant of *sallow* 'a willow'. As mentioned in Chapter 1, Australian languages have no *s* sound.]
Any of several trees of the genera *Eucalyptus* and *Acacia*, which resemble the willow in habitat or foliage. [1826]

tallerack /ˈtæləræk/
[Nyungar, Perth–Albany region, probably *dalarag*.]
The tree *Eucalyptus tetragona* of scrubland on the southern coast of Western Australia, a mallee growing to about three metres tall, and having cream flowers in spring and summer; also called *silver marlock*. [c 1894]

> **1969** S. KELLY, *Eucalypts*, 9. Tallerack … A feature of the sandy, low scrub within thirty to forty miles of the southern coast of Western Australia, and also occurring north of Perth in the area near Jurien Bay.

tamma /ˈtæmə/
[Probably from a Western Australian language.]
A vegetation community consisting of low, thick, scrubby growth. [1905]

> **1979** R. ERICKSON et al., *Flowers and Plants of Western Australia*, 148. Another vegetation type is tamma which is also a shrub formation but is less than 2 m. high and is dominated by *Casuarina campestris*.

tuart /'tjuat/
Formerly also **tewart**, **tooart**, **tooat**, and **touart**.
[Nyungar, Perth–Albany region, probably *duward*.]
The medium to tall tree *Eucalyptus gomphocephala* of coastal south-west Western Australia. It provides one of the heaviest and most durable timbers in Australia, which is not liable to splinter. Tuart has been mainly used for railway carriage construction, and is in limited supply. [1833]

> **1928** J. POLLARD, *Bushland Vagabonds*, 157. The railways use plenty of it. They replaced the steel under-carriages of the trucks with tuart. So it must be pretty strong.

tuckeroo /tʌkə'ru/
[Probably Yagara, Brisbane region *dagaru*.]
The tree *Cupaniopsis anacardioides* of north and east Australia, cultivated as an ornamental. Also called *green-leaved tamarind* and *bead tamarind*. [1889]

> **1994** I. G. READ, *The Bush*, 153. Tuckeroos are slender trees with spreading branches that may reach to the ground.

waddywood /'wɒdiwʊd/
Also **waddy tree**.
[Probably Midhaga, north-east of Birdsville, Queensland *wadi*.]
Any of several trees yielding a hard wood, especially the rare *Acacia peuce*, which occurs in two small areas, one in south-west Queensland and the other around Andado in the Northern Territory. Note that *waddy* is also the name for a type of club (pp. 181–2). [1912]

> **2003** *Outback*, April, 86. Tall and slender, the graceful casuarina-like waddy-woods tower over the sparse grasses and stunted shrubs that share their desolate habitat.

wallum /'wɒləm/
Formerly also **wallom**.
[Gabi-gabi, south-east Queensland *walum* or *walam*.]
The shrub or tree *Banksia aemula* of south-east Queensland and eastern New South Wales; also called **wallum banksia** and *bottlebrush*. **Wallum** or **wallum country** also refers to the sandy coastal heathland in which the plant grows, or, more generally, an area of coastal heath. [1861]

> **1975** *Wildlife Australia*, December, 135. The banksias the Aborigines called Wallum were the tall, saw-tooth leaved, flowering species of *Banksia aemula* and *Banksia serrata*. Few Europeans have savoured the delight of Wallum honey, instead we have applied the name Wallum contemptuously to the infertile coastal lowlands where these particular Wallum banksias thrive.

The **wallum froglet**, *Crinia tinnula*, is so called because it lives in the wallum country of south-east Queensland, from Tweed River to Fraser Island.

> **2004** *Courier-Mail* [Brisbane], 6 March, 12. Another endangered frog in the area, the Wallum froglet, was even harder to find because it was as small as a fingernail.

wandarrie /wɒnˈdæri/
Also **wanderrie**, **wanderry**.
[Ngarla, De Grey River, Western Australia, *warndarri* 'sand-dune, sandhill'.]
A native drought-resistant perennial grass of sandy soils, found mainly in the Gascoyne, Murchison and Goldfields regions, principally *Eriachne triodioides*. There are a dozen or so further species within *Eriachne*, each termed a kind of wandarrie; they include **northern wandarrie** (*E. obtusa*) and **long-awned wandarrie** (*E. armitii*). The terrain in which these occur is **wandarrie country**. [1947]

> **1947** *Journal of the Department of Agriculture of Western Australia*, 17. Associated with the Bowgada is a perennial tussocky grass (Wandarrie grass) *Eriachne* spp., which was seen only to occur in this habitat. The Wandarrie country appears particularly suited to the growth of perennial grasses.

wandoo /wɒnˈdu/
Formerly also **wando**.
[Nyungar, Perth–Albany region *wandu*.]
The tree *Eucalyptus wandoo* of south-west Western Australia, usually having a smooth, mottled, white or grey bark. The wood of the tree is very hard, strong, and durable, and is much prized by wheelwrights. [1837]

> **1842** G. F. MOORE, *Descriptive Vocabulary of the Language … of Western Australia*, 72. Wando … Eucalyptus; the white gum-tree. In hollow trees of this sort, water is frequently retained, which forms the only resource for natives in summer, in many districts. It is discovered by a discoloration of the bark. A hole is opened with a hammer and carefully closed again.

wilga /ˈwɪlgə/
[Wiradhuri, south-west New South Wales (and nearby languages) *wilgarr*.]
A drought-resistant shrub or small tree of the genus *Geijera*, especially *Geijera parviflora* of inland eastern Australia, having a spreading crown and pendulous white foliage. Also called *sheep bush* (because it is a favourite fodder for sheep), *dogwood*, and *green heart*. [1887]

> **1936** F. CLUNE, *Roaming Round the Darling*, 120. The wilga is specially suited for sheep, who … squat on their haunches and nibble the leaves overhead.

wirilda /wə'rɪldə/

[Yaralde, mouth of the Murray River, South Australia, probably *wurrulde*.]
The shrub or small tree *Acacia retinodes* of South Australia, Victoria, and Tasmania, cultivated as an ornamental. Also called **wirilda wattle**. [1843]

> **1939** J. GALBRAITH, *Garden in a Valley* (1985), 107. The Wirilda … is shining through the rain, a lovely tree with blue-green leaves and primrose flowers.

wirra /'wɪrə/

[Diyari, Lake Eyre region, South Australia *wirra* for *Acacia ligulata*. T. H. Johnston and J. B. Cleland (*Transactions of the Royal Society of South Australia*, LXVII, 1943, p. 154) state that there has been confusion between *Acacia salicina*, which prefers a sandy habitat, and *A. ligulata*, which prefers alluvial flats or situations near water. The Diyari name *wirra* referred to *A. ligulata*, but is used in English for *A. salicina*.]
The plant *Acacia salicina*: see *cooba*. Note that *wirra* is also the name for a kind of vessel (p. 185). [1906]

> **1941** I. L. IDRIESS, *Great Boomerang*, 102. Burned leaves of the wirra (a species of acacia, the leaves of which when burned yield a powder of potash).

wodgil /'wɒdʒəl/
Also **wodjil**.
[Probably from a Western Australian language.]
A vegetation community of tall, shrubby growth dominated by *Acacia* plants, especially *Acacia neurophylla*. Also called **wodgil scrub**. [1948]

> **1962** B. W. LEAKE. *Eastern Wheatbelt Wildlife*, 103. The mountain devil likes gravelly scrub and wodgil country but will wander far from this.

yacca /'yækə/
Also **yacka**. Chiefly used in South Australia.
[Gaurna, Adelaide region, *yagu* 'gum obtained from a type of native pine tree'.]
The *grass-tree* or *blackboy*, any of many small trees of the genus *Xanthorrhoea*, having a crown of grass-like leaves. **Yacca gum**, or *grass-tree gum*, is the resin exuded by the tree, rich in picric acid, usually red, and formerly much used as an adhesive. Aborigines used the flower stalk of the tree to make spears as well as to obtain fire by friction. [1840]

> **1906** *Emu*, V, 132. The 'yacca', as the grass-tree is often called, exudes from the lower portion of its trunk a rust-coloured resinous gum.

yapunyah /yə'pʌnyə/
Also **lapunyah** and **napunyah**.
[Gunya, Cunnamulla region, Queensland, *yapañ*.]

Any of various trees of the genus *Eucalyptus* that occur along watercourses in Queensland and the Northern Territory, especially *Eucalyptus ochrophloia* and *Eucalyptus thozetiana* (also known as *Thozet's box* and *Thozet's iron-box*). [1878 *yapunyah*, 1940 *lapunyah*, 1949 *napunyah*]

> **1976** N. V. WALLACE, *Bush Lawyer*, 129. There were also beefwood, box, and wild orange, but the most beautiful of all was the tan-barked yapunyah, a species of eucalypt.

yarra /'yærə/
Also **yara**, **yarrah**, and **yarrow**.
Obsolete.
[Possibly Wiradhuri, south-west New South Wales *yara*; or possibly from Baagandji, Darling River, where *yarra* is the general word for 'tree'.]
A name given to any of several trees occurring near watercourses, perhaps chiefly *Eucalyptus camaldulensis*. Also called *river red gum* and *Murray red gum*. [1834]

> **1861** J. D. LANG, *Queensland, Australia*, 106. No longer a chain of dry ponds in brigalow scrub, but a channel shaded by lofty yarra trees.

yarran /'yærən/
Also **yarren**.
[Kamilaroi, east New South Wales, and nearby languages *yarraan* for 'a river gum tree'.]
The small to medium tree *Acacia omalophylla* of inland New South Wales, Queensland, and northern Victoria, having a rough bark, smooth foliage, and an unpleasant odour. The wood is dark brown and durable; it was used for boomerangs and spears. [1882]

> **1887** W. H. SUTTOR, *Australian Stories Retold and Sketches of Country Life*, 117. The yarran, an acacia, like the myall having violet-scented wood, is widely dispersed, and frequently fringes the myall patches with its olive green foliage.

yate /yeɪt/
Formerly **yeit**.
[This has been said to be a borrowing from an Australian language. If so, it must come from Nyungar, Perth–Albany region, since the tree only grows in Nyungar territory. No trace of a word similar to *yate* has been found in the extensive materials on Nyungar. At least in some dialects of Nyungar this tree was called *ma*. It thus seems unlikely that *yate* does originate in an Australian language.]
Any of several eucalypts of southern Western Australia, especially the rough-barked *Eucalyptus cornuta*, yielding a remarkably hard, strong timber. Also called **yate tree**. [1833]

> **1938** *Bulletin* [Sydney], 6 July, 21. The comparatively small yate tree, which occurs in forests in W.A.'s extreme sou'-west, produces one of the world's strongest timbers.

RELIGION AND CEREMONY

Almost all aspects of the life of Aboriginal people were closely entwined with their religious beliefs. They believed that ancestral spirits had created the country, the places, and foodstuffs in it, and knowledge about them which was handed down from generation to generation. Aboriginal religion was concerned with the preservation and continuation of life, which was under the authority of the spirits of recent and long-distant ancestors. Religious practice involved understanding the sacred traditions of one's group, their relationship to the land and to totems; and organising one's life in the way that tradition demanded. There was a sense of mystery concerning the spirit world, which was believed to show itself through subtle signs and symbols.

SOURCE: W. E. H. STANNER, 'Some aspects of Aboriginal religion', *Colloquium*, IX, 19–35, 1976.

alcheringa /æltʃə'rɪŋgə/
Also **alchuringa**.
[Aranda, Alice Springs region *aljerre* 'dream' + *-ŋe* 'from, of', together meaning 'in the dreamtime'.]
The dreamtime, that collection of events beyond living memory, which shaped the physical, spiritual, and moral world of the Aborigines; the era in which these occurred; an Aborigine's consciousness of the enduring nature of the era. [1891]

> **1899** B. SPENCER & F. J. GILLEN, *The Native Tribes of Central Australia*, 645.
> *Alcheringa*—Name given to the far past times in which the mythical ancestors of the tribe are supposed to have lived.

bora /'bɔrə/
Formerly also **boorah**, **borah**, **boree**, and **borer**.
[Kamilaroi, east New South Wales *buurr* 'initiation rite, initiation belt' plus locative case *-a*, i.e. *buurr-a* 'at the initiation, place of initiation'.]
An initiation ceremony at which an Aboriginal youth is admitted to the privileges and responsibilities of manhood; the site at which a bora is held. In the bora initiation grounds of south-eastern Australia, there were often moulded figures of earth representing the ancestral spirits. Bora is also used in the compounds **bora ceremony**, **bora circle**, **bora ground**, and **bora ring**, and is sometimes applied to *corroboree ground*. [1851]

> **1937** D. GUNN, *Links with the Past*, 17. All the boras I know consist of two round patches of ground cleared of grass and sticks. The larger ring is where the men of the tribe meet and pass laws, which are confirmed by the old men who meet at the smaller ring.

1969 A. A. ABBIE, *The Original Australians*, 134. Special ceremonies are sometimes held on a particularly sacred piece of ground called a bora; this title may also be applied to the ceremony itself. The bora ground is usually defined by a circular earthen bank or by a ring of large stones, hence the common name of 'bora ring'.

boylya /'bɔɪlyə/
Also **bolya**, and **bullya**.
[Nyungar, Perth–Albany region, probably *bulʸa* 'sorcery'.]
A name for a 'clever man': see *koradji*. [1837]

> **1842** G. F. MOORE, *Descriptive Vocabulary of the Language … of Western Australia*, 13. Boyl-ya … a certain supposed power of witchcraft, sorcery … Boylya Gădăk … one possessed of Boylya; a wizard; a magician. The men only are believed to possess this power. A person thus endowed can transport himself through the air at pleasure, being invisible to everyone but his fellow-Boylyagădăk. If he have [sic] a dislike to another native, he is supposed to be able to kill him, by stealing upon him at night, and secretly consuming his flesh; entering into his victim like pieces of quartz, and occasioning much pain. Another Boylyagădăk can, however, disenchant the person thus afflicted. When this is done the Boylya is drawn out from the patient in the form of pieces of quartz, which are kept as great curiosities.

bucklee /'bʌkli /
Also **bucklegarroo**.
[Yindjibarndi, Hamersley Range, Western Australia *bagarli* 'initiation ceremony'.]
An initiation rite. The word has also been used as a verb, meaning 'to undergo initiation'. [1929]

> **1929** K. S. PRICHARD, *Coonardoo* (1961), 17. The older men took the boys off into the mulga thickets … for the bucklegarroo ceremonies which no woman was allowed to see.

bugeen /'bʌgin/
Also **buckee** and **buggeen**.
[Probably Wiradhuri, south-west New South Wales *bagiñ*, 'clever man, sorcerer, ghost'; but it may possibly come from British English *bugan*, 'evil spirit'.]
A devil or evil spirit. [1834]

> **1834** G. BENNETT, *Wanderings in New South Wales* I, 126. They were afraid, if they buried them, the *Buckee*, or devil devil would take them away.

churinga /tʃə'rɪŋgə/
Also **tjuringa**.
[Aranda, Alice Springs region *jʷerreŋe*, 'object from the dreaming'.]

A sacred object (normally carved or painted) of Aboriginal ceremonial. Also **churinga stone** [1886]

> **1896** B. SPENCER, *Report on the Work of the Horn Scientific Expedition to Central Australia*, IV, 76. Ceremonial sticks and stones. Under this head I deal with a class of objects of some symbolic import which are common to a large group of natives in the interior. Concerning them a good deal of secrecy and mystery exists among the blacks, and very little has been said, or seems to be known of their true significance. Collectively, the term 'Churiña' (*sic*) is applied to them in the Arunta (Gillen).

cobba-cobba /ˈkɒbə-kɒbə/
[Bardi, north-west of Derby, Western Australia, probably *goba-goba*.]
A corroboree. [1914]

> **1923** E. J. STUART, *A Land of Opportunities, being an account of the author's recent expedition to explore the northern territories of Australia*, 16. Subsequently we lined up all the natives, who were just about to visit Hadley's Mission on Sunday Island, and we induced them to get into their war-paint, after which they entertained us with a Cobba Cobba dance, which in the east of Australia is better known as a Corroboree.

corroboree /kəˈrɒbəri/
Formerly with much variety, as **coroborey**, **corrobbaree**, **corrobboree**, **corrobara**, **corroberee**, **corrobora**, **corrobori**, and **corrobory**.
[Dharuk, Sydney region, probably *garabari*, 'a style of dancing'.]
A dance ceremony, of which song and rhythmical musical accompaniment are an integral part, and which may be sacred and ritualised or non-sacred, occasional, and informal. Several groups would come together for a corroboree. In corroborees of ritual significance, the dancers act out ancestral scenes, whereas for the non-sacred ceremonies the dancers usually dramatise everyday occurrences. For both types, the dancers are decorated with clay in traditional designs. Music is provided by chanting and singing as well as clapping sticks and didgeridoos. **Corroboree** is often used loosely, in extended senses, especially with reference to a meeting or assembly, or to festivity generally. A **fighting corroboree** amounts to organised combat between two groups to settle some grievance, and would often be concluded by singing and dancing. [1790]

> **1825** B. FIELD, *Geographical Memoirs of New South Wales*, 433. The corrobory, or night-dance, still obtains. This festivity is performed in very good time, and not unpleasing tune. The song is sung by a few males and females who take no part in the dance. One of the band beats time by knocking one stick against another. The music begins with a high note, and gradually sinks to the octave, whence it rises again immediately to the top.

1826 S. MACARTHUR ONSLOW, *Some Early Records of the Macarthurs of Camden* (1914), 455. Let me give you some account of one of our native dances—a 'Corroboree' as they call it, when it is not unusual for two or three hundred to collect, to paint and deck themselves with green boughs, and in sets perform various grotesque figure dances, in most excellent time, which is given by others who sit apart and chant a sort of wild cadence.

The word **corroboree** is used in several other ways.

1. To refer to any social gathering, especially of a boisterous nature.

1952 H. E. BOOTE, *Sidelights on Two Referendums*, 9. The monthly corroboree of the Artists' Union on Saturday night. A nice little crowd there, and the beer flowing.

2. In a transferred sense:

1833 *Perth Gazette*, 24 August, 135. Several natives ... expressed some alarm when they perceived the preparations ... for the parade. They were given however to understand, that it was only a corrobora; it seemed to amuse them greatly to find that we had also our corroboras.

3. In the combinations, **corroboree dance**, **corroboree ground**, and **corroboree stick**.

1997 N. OLIVE, *Karijini Mirlimirli*, 87. They'd have a big corroboree dance and all go back to the stations when it was over.

1898 D. W. CARNEGIE, *Spinifex and Sand*, 421. Near the spring in the scrub was a cleared corroboree ground, twenty feet by fifty yards, cleared of all stones and enclosed by a fallen brush-fence.

1939 *Wild Life* [Melbourne], December, 13. The singing changed to a mournful chant accompanied by the slow tapping of corroboree sticks as two lithe maidens gracefully acted the tragedy of the rock wallaby.

4. As a verb meaning 'to perform a corroboree'.

1998 G. ALLEN, *The Gun Ringer*, 183. The stockcamps. Places of wild exciting days but long lonely nights for the white head stockman alone with the blacks. And made doubly lonesome by the singing, laughing and dancing of their black workmates corroboreeing nearby.

5. In the name of the **corroboree frog**, the small frog *Pseudophryne corroboree* of mountainous south-east New South Wales.

1953 *Proceedings of the Linnean Society of New South Wales*, LXXVIII, 180. *Pseudophryne corroboree* ... The specific name was suggested by the resemblance of the dorsal pattern of *P. corroboree* to the body paintings used by some Australian aboriginal tribes in their corroborees.

cunmerrie /ˈkʌnməri/
[Pitta-pitta, Boulia district, Queensland (and languages to the south-west well into South Australia) *ganmarri*.]
A spirit believed to carry off people and animals, variously described as a large bird or a three-eyed snake. [1897]

> **1897** W. E. ROTH, *Ethnological Studies among the North-west-central Queensland Aborigines*, 33. kăn-mă-rĕ = huge supernatural water snake.

> **1959** D. LOCKWOOD, *Crocodiles and Other People*, 59. They're especially scared of the cunmerrie, a ghastly, ghostly bird with enormous wings, talons, and beak—a bird that can swoop down on a mob and carry away the fattest bullock.

douligah /ˈduləga/
Also **dulagar**.
[Dhurga, Jervis Bay to Wallaga Lake, south coast of New South Wales, probably *dulaga*.]
See quotations. [1918]

> **1918** *Bulletin* [Sydney], 4 April, 24. The existence of 'douligahs' the wild men covered with hair … was firmly believed in … on the N. S. Wales South Coast 30-odd years ago.

> **1984** D. BYRNE, *The Mountains Call Me Back*, 15. People from Wallaga point out the 'dulagar' track, the route believed to be followed even today by a powerful spirit-being when it travels from the inland ranges to the coast.

jingy /ˈdʒɪndʒi/
Also **chingah**, **chingi**, **jinga**, and **jingie**.
[Nyungar, Perth–Albany region *jan-ga*, 'spirit of a dead person'; this was also the original form for *djanga*, p. 165.]
A devil or spirit. [1837]

> **1851** MRS R. LEE, *Adventures in Australia*, 243. Everybody believed in an evil spirit, which haunts dark caverns, and gloomy plains; that its name is Jinga, and that they are afraid of him at night.

kipper /ˈkɪpə/
Formerly also with much variety, as **kebah**, **kebarra**, **kebarrah**, **keepara**, **keeparra**, and **kippa**.
Obsolete.
[Dharuk, Sydney region, and neighbouring languages *gibarra*, 'an initiated boy', possibly related to *giba*, 'stone' (1798 quotation). Note also that in Yagara, Brisbane region, *giba* is 'initiated boy'. Contact with this Brisbane word reinforced the borrowing in English.]

An Aboriginal male who has been initiated into manhood; the ceremony in which such an initiation takes place, which is also referred to as a **kipper ceremony** or **kipper making**. [1798]

> **1798** D. COLLINS, *Account of the English Colony of New South Wales*, I, 580. [Boys who had had a tooth extracted, as an initiation rite] were also termed *Ke-bar-ra*, a name which has reference in its construction to the singular instrument used on this occasion, *ke-bah* in their language signifying rock or stone.

> **1885** MRS C. PRAED, *Australian Life Black and White*, 24. The great mystery of the Blacks is the Bora—a ceremony at which the young men found worthy receive the rank of warriors and are henceforth called *kippers*.

The word **kipper** is also used as a verb, meaning 'to initiate (an Aboriginal male) into manhood'.

> **1972** M. CASSIDY, *The Dispossessed*, 174. Murac … had broken the tribe's law by marrying a girl before he was kippa-ed.

The **kipper ground** or **kipper ring** is the place reserved for the holding of an initiation ceremony.

> **1851** *Empire* [Sydney] 22 October, 284. Nor are they treated in any manner as men, nor allowed to take to themselves a wife or wives (for Polygamy is allowed among them) until they have their allotted probation at the Kipper ground.

> **1872** 'EIGHT YEARS RESIDENT', *The Queen of Colonies*, 328. 'Kipper rings' may be seen, where these mysteries are performed and the initiations take place.

kobong /ˈkoʊbɒŋ/
Obsolete.
[Nyungar, Perth–Albany region, probably *gubuŋ*.]
See quotation. [1840]

> **1840** G. GREY, *Vocabulary of the Dialects of South-Western Australia*, 64. Ko-bong—a friend, a protector … This name is generally applied to some animal or vegetable which has for a series of years been the friend or sign of the family, and this sign is handed down from father to son, a certain mysterious connection existing between a family and its ko-bong, so that a member of the family will never kill an animal of the species to which his ko-bong belongs, should he find it asleep; indeed he always does it reluctantly, and never without affording it a chance of escape. This arises from the family belief that some one individual of the species is their nearest friend, to kill whom would be a great crime, and is to be carefully avoided.

koradji /kəˈrædʒi/
Also formerly in a wide variety of unfixed spellings including **coradgee**.

[Dharuk, Sydney region *garraaji* 'doctor' (*garraaji-gan* may have been the plural form).]

An Aborigine having recognised skills in traditional medicine and (frequently) a role in ceremonial life. For words taken from other Australian languages, see *boylya* and *warra-warra*. The words applied by the colonists to denote a perceived function or power of such a person include *clever man, conjuror, medicine man, (native) doctor, priest, sorcerer, wise man, witch doctor,* and *wizard.* [1790]

1790 W. DAWES, *Grammatical Forms of the Languages of N. S. Wales.* Car-rah-dy-gan, car-rah-dy, a person skilled in healing wounds; they call our surgeons by this name.

1793 W. TENCH, *A Complete Account of the Settlement at Port Jackson,* 232. Yellomundee was a Cár-ad-yee, or Doctor of renown.

1878 R. BROUGH SMYTH, *The Aborigines of Victoria,* I, 62. When a lad has to be initiated, he is removed to some remote and secluded spot, and when it is night, the coradjes (priests and doctors), painted and decorated with feathers, &c., begin their operations.

1946 A. P. ELKIN, *Aboriginal Men of High Degree,* 19. I have known white persons almost fear the eyes of a *karadji,* so all-seeing, deep and quiet did they seem. This 'clever man' was definitely an outstanding person.

kurdaitcha /kəˈdaɪtʃə/

Also **coordaitcha, goditcha, kadaicha, kadaitcha, kaditcha,** and **kooditcha.**

[There is a word *gʷerdaje* in Aranda, the Alice Springs language, but it may have come into this language quite recently. Pastor Carl Strehlow called it an 'English word introduced'. If this is so, the ultimate origin of the word is not known.]

A malignant spirit (also known as a **kurdaitcha spirit**); a man who has either been formally selected or who goes out on his own initiative on a mission of vengeance against some individual accused of having injured someone by magic (also known as **kurdaitcha man**). [1886]

1886 E. M. CURR, *The Australian Race,* I, 148. It was discovered in 1882, or there-abouts, that the Blacks to the westward of Lake Eyre, on the Musgrave Ranges, and, it is believed, in some other portions of Central Australia, wear a sort of shoe when they attack their enemies by stealth at night. Some of the tribes call these shoes *Kooditcha,* their name for an invisible spirit. I have seen a pair of them. The soles were made of the feathers of the emu, stuck together with a little human blood, which the maker is said to take from his arm. They were about an inch and a half thick, soft, and of even breadth. The uppers were nets made of human hair. The object of these shoes is to prevent those who wear them from being tracked and pursued after a night attack. It is only on the softest ground that they leave any mark, and even then it is impossible to distinguish the heel from the toe, so that the Blacks say they can track anything that walks, except a man shod with *Kooditcha.*

1927 B. SPENCER & F. J. GILLEN, *The Arunta*, 458. We have met several Kurdaitcha men who claim to have killed their victim.

1936 L. KAYE, *Black Wilderness*, 108. 'Kaditcha' he said in fear, as he trekked not through darkness filled with spearmen merely, but with things supernatural and terrible.

The word **kurdaitcha** is used in several other ways.

1. As the name for an emu-feather shoe, worn especially on a mission of vengeance and so made as to leave no trace of the wearer's movements (see 1886 quotation, above). In full, this is known as a **kurdaitcha boot (shoe, slipper)**.

1977 J. CARTER, *All Things Wild*, 61. They seek out their victim by stealth, wearing magic kurdaitcha shoes, fashioned from kangaroo fur, string and emu feathers. These leave no tracks.

2. To refer to the mission of vengeance itself, or to the ritual accompanying this.

1896 B. SPENCER, *Report on the Work of the Horn Scientific Expedition to Central Australia*, 110. When a native for some reason desired to kill a member of another camp or another tribe he consulted the medicine man of his camp, and arrangements were made for a kurdaitcha luma.

3. In the phrase, **to go kurdaitcha**, which means 'to embark on such a mission'.

1901 F. J. GILLEN, *Gillen's diary: the camp jottings of F. J. Gillen on the Spencer and Gillen Expedition across Australia* (1968), 88. The members of a group fully realise that they cannot go Kurdaitja, that they cannot in fact impart to the feather shoes the magic properties which make them leave no track.

makarrata /mækə'ratə/
Also **makharata**, **makarata**, and **makkarata**.
[Yolngu languages, north-east Arnhem Land *makarrata*.]
A ceremonial ritual symbolising the restoration of peace after a dispute; the name given to a proposed treaty between 'the Aboriginal nation' and the Australian government, for which a group of distinguished white Australians began campaigning in 1979. [1937]

1937 W. L. WARNER, *A Black Civilisation*, 174. The makarata is a ceremonial peacemaking fight. It is a kind of general duel and partial ordeal which allows the aggrieved parties to vent their feelings by throwing spears at their enemies or by seeing the latter's blood run in expiation.

1987 L. R. HIATT, *Oceania*, Vol. 58, 144. The predominant purpose of a makarrata was to expunge guilt rather than to exact revenge.

1988 *Mercury* [Hobart], 21 August, 13. Six years ago the Fraser Government agreed that some form of compact or 'makarrata' with Aborigines should be pursued.

malgun /mæl'gun/, /mæl'gʌn/
Obsolete.
[Dharuk, Sydney region *malgun.*]
The ceremonial amputation of the first two joints from the little finger of the left hand of a female Aboriginal infant. [1790]

> **1790** W. DAWES, *Grammatical Forms of the Languages of N. S. Wales*, 60. Malgun, the little finger of the left hand of the woman when the two joints are cut off.

> **1878** R. BROUGH SMYTH, *The Aborigines of Victoria*, I, xxiii. The practice of mutilating the body prevails in all parts of Australia. In New South Wales, at an early age, the women are subjected to an uncommon mutilation of the first two joints of the little finger of the left hand. This operation is performed when they are very young, and is done under an idea that these little joints of the left hand are in the way when they wind their fishing lines over the hand. This amputation is termed *Malgun.*

mimi /'mimi/
[Gunwinygu, central Arnhem Land, Northern Territory *mimi?* (the word ends in a glottal stop, which is a contrastive sound in this language).]
A category of spirit people depicted in rock and bark paintings of western Arnhem Land. [1949]

> **1956** C. P. MOUNTFORD, *Records of the American-Australian Scientific Expedition to Arnhem Land*, I, 112. The *Mimi* artists had a feeling for composition and movement which the x-ray artists lacked. Their main subject was man in action, running, fighting, throwing spears. All *Mimi* paintings were executed in red which, according to the myth, was made up of blood and red ochre.

> *Ibid.* 181. The general term *Mimi* covers a large group of spirit people. Some … live under similar conditions to the aborigines; that is, they have the same hunting implements, eat the same foods, and know the way to make fire … The cave-painting *Mimi*, whose specific name I did not find out, are supposed, by the aborigines, to have been responsible for the single-line rock paintings in the caves of the Arnhem Land plateau, adjacent to Oenpelli, particularly those of human beings.

> **1981** J. MULVANEY et al., *Aboriginal Australia*, 163. Mimi spirits are characterised by their elongated and slender form. They are trickster spirits, sometimes cannibalistic, which inhabit rocky places. Where they disappear into the rock walls of caves and shelters, they sometimes leave their shadows behind, which appear as paintings on the rock surfaces.

mokani /mə'kani/
Obsolete.
[Yaralde, mouth of Murray River, South Australia, probably *mogani.*]
See quotation, below. [1843]

1843 H. A. E. MEYER, *Vocabulary of the Language ... in the Vicinity of Encounter Bay*, 81. Mōkani ... black stone, something like a hatchet, the head fastened between two sticks, which are bound together, and form a handle. There is a sharp edge, which is used to charm men, while the other end of the stone is blunt and rough, and is used to charm women. It is used for the same purpose and in the same manner as the plongge.

mudlo /ˈmʌdloʊ/
Also **muddlo**. *Obsolete.*
[Probably Yagara, Brisbane region *mulu* (often pronounced [mudlu]) 'stone'.]
See quotation for definition. [1861]

1876 'EIGHT YEARS' RESIDENT', *Queen of Colonies*, 333. When one of the tribe is sick he is said to have a 'mudlo'. Mudlo is a stone, and their belief is that death is caused by some hostile black placing a stone in that portion of the body which is affected. We have seen blacks with mudlos in their heads, some in their stomachs or breasts, and some in the legs. They will tell you with the greatest composure whether the mudlo will be got out, or whether the patient will 'go bong'.

mundie /ˈmʌndi/
Also **mundy**. *Obsolete.*
[Probably Kattang, Taree region, New South Wales *mundi*.]
See quotation for definition. Also called **mundie stone**. [1847]

1847 G. F. ANGAS, *Savage Life and Scenes*, II, 224. Mundie is a crystal, believed by the natives to be an excrement issuing from the Deity, and held sacred. It is worn concealed in the hair, tied up in a packet, and is never shown to the women, who are forbidden to look at it under pain of death.

plongge /ˈplɒŋgi/
Obsolete.
[Yaralde, mouth of Murray River, South Australia, probably *blonge*.]
A club used in ritual. See also *mokani*. [1843]

1846 H. A. E. MEYER, *Manners and Customs of the Aborigines of the Encounter Bay Tribe*, 8. The plongge is a stick about two feet long, with a large knob at the end. They believe that if a person is tapped gently upon the breast with this instrument he may become ill and die, or if he should shortly afterwards receive a wound that it will be mortal.

prun /prun/
Used in North Queensland.
Also **brun**.

[Nyawaygi, just south of Ingham, North Queensland *burun*, 'fighting ground'.]
A fighting corroboree; also **prun-ground**. [1902]

> **1902** W. E. ROTH, *Games, Sports and Amusements* (*North Queensland Ethnography. Bulletin*, 4), 15–16. The tribe on whose territory the prun-ground happens to be is always the first to arrive there on the day appointed … some few days previously a messenger has been sent round to the various camps reminding them of the date … The prun helps both to settle old scores and at the same time promotes social intercourse and amusement.

Quinkan /'kwɪŋkən/
Also **Quinkin**.
[Kuku-Yalanji, Bloomfield River, North Queensland *guwin-gan*, 'ghost, spirit'.]
A category of spirit people depicted in rock paintings of northern Queensland. [1969]

> **1969** P. J. TREZISE, *Quinkan Country*, 29. Supernatural spirits and spirits of dead people are called Quinkans by all Cape York Aborigines of today. This name probably originated in the Mareeba area, a great meeting place of present-day Aborigines, and now replaces all the individual tribal names for such spirits.

> **1969** D. BAGLIN & B. MULLINS, *Aborigines of Australia*, 22. Many of these galleries feature Quinkans, a phenomenon of northern Queensland. According to the Aborigines, these strange creatures live in rock crevices and emerge at night, waiting just outside the light of the campfire to grab the unwary.

> **1979** *Commonwealth Parliamentary Papers*, VIII, 2. The Quinkan galleries, which were discovered in 1960 and located in the Laura region of the Cape York Peninsula, contain several hundred Aboriginal rock art galleries which have been described as one of the largest and most exciting bodies of prehistoric art in the world.

wagyl /'wɒgl/
Used in Western Australia.
[Nyungar, Perth–Albany region *waagul*.]
A carpet snake; the rainbow serpent; a mythical monster. [1831]

> **1841** G. F. MOORE, *Colonial Magazine and Maritime Journal*, No. 5, 20. They have a horror of some imaginary creature, called Waukal which inhabits deep waters and dark places, the description of which is that of a snake of monstrous shape.

> **1989** *Weekend Australian* [Sydney], 22/23 July, 20. WAGYL, the rainbow serpent, is the creator of all the waterways. In the beginning, there was no water and the rainbow serpent circled the land in search of water. Where he went the rains came and over the years he carved out lakes and rivers.

Wandjina /ˈwɒndʒinə/
Also **Wondjina**.
[Ungarinyin, north Kimberley, Western Australia *wanjina* (several etymologies have been suggested for this word in Ungarinyin, but none is plausible—see pp. 17–18, above).]
An ancestral spirit, connected with fertility and rain, depicted in rock paintings of the Kimberley Ranges in Western Australia. [1930]

> **1969** R. EDWARDS & B. GUERIN, *Aboriginal Bark Paintings*, 23. The Wandjinas of the Kimberleys are creative ancestral beings. When first discovered their white bodies and halo-like head-dresses led to some fanciful theories linking them with Christian myths … To the Aborigines, the Wandjinas are not just paintings, but spirits.

warra-warra /ˈwɒrə-wɒrə/
Obsolete.
[Gaurna, Adelaide region *warra-warra*.]
A name for a 'clever man': see *koradji*. [1840]

> **1843** J. F. BENNETT, *Historical and Descriptive Account of South Australia*, 67. They think to counteract the influence of the bad men who possess supernatural powers, by charms and other magic evolutions, for which purpose there are among them professed sorcerers, called *warra-warra*.

witarna /wɪˈtanə/
[Parnkalla, Port Lincoln area (and many other languages in South Australia) *widarna*.]
A ceremonial object. Also called *bullroarer* (see p. 241) [1844]

> **1846** C. W. SCHÜRMANN, *The Aboriginal Tribes of Port Lincoln*, 5. The witarna, an oval chip of wood, say eighteen inches long and three or four broad, smooth on both sides and not above half an inch thick. By a long string which passes through a hole at one end, the native swings it round his head through the air, when it gradually, as the string becomes twisted, produces a deep unearthly sound.

wonga /ˈwɒŋgə/
[Pajamal (spoken to the west of Darwin) and languages in the Daly River area *waŋga*.]
A corroboree. Note that *wonga* is also the name for a kind of plant (p. 125). [1946]

> **1946** W. E. HARNEY, *North of 23°*, 220. The Aboriginals are singing and stamping their feet down in the camp, for they are dancing a wonga, the trade dance of these people.

yahoo /ˈyahu/
Obsolete.
[This is probably a loan word into Australian languages from English, although it may possibly be an original word from a New South Wales language (if so, probably Awabakal or Wiradhuri or both).]
A name given to an evil spirit, monster, or 'hairy man'. Note that *yahoo* is also the name of a bird (p. 89). [1835]

> **1835** J. HOLMAN, *A Voyage Round the World, including Travels in ... Australia*, IV, 480. The natives are greatly terrified by the sight of a person in a mask calling him 'devil' or *Yah-hoo*, which signifies evil spirit.

> **1844** MRS C. MEREDITH, *Notes and Sketches of New South Wales*, 95. They have an evil spirit, which causes them great terror, whom they call 'Yahoo' or 'Devil-devil': he lives in the tops of the steepest and rockiest mountains, which are totally inaccessible to all human beings, and comes down at night to seize and run away with men, women or children, whom he eats up, children being his favourite food ... The name Devil-Devil is of course borrowed from our vocabulary ... that of Yahoo, being used to express a bad spirit, or 'Bugaboo', was common also with the aborigines of Van Dieman's Land, and is as likely to be a coincidence with, as a loan from, Dean Swift; just as their word '*collar*', for anger, very nearly approaches in sound our word *choler*, with a like meaning.

> **1854** L. E. THRELKELD, *Christian Herald*, 23 December, 362–3. *Kurriwilbán* ... has a long horn on each shoulder, growing upward, with which she pierces the aboriginal children, and then shakes herself until they are firmly impaled on her shoulders, when she carries them to the deep valley, roasts and eats them ... By some unaccountable means *Yarhoo* has been given as a name to this Demoness, most likely introduced by some way from Dean Swift's travels of Gulliver.

yoolang /ˈyulæŋ/
Also **yoolahng** and **yoolangh**.
[Dharuk, Sydney region *yulaŋ*, 'place where initiation ceremonies take place'.]
A ceremony during which a youth is initiated into manhood; the place where such ceremonies take place. [1796]

> **1796** D. COLLINS, *An Account of the English Colony in New South Wales* (1798), I, 563–4. Between the ages of eight and sixteen, the males and females undergo the operation which they term Gnahnoong, viz. That of having the *septum nasi* bored ... Between the same ages also the males receive the qualifications which are given to them by losing one of the front teeth ... The place selected for this extraordinary exhibition was at the head of Farm Cove, where a space had been for some days prepared by clearing it of grass, lumps etc.; it was of an oval figure, the dimensions of it 27 feet by 18, and was named *Yoo-lahng*.

PEOPLE

There are a number of words borrowed from Australian languages into Australian English to name Aboriginal people. These frequently reflect relations between Aborigines and white Australians. Some are derogatory, like *binghi*, *gin*, and *lubra*. Others—which were borrowed from Australian languages into the English used by Aboriginal people and have only recently come into the English used by other Australians—are more positive in their connotations, exhibiting pride in Aboriginality. Varying labels are used in different parts of the continent.

In 1990, the University of Melbourne advertised a 'Stewart Murray Memorial Fellowship' for

> a scholar working on any aspect of the culture and society of the Koorie, Murrie, Nyungar, Nunga, Yolngu, Yura, Anangu, Yuin or Torres Strait Island people.

However, this list omitted a fair number of regional labels—for example, it made no mention of Bama (from North Queensland), Mardu (from the Western Australian desert fringe), Mulba (from the Pilbara), Wongi (from the Kalgoorlie region), or Yammagi (from the Murchison River region). We include all these terms below, but the list is not held to be exhaustive; there are certainly further terms in small regional pockets.

Most terms have a purely regional currency. However, *koori* experienced something of a geographical expansion. It was originally used on the coast north of Sydney, but then expanded over southern New South Wales and down into Victoria. It has recently been suggested (by some Koories from New South Wales and Victoria) that the term *Koori* be used nationally in place of *Aboriginal*, or *Aborigine*, which is in some contexts mildly derogatory (in other countries, *aborigine* is a common noun used, sometimes unflatteringly, to describe an original inhabitant of a land). As sections of the media began to adopt this suggestion, indigenous people in various parts of the country protested against such an idea. Indeed, on 18 September 1994, the *Sunday Herald Sun* ran an article (on page 10) under the heading CLAN: WE'RE NOT KOORIES, which began:

> The use of the term 'koorie' to describe native Australians has been condemned. Members of the Wurundgeri tribe—the traditional inhabitants of the Melbourne region— say the term is offensive and should be changed. They say it comes from a NSW Aboriginal dialect and is not appropriate for Victorian use. A spokesman for the Nevin clan of the Wurundjeri tribe, Ian Hunter, said that the closest word in local dialect was 'koonie', which meant dung … Mr Hunter has written to the Aboriginal and Torres Strait Islander Commission (ATSIC) and the Victorian Aboriginal Education Association, asking them to

ban the use of the term. Instead, he has asked that traditional local words be used. They are 'woongie' or 'kulin' which translate as 'people'.

anangu /ˈanaŋu/

Used in Central Australia.
[Western Desert language *arnaŋu*.]
An Aborigine. [1937]

> **2001** *Australian*, 24 November (Magazine Supplement), 28. You think Anangu care about junkies in Melbourne? No. And people don't care about sniffers in the bush.

bama /ˈbæmə/, /ˈpæmə/

Also **pama**. Used in North Queensland.
[From many North Queensland languages *bama*, 'person' or 'man'.]
An Aborigine. [1770]

> **1978** *Bloomfield River News*, August, 13. *Bama* have lived at Bloomfield and indeed all over Australia, for more than 40,000 years.

binghi /ˈbɪŋgi/

Also **bing-eye**.
[Awabakal, Newcastle region (and neighbouring languages), *biŋay* '(elder) brother'.]
A somewhat demeaning term for an Aborigine, formerly used as a name for the 'typical' Aborigine. In early Australian English, it meant 'brother', and was used patronisingly, like *black brother*. [1830]

> **1830** R. DAWSON, *Present State of Australia*, 221. I was received by them with the greatest cordiality, and greeted by the term bingeye, or brother.

> **1925** *Bulletin* [Sydney], 23 April, 23. So long as the witch-doctor leaves him alone, Binghi in his wild state is a hardy customer.

> **1985** J. MILLER, *Koori: a Will to Win*, 156. The popular Press of Australia makes a joke of us by presenting silly and out-of-date drawings and jokes of 'Jacky' or 'Binghi', which have educated city-dwellers and young Australians to look upon us as sub-human.

boko /ˈboʊkoʊ/

Also **boco**.
[Possibly from an Australian language.]
An animal or person who is blind in one eye. Also used as an adjective. [1847]

> **1953** H. G. LAMOND, *Big Red*, 154. As horses, men and other animals, were liable to infection, it can be assumed 'roos also ran the risk. If they did, the curse never got beyond the initial stages—boko, scummy-eyed kangaroos were unknown.

boong /bʊŋ/
[Although it has been suggested that this may be an Aboriginal word, it is more likely not to be a borrowing from an Australian language. One possible origin is *bung*, the word for 'elder brother' (also used as a general term of address) in the Jakarta dialect of Indonesian.]
A highly derogatory name for an Aborigine. The word is also applied to an indigenous inhabitant of New Guinea, Malaysia, etc. **Boong line** is a term for a team of native bearers, as employed in Papua New Guinea during the war of 1939–45. [1924]

> **1997** MUDROOROO, *Indigenous Literature of Australia*, 81. Freedom is not the birth-right of the Australian Indigenous person and too often, if he or she ends up at the receiving end of the white law, he or she is never treated as a common Australian citizen, but as a boong.

boorie /ˈbʊri/
Also **burry**.
[Wiradhuri, south-west New South Wales (and neighbouring languages) *burraay*, 'boy, child'.]
A derogatory name for an Aborigine. [1955]

> **1972** K. WILLEY, *Tales of the Big Country*, 170. Some Queenslanders still disparage Aborigines as 'abos' and 'boories'.

bunji-man /ˈbʌndʒə-mən/
Also **bunjamun, bunji**.
[Possibly from a Western Australian language; or possibly from the English *fancy-man*.]
A white man with a predilection for Aboriginal women. [1975]

> **1985** *National Times* [Sydney], 12 April, 20. The origins of the term are unclear, but could be related to Bun-gyte, meaning an unbetrothed girl. Today the term, widely used by Aboriginal people around Perth, refers to lonely, alcoholic, old, white men who wander the parks and back streets seeking 'black velvet'—sexual solace from Aboriginal women ... The best free translation of Bunji is 'dirty old man'.

[Note: Over much of Queensland, Aborigines use a term *banji* or *bunji* meaning 'cousin' or 'friend', someone with whom one is on easy terms. This may have come from a Queensland language, although its origin has not yet been traced. It is unlikely to be related to the Western Australian term *bunji-man*.]

burka /ˈbɜkə/
Obsolete.
[Gaurna, Adelaide region *burga*, 'old (adj.); old man'.]

A South Australian word for an old man, one who is completely knowledgeable about religious matters. [1839]

> **1858** W. A. CAWTHORNE, *Legend of Kupirri*, 30. 'Burka.'—An aged man, the last stage through which men pass, and in whom the knowledge of all charms, ceremonies, etc., is deposited.

cooboo /'kubu/
Mainly used in Western Australia.
[Probably Ngarluma, Yule and Fortescue Rivers, Western Australia *gubuyu*, 'small'; 'child' (with similar forms in neighbouring languages).]
'(Aboriginal) baby'. The word was given currency by the novelist Katherine Susannah Prichard. [1903]

> **1929** K. S. PRICHARD, *Coonardoo* (1961), 10. Their skins darken with exposure to the air and sunshine, so that by the time they are toddling, the cooboos are as bronzed and gleaming as pebbles lying on the red earth.

coolie /'kuli/
Also **kooli**. *Obsolete.*
[Wemba-wemba, Wuywurung, and Wathawurung, Victoria *guli*, 'person'.]
A derogatory name given by white Australians to the consort of an Aboriginal woman; also applied, usually in the plural form, to Aboriginal men in general. [1842]

> **1884** J. BONWICK, *Lost Tasmanian Race*, 41. The stock-keepers at Mr Stocker's of Salt Pan Plains, were guilty of abominable conduct toward two Native women. These afterwards told their Coolies or husbands, and the tribe surrounded the hut, and killed two men out of the three.

djanga /'dʒæŋə/
Primarily used in Western Australia. *Now obsolete.*
[Nyungar, Perth–Albany region *jan-ga*, 'spirit of a dead person' (this was also the original for *jingy*, p. 153).]
A term applied by Aborigines to a white person. [1838]

> **1842** G. F. MOORE, *Descriptive Vocabulary of the Language … of Western Australia*, 20. Djandga … The dead. The re-appearance of deceased persons. A term applied to Europeans, who are supposed to be aborigines, under another colour, restored to the land of their nativity. This idea prevails equally on the eastern as on the western coast of Australia, in places 2000 miles apart from each other.

gin /dʒɪn/
Formerly also **din**, **ding**, and **jin**.
[Dharuk, Sydney region *diyin*, 'woman, wife'.]

An Aboriginal woman or wife. Today, the term is almost always derogatory. [1790]

> **1790** R. CLARK, *Journal*, 15 February, 133. I heard the crying of children close to me I asked them to go and bring me there (Dins) which is there [*sic*] woman.

The word **gin** has been used in a number of other ways.

1. Attributively, in expressions like **gin burglar**, **gin hunter**, **gin jockey**, and **gin stealer**, to designate a white man who sexually exploits an Aboriginal woman or, in expressions like **gin burglary**, the activity of so doing.

> **1971** K. WILLEY, *Boss Drover*, 45. Now and then you would meet fellows who … would go from station to station, scrounging feeds and hanging about the blacks' camps looking for girls. They were known as combos, murlongers, or gin burglars.

2. In combination with other words.
gin's piss, beer deemed to be of inferior quality.

> **1972** J. O'GRADY, *It's your Shout, Mate!*, 43. Yeah, but you come from England. That's gin's piss country. Any kind o'beer'd be better than that English muck.

gin shepherd, (like *gin burglar*, etc.) a white man who cohabits with an Aboriginal woman; but used also, with a quite different meaning, of one who seeks to prevent the sexual exploitation of Aboriginal women by white men.

> **1946** W. E. HARNEY, *North of 23°*, 77. In those old days we had the eternal clash of 'gin burglar' versus 'gin shepherd'.

gin's sister

> **1878** R. BROUGH SMYTH, *The Aborigines of Victoria*, I, 64. *Djee-gun* is the superb warbler; the *eering* the *emu wren*; the former is called the 'gins' sister', the latter the 'blackfellows' brother'.

jackeroo /dʒækəˈru/
Also **jackaroo**.
[Of unknown origin. The 1895 quotation (from Archibald Meston, who is not a reliable source) has often been mentioned, but the etymology proposed appears to be without foundation. There is no confirmatory evidence of a bird name *tchaceroo* in the Brisbane language. The 1840 quotation in which missionaries are called 'jackaioos' may possibly relate to a different word.]
Originally, this was a Queensland term referring to a white man who lived beyond the bounds of close settlements. Later, a 'jackeroo' was 'a young man (frequently English and of independent means) seeking to gain experience by working in a supernumerary capacity on a sheep or cattle station'. A jackeroo is now 'a person working on such a station with a view to acquiring the practical experience and

management skills desirable in a station owner or manager'. The word can also be used as a verb, meaning 'to work as a jackeroo'. The term *jillaroo* is used for a female jackeroo. [1840]

> **1840** H. H. J. SPARKS, *Queensland's—First Free Settlement, 1838–1938* (1938), 24–5. Letter from Commandant's Office, Moreton Bay, March 30, 1840. We found one man belonging to the Duke of York's tribe, that appeared to have got a few grains of shot about the forehead and chest, and on inquiry from how he got wounded, he said that the jackaioos (meaning the missionaries) had fired on him and others.

> **1895** A. MESTON, *Geographic History of Queensland*, 32. Another word used throughout Australia is 'jackeroo', the term for a 'newchum', or recent arrival, who is acquiring his first colonial experience on a sheep or cattle station. It has a good-natured, somewhat sarcastic meaning, free from all offensive significance. It is generally used for young fellows during their first year or two of station life. The origin of the word is now given for the first time. It dates back to 1838, the year the German missionaries arrived on the Brisbane River, and was the name bestowed upon them by the aboriginals. The Brisbane blacks spoke a dialect called 'Churrabool', in which the word 'jackeroo' or 'tchaceroo' was the name of the pied crow shrike, *Stripera graculina*, one of the noisiest and most garrulous birds in Australia. The blacks said the white men (the missionaries) were always talking, a gabbling race, and so they called them 'jackeroo', equivalent to our word 'gabblers'.

Jindyworobak /dʒɪndiˈwɒrəbæk/
[Wuywurung, Melbourne region.]
A member of a literary group formed in 1938 by the poet R. C. Ingamells (1913–1955), to promote Australianism in art and literature. It is likely that Ingamells found the word *Jindy-worabak* in the miscellaneous list of words from Australian languages at the end of *The Vanished Tribes* by J. Devaney, 1929 (p. 240). Devaney had taken it from Daniel Bunce's vocabulary of the Melbourne language in his *Language of the Aborigines of the Colony of Victoria and other Australian Districts* (1851, p. 2), where the spelling *Jindi woraback* was used. [1851]

> **1938** R. INGAMELLS, *Conditional Culture*, 4. 'Jindyworobak' is an aboriginal word meaning 'to annex, to join', and I propose to coin it for a particular use. The jindyworobaks, I say, are those individuals who are endeavouring to free Australian Art from whatever alien influences trammel it, that is, to bring it into proper contact with its material.

koori /ˈkʊri/, /ˈkuri/
Also **kooree**, **koorie**, and formerly **coorie**, **kuri**, and **kurri**. Used in New South Wales and Victoria.
[Awabakal, Newcastle region, and neighbouring languages *guri*.]
An Aborigine. [1834]

Koori comes from the north coast of New South Wales. It is believed to have spread as far as the Murray River by early in the twentieth century and is now in use through much of New South Wales and Victoria. It is a name that expresses pride in Aboriginality. The term was until recently employed only among Aborigines for referring to themselves, but many people in the south-east now ask to be called *Kooris*, rather than *Aborigines*, by the media and by white people generally. However, some indigenous people are objecting to the use of Koori as a general term for all Aborigines (see the quote at the beginning of this section and one below).

> **1973** D. WOLFE, *The Brass Kangaroo*, 306. You should get rid of the white bosses here and let us koories run the station.

> **1992** K. COOKE, *The Crocodile Club*, 167. The Minister beamed at Chloe ... 'It's always such a marvellous treat to come all the way here for some Koori culture. Marvellous.'

> 'They're not Koori, they're from Nyampuju,' she said.

> 'Oh well, of course, let me just say that I mean Koori in the wider sense, as you people have asked to be addressed.'

> 'I've never asked to be called Koori in my life,' said Chloe. 'That's a word used for Aboriginal people in the south-eastern states. There's Murris in Queensland and Nungas in South Australia and a whole lot of different names for groups all over.'

> 'Extraordinary,' said the Minister.

A complementary term, which Kooris use among themselves to describe white people is *Guba* or *Gubba*, sometimes abbreviated to *Gub* or *Gubb* (this may possibly be derived from the English *governor* or *government man*).

koori /'kʊri/
[Probably from Panyjima, Tom Price area, Western Australia *kurri*, 'marriageable teenage girl', or possibly from the Western Desert language *kurri*, 'spouse, sexual partner'.]
A young Aboriginal woman. [1886]

> **1985** H. MARIS & S. BORG, *Women of the Sun*, 94. If you were a koori, what chance did you have of finding a job—except ... cleaning up whitefeller's dirt?

lubra /'lubrə/
Formerly also with some variety, as **leubra** and **loubra**.
A derogatory term for an Aboriginal woman. [1829]

 There has been considerable controversy as to the origin of this word. Most people consider it to be Tasmanian, but others suggest it may have come from a mainland Australian language. Certainly, after its introduction into English, it spread rapidly and widely and was used by both white and Aboriginal people in many localities for 'black woman', which makes it difficult to pinpoint the source of the word; the earliest quotations, from 1829 and 1830, involve G.A. Robinson, who undoubtedly used a form of pidgin to communicate with the Tasmanians. Although we cannot be certain, it is most likely to have originally come from one of the languages of south-eastern Tasmania, but it certainly was not the regular word for 'woman', which was *lowana*. (In the Oyster Bay language, 'penis' was *lubara*. It is not impossible that this was borrowed into English as the term for 'Aboriginal woman'.)

> **1829** G. A. ROBINSON, in N. J. B. PLOMLEY, *Friendly Mission* (1966), 18 May, 59. The husband soon followed me, his cheeks wet with tears. Said *leuberer lowgerner unnee* (his wife asleep by the fire).

> **1830** *Ibid.*, 19 March (1966), 133. Dray told me that the natives had gone away last night and that Woorrady and *lubra* or *lore* went after them.

Lubra has also been applied to a non-Aboriginal woman, and used figuratively.

> **1971** D. WILLIAMSON, *Don's Party* (1973), 49. Any man who isn't married with four kids is a lecher in your book, you flop-bellied, breast-sucked old lubra.

maluka /məˈlukə/
Also **maluga**.
[Djingulu, Newcastle Creek, Northern Territory *marluga*, 'old man: old'; *marluga*, 'old man', also occurs in neighbouring languages.]
The person in charge; the boss. [1905]

> **1908** MRS A. GUNN, *We of the Never-Never*, 340. The tribe mourned for their beloved dead—their dead and ours—our Maluka, 'the best Boss that ever a man struck'.

mardu /ˈmadu/
Also **martu**. Used in the Western Desert fringe of Western Australia.
[Western dialects of the Western Desert language, *mardu*.]
An Aborigine. [1966]

> **1980** *Mikurrunya* [Strelley, Western Australia], 23 April, 16. The whiteman brought in their animals; cattle, sheep and horses, and the martu were taught how to muster, and how to cut posts and build fences and yards.

marla /ˈmalə/
Used in Central Australia.
[Aranda, Alice Springs region *marle*, 'young female person or animal'.]
A girl. [1845]

migaloo /ˈmɪɡəlu/
Also **micolo**, **miguloo**, and **mikulo**. Used in North Queensland.
[Biri, Mackay region *migulu*, 'ghost, spirit'.]
A white person. Originally used in Aboriginal English, then borrowed into many Aboriginal languages of the region with this meaning, and also into the everyday English of the area. [1887]

> **1978** B. ROSSER, *This is Palm Island*, 20. 'I could see he's not a migaloo …' Fred winked at me. 'With a nose like his, he'd have to be a murrie'.

monaych /ˈmɒnaɪtʃ/
Also **monarch**.
[Nyungar, Perth–Albany region *manaj*, 'white cockatoo'; by transference, 'a police officer'.]
A police officer; the police. [1842]

> **1979** N. BRAHAM (ed.), *The Dwarf: selections from the McGregor Literary Competitions 1978–79*, 28. When I'm broke I'm just Tommy Caylun, the boong, shuffling down the street, with an eye out for the monaych—coppers.

mulba /ˈmʊlbə/
Used in the Pilbara region of Western Australia.
[Panyjima, Tom Price area, Western Australia *marlba*.]
An Aborigine. [1903]

> **1989** S. MORGAN, *Wanamurraganya, the story of Jack McPhee*, 136. It seemed that you had to choose one way or the other, no one would let you be both. The problem was, if you chose to be a Mulba you and your family never had any rights at all and you could kiss any hopes of getting on goodbye. Yet if you chose to be a whiteman, you had rights, but you couldn't mix with everyone. It was hard, very hard.

munjon /ˈmʌndʒən/
Also **mungus**, **munjong**, and **murndong**. Used in Western Australia.
[Yindjibarndi, Hamersley Range, Western Australia, and nearby languages *mañjaŋu* 'stranger'.]
An Aborigine who has had little contact with white society. The word has also been applied to an Aborigine brought up in white society and unfamiliar with the traditional way of life. [1948]

> **1998** G. ALLEN, *The Gun Ringer*, 53. The munjons were the natives who refused to come into the stations and work for the whites. They still lived in the bush the old free way and were the only people, apart from the outlaws, who inhabited the Underworld. The country was too isolated and poorly grassed to attract settlers.

murlonga /mɜˈlɒŋɡə/
Also **myrnonga**.
[Possibly from an Australian language.]
A white man who sexually exploits Aboriginal women; see also *gin burglar*.
[1912]

> **1912** *Bulletin* [Sydney], 15 February, 13. There is the much less widely known aboriginal term 'myrnonga'. The myrnonga is a person of more promiscuous habits [than the combo] who … prowls with furtiveness when the moon is young.

murri /ˈmʌri/
Also **mari**, **murrie**, and **murry**. Used over northern New South Wales and most of Queensland, almost as far north as Cairns.
[Kamilaroi, east New South Wales (and many languages in south and central Queensland) *mari*.]
An Aborigine. [1844]

> **2000** *Courier-Mail* [Brisbane], 19 February (Weekend Supplement), 2. 'I'd never known much about my own culture before that,' she says. 'Only that it was problematic. Could get you into trouble. So I stayed away from it, stayed away from other Murri kids, too.'

myall /ˈmaɪəl/, /ˈmaɪɔl/
Formerly also **mial**, **miall**, and **myal**.
[Dharuk, Sydney region *mayal* or *miyal* 'a stranger, an Aborigine from another tribe'. *Myall* is also a name for a tree (p. 143)]
Myall meant 'stranger' in Dharuk and was first used in English in the same sense. As the Aborigines who were 'strangers' were those who lived at a remove from white settlements, the word came to be applied by whites, as it is now, to Aborigines who live in the traditional manner and who are unaccustomed to white society. *Warrigal* is used similarly. [1798]

> **1976** s. WELLER, *Bastards I Have Met*, 98. Charlie's people were Myalls and never saw a white man.

Myall is used in several other ways.

1. As an adjective in the above sense (it formerly meant 'strange' or 'hostile').

> **1845** *Sydney Morning Herald*, 10 June, 2. On my return … I found that some myall blacks, belonging to the north-west … had been in.

2. As an adjective, used of a plant or animal, to mean 'wild'.

> **1888** 'R. BOLDREWOOD', *Robbery Under Arms* (1937), 12. Didn't like the thought of his children growing up like myall cattle.

3. By Aboriginal people in central Australia to describe an Aboriginal person, with the meaning 'ignorant of one's own culture'.

> **1983** P. NATHAN & D. L. JAPANANGKA, *Settle Down Country*, 17. Does the researcher think I'm *myall* [stupid]. She knows the answers. What is she asking me these things for?

4. In the name of the **myall snake**, *Denisonia suta*.

> **1848** *Atlas* [Sydney], IV, 359. Occasionally they tell of someone 'tumble down' from bite of myall snake.

nunga /'næŋgə/
Also **nanga**. Used in the southern part of South Australia.
[Wirangu, Port Lincoln to Head of Bight, South Australia *nhaŋga*.]
An Aborigine. [1917]

> **1987** N. BARBER, *How to Become a Successful Derelict in Adelaide*, 22. Aboriginal is the white people's name for Nungas. They call themselves Nungas. Always have.

A complementary term used among Nungas in South Australia to refer to white people is Goonya (this is of uncertain etymology).

nyoongah /'nyʊŋə/, /'nyuŋə/
Also **noongah**, **noongar**, and **nunga**. Used in the south-west of Western Australia.
[Nyungar, Perth–Albany region *ñuŋar*.]
An Aborigine. [1831]

> **1977** K. GILBERT, *Living Black*, 88. The most effective means of communication … we call … the 'noongar grapevine' … It used a sort of communication that can only be understood by Aborigines and it's highly functional.

pinnaroo /pɪnə'ru/
[Diyari, Lake Eyre region, South Australia and neighbouring languages *pinarru*, 'an elder'.]
An Aboriginal elder. [1873]

> **1966** K. WALKER, *The Dawn is at Hand*, 42.
>
> > I look at you and am back in the long ago,
> > Old pinnaroo lonely and lost here,
> > Last of your clan.

queeai /'kwiaɪ/
Also **kwee-ai**, **quee-eye**, and **qui-ai**.
[Aranda, Alice Springs area *gʷeye* 'girl'.]
An Aboriginal girl. [1886]

1976 C. D. MILLS, *Hobble Chains and Greenhide*, 12. I would look at one of the 'queeais', who, like little girls the world over, would turn her head away, suddenly overcome with the giggles.

waddy /'wɒdi/
[Western Desert language *wadi*, 'initiated man'.]
An Aboriginal male. [1935]

> **1935** H. H. FINLAYSON, *The Red Centre*, 68. Over large portions of the interior the aborigine distinguishes himself from the white man by the term 'waddi' and this might perhaps serve as a name for the race.

weei /'wiaɪ/
Also **weeai**, **weeay**, and **wei**.
[Aranda, Alice Springs region *aweye*, 'a young male person or animal'.]
An Aboriginal boy. [1886]

> **1976** C. D. MILLS, *Hobble Chains and Greenhide*, 72. The 'weeais' usually scored knives and mouth organs. A pocket knife was highly prized and carefully guarded.

wongi /'wɒŋgaɪ/
Used in the vicinity of Kalgoorlie, Western Australia.
[*Waŋgayi*, originally the term used by the Mount Margaret group of speakers of the Western Desert language for the Warburton group, now generalised as a term to refer to any Aborigine. Probably based on *waŋga* 'language'.]
An Aborigine. Note that *wongi*, with a different pronunciation, is also a verb, 'to talk or tell' (p. 202). [1929]

> **1981** A. WELLER, *The Day of the Dog*, 61. Charley's woman, a shy dark wongi from Kalgoorlie, comes out and takes the baby … [Note] Really the people from Kalgoorlie way, but any full-blood Aboriginal.

yammagi /'yæmədʒi/
Also **yamager**, **yamagi**, **yamidgee**, **yammagee**, and **yammogee**. Used in the Murchison River region of Western Australia.
[Watjarri, Murchison River, Western Australia *yamaji*, 'person, man'.]
An Aborigine. [1893]

> **1983** G. E. P. WELLARD, *Bushlore*, 55. I was standing outside the humpy discussing the days work with three of the Yamagee musterers. I use the word 'Yamagee' because that is the name they call themselves in that district. They never say 'Blackman' or 'Aborigine', it is always 'Yamagee'.

yolngu /'yʊlŋu/
Also **yolnu**. Used in north-eastern Arnhem Land.
[Yolngu languages, north-east Arnhem Land, Northern Territory *yuulŋu*.]
An Aborigine. [1980]

> **1980** *Canberra Times*, 5 July, 2. Anthropologists tell me that Yolnu is not strictly a language, but the word used by the people of north-east Arnhem Land to describe themselves. This, again, means that it is not the name of a tribe or clan, because many groups of people live in the whole area.

yuin /yuən/
Used on the New South Wales south coast.
[Dharawal and Dhurga, New South Wales south coast *yuwiñ*.]
An Aborigine. [1904]

> **2004** *Koori Mail*, 18 September, 9. It is a woman's mountain and a teaching place, and is the centre of creation for all Yuin people.

yura /'yurə/
Used in the Flinders Ranges area of South Australia.
[Adnyamathanha, the Flinders Ranges, and Parnkalla, lower Eyre Peninsula, *yura*, with similar words in neighbouring languages.]
An Aborigine. [1844]

> **2000** *Outback*, December, 121. Within five minutes you can sense that his place means more than just tucker to this indigenous Australian, or Yuras, which he says is the more politically-correct term.

IMPLEMENTS

An Aboriginal woman traditionally possessed only a few tools for collecting and processing food. Men also had only a small number of weapons for hunting. Even though the possessions of an Aboriginal family were few, they were designed to be lightweight and efficient, and commonly were useful for a variety of activities. One multi-purpose desert artefact was used as a spear-thrower, as a cutting implement, as a fire-making tool, as a hook for reaching high berries, as a tray in which to mix tobacco or ochres, and as a percussion instrument for song accompaniment. A 'tool kit' generally included digging sticks, coolamons, dilly bags, stone hatchets, spears, and spear-throwers. Canoes were made from bark, heated and bent to shape, sewn, and their joints made waterproof with wax; blankets were also made from bark. Sacred, musical, and artistic objects were usually produced by men.

Some Aboriginal weapons and implements were similar to those used outside Australia, and established names like *spear* and *shield* could be used by the colonists.

There were a number of Aboriginal artefacts, such as the boomerang and woomera, that were of unfamiliar design to the colonists, and for these a name was taken over from an Australian language.

Hunting or warfare

bondi /ˈbʌndi/, /ˈbʊndi/, /ˈbʊndaɪ/
Also **boondie**, **bundi**, and **bundy**.
[Wiradhuri, south-west New South Wales, and nearby languages, *bundi*.]
A heavy club with a knob on the end. [1844]

> **1976** C. D. MILLS, *Hobble Chains and Greenhide*, 98. A coon doesn't like fighting with his hands, 'finger-fight' he calls it, and doesn't give *you* any points if *you* do. He is brought up with a bundy in his hand as soon as he can toddle.

boomerang /ˈbuməræŋ/
Formerly also with much variety as **bomerang**, **bommerang**, **bomring**, **boomer-eng**, **boomering**, **bumerang**, and **womerang**.
[Dharuk, Sydney region, probably *bumariñ*.]
A crescent-shaped wooden implement used as a missile or club, in hunting or warfare, and for recreational purposes. The best-known type of boomerang, used primarily for recreation, can be made to circle in flight and return to the thrower. The boomerang was originally believed (in error) to be a type of sword (see the 1790 quotation, below). Although boomerangs were known in other parts of the world, the earliest examples and the greatest diversity of design is found in Australia. A specimen of a preserved boomerang has been found at Wyrie Swamp in South Australia, and is dated as 10,000 years old. The boomerang as a hunting weapon was not known throughout the entirety of Australia, being absent from the Lower Murray River and Adelaide region, from the west of South Australia, from the north Kimberley region of Western Australia, from parts of Arnhem Land, from the northern part of the Cape York Peninsula in Queensland, and from Tasmania—see the map on page 14 of *Australian Languages: Their Nature and Development* by R. M. W. Dixon (Cambridge University Press, 2002). In some areas, boomerangs are mentioned in myth and ritual. In some regions, they are decorated with designs that are either painted or cut into the wood. The boomerang is also known as *kirra*, *kylie*, or *wonguim*. The volume *Boomerang, Behind an Australian Icon* by Philip Jones (Wakefield Press, 1996) provides an authoritative and engrossing account of this artefact. [1790]

> **1790** W. DAWES, *Grammatical Forms of the Languages of N. S. Wales*, Boo-mer-it, the Scimiter.

> **1825** B. FIELD, *Geographical Memoirs on New South Wales*, 292. The spear is universal, as is also the throwing-stick; the *boomerang* or *woodah* … a short crested weapon

which the natives of Port Jackson project with accurate aim into a rotary motion, which gives a precalculated bias to its forcible fall … was also seen on the east coast, and at Goulburn Island on the north.

The word **boomerang** is used in several other ways.

1. Figuratively, especially with reference to something which returns to or recoils upon its author.

> **1846** *Boston Daily Advertiser*, 5 May.

> > Like the strange missile which the Australian throws,
> > Your verbal *boomerang* slaps you on the nose.

> **2003** B. RANDALL, *Songman*, 232. Aboriginal people have this idea of boomerang Law. Whatever you throw out will come back to you. If you throw out negative things from your mind, they will come back … This is the real meaning of payback.

2. In combination with other words:

boomerang thrower, throwing

> **1956** S. HOPE, *Diggers' Paradise*, 32. The expert boomerang throwers … still make their own by hand for competitive displays.

> **2001** *Manly Daily*, 13 July, 11. A NAIDOC Week celebration with aboriginal artefacts, didgeridoo playing and boomerang throwing demos.

boomerang cheque, a cheque that 'bounces'.

> **1958** T. RONAN, *Moleskin Midas*, 286. Bob was good with the pen in his day, mainly for signing boomerang cheques.

boomerang leg, a disease characterised by flattening and forward bowing of the shinbone, a leg affected by the disease.

> **1915** *Journal of Tropical Medicine and Hygiene*, XVIII, 218. The disease has for some time been known as 'boomerang leg' on account of the similarity of shape of the leg to that of a boomerang.

boomerang legged, used of a person affected by the above disease.

> **1894** *Intercolonial Quarterly Journal of Medicine and Surgery* [Melbourne], I, 223. The condition is well recognised by the residents who, not inaptly, describe the natives so affected as 'boomerang-legged'.

boomerang propeller, a steamship propeller, the design of which was inspired by the Aboriginal weapon, invented by the explorer Thomas Mitchell (1792–1855), but never developed commercially.

1913 J. C. L. FITZPATRICK, *The Good Old Days of Molong*, 38. He was a man of most versatile type—for instance, he published a trigonometrical survey of Port Jackson, patented a boomerang-propeller for steamers, and translated 'The Lusiad' of Camoens.

3. As a verb meaning 'to return in the manner of a boomerang', 'to recoil (upon the author)', 'to ricochet'.

1979 *Canberra Times*, 13 November, 28. Greg Chappell's decision to send England in appeared to have boomeranged.

4. As the verbal noun **boomeranging**, 'the throwing of the boomerang'.

1899 *Longman's Magazine* [London], XXXIII, 475. Boomeranging is dangerous to on-lookers, till the thrower is a perfect master of his weapon.

dowak /ˈdaʊæk/
Also **dowuk**.
[Nyungar, Perth–Albany region, probably *duwag*.]
A weapon used by Aborigines, described as a straight stick, about eighteen inches long, about an inch thick and abruptly pointed at each end. [1831]

1841 G. GREY, *Journals of Two Expeditions of Discovery*, II, 265. With the dow-uk, a short heavy stick, they knock over the smaller kinds of game.

1962 B. W. LEAKE, *Eastern Wheatbelt Wildlife*, 55. The male would carry a … dowak, which was a waddy about thirty inches long, and one and a quarter inches thick sharpened slightly at one end.

gidgee /ˈgɪdʒi/
Also **gidgie**. Chiefly used in Western Australia.
[Nyungar, Perth–Albany region *giji*.]
An Aboriginal spear. Also used as a transitive verb, 'to spear'. *Gidgee* is also the name for a tree (p. 132). [1833]

1878 *Catalogue of Objects Ethno-typical at the Australian National Gallery, Melbourne*, 46. *Gid-jee*, a hardwood spear, with fragments of quartz set in gum on two sides and grass-tree stem. Total length, 7 feet 8 inches.

1979 H. WILSON, *Skedule*, 192. Mr Brent gidgied a section of bakewell tart which had bounced off his plate.

hielaman /ˈhiləmən/
Also with much variety, especially formerly as **yeelaman** and **yelaman**.
[Dharuk, Sydney region *(y)ilimaŋ* 'bark shield'.]
A shield made from bark or wood. [1793]

1793 W. TENCH, *A Complete Account of the Settlement at Port Jackson*, 191. Their shields are of two sorts: that called *il-ee-mon*, is nothing but a piece of bark, with a handle fixed in the inside of it. [The other sort was a wooden shield: see *tawarang*.]

1848 H. W. HAYGARTH, *Recollections of Bush Life in Australia*, 113. The heeloman is a sort of shield, made of the toughest wood procurable, about three feet in length, and six inches in breadth at the centre, whence it gradually tapers off to a point at either extremity. The handle is in the middle, and is merely a small aperture, just large enough to admit the hand.

kirra /ˈkɪrə/
Chiefly used in South Australia.
[Diyari, Lake Eyre region, South Australia (and neighbouring languages) *kirra*.]
A boomerang. [1873]

1905 *Steele Rudd's Magazine*, April, 363. Every dialect had usually its own word for the boomerang and all other weapons. 'Kylie' is a common name in West Australia, and 'Kirra' in South Australia.

1965 A. UPFIELD, *The Lure of the Bush*, 69. 'There are three kinds of boomerang', he went on. 'The Wonguim, which returns in its flight to the thrower; the Kirras, which does not return; and the very heavy Murrawirrie.

kylie /ˈkaɪli/
Also **kiley** and **koilee**. Chiefly used in Western Australia.
[Nyungar, Perth–Albany region (and other Western and central Australian languages) *garli*.]
A boomerang. The girl's name *Kylie* may be based on this word. [1833]

1872 MRS E. MILLETT, *An Australian Parsonage*, 22. The flat curved wooden weapon, called a *kylie* … the natives have invented for the purpose of killing several birds out of a flock at one throw.

1885 M. A. BARKER, *Letters to Guy*, 177. There are heavier 'ground kylies', which skim along the ground, describing marvellous turns and twists, and they would certainly break the leg of any bird or beast they hit.

leangle /liˈæŋɡəl/
Formerly with much variety as **langeel**, **leangil**, **leawill**, **leeangle**, **liangel**, and **liangra**.
[Wemba-wemba and Wuywurung, Victoria *liengel*, related to *lia* 'tooth', describing the head of the implement.]
A fighting club with a hooked striking head. [1838]

1878 R. BROUGH SMYTH, *The Aborigines of Victoria*, II, 299. The Murray and Lower
Goulburn natives ... use ... the leangle—a peculiar weapon not unlike the miner's pick.

leonile /'liənil/
Obsolete.
Probably a variant of *leangle*, but possibly from a related language. [1894]

> **1894** *Journal of the Anthropological Institute* [London], XXIII, 317. The *Australian
> Aboriginal weapon*, termed the *leonile, langeel, bendi* or *buccan* ... The *leonile* con-
> sists, speaking generally, of a more or less long straight handle, or shaft, and a
> sharp pointed head, of greater or less length, either at right angles to the former, or
> opposed to the shaft at an angle somewhat greater than a right angle.

lil-lil /'lɪl-lɪl/
[Probably Wemba-wemba, western Victoria *liəwil* (a dialect variant of *liɲgel*, see
leangle), formed from *lia* 'tooth' and the affix *-wil* 'having'.]
A weapon used both as a missile and in close combat. [1878]

> **1974** M. TERRY, *War of the Warramullas*, 121. Boomerang-shaped clubs were used in
> eastern and central Australia. The lil-lil, a short, bladed weapon with a curved handle,
> was much used in New South Wales and Victoria for hand-fighting or throwing.

malka /'mælkə/, /'mʌlkə/
Also **malga**, and now usually **mulga**.
[Wuywurung, Melbourne region, and other Victorian languages, *malga, malgarr*.]
A shield. [1839]

> **1856** J. BONWICK, *William Buckley*, 71. Buckley tells us that the Yarra Blacks called
> ... the two shields, Malka and Seaugwel ... The Malka, to ward off blows, is two or
> three feet long, and is provided with a handle.

meera /'mirə/
Also **meara**, **merro**, and **meru**. Chiefly used in Western Australia.
[Nyungar, Perth–Albany region *mirra* (in south-western dialects) *mirru* (in north-
ern dialects).]
A woomera. [1821]

> **1841** G. GREY, *Journals of Two Expeditions in North-west and Western Australia* I, 304.
> The old lady ... went up to him ... seizing his merro, or throwing stick.

midla /'mɪdlə/
Also **middla** and **midlah**. *Obsolete.*
[Gaurna, Adelaide region (and neighbouring languages) *midla*.]
A woomera. [1839]

1842 *South Australian News* [London], 15 October, 46. The weapon is thrown by the midla (propelling stick) a distance of sixty or eighty yards with considerable precision.

mogo /ˈmoʊɡoʊ/
Also **maga**, **mago**, **mogin**, and **moko**. *Obsolete.*
[Dharuk, Sydney region, and neighbouring languages *mugu*.]
A stone hatchet. Also the name of a small town near Bateman's Bay, in southern New South Wales. [1793]

> **1820** J. OXLEY, *Journals of Two Expeditions into the Interior of New South Wales*, 175. They were entirely unarmed, and there was but one mogo, or stone-hatchet, among them.

mungo /ˈmʌŋɡoʊ/
[Probably Ngiyambaa, central New South Wales *maŋgar* 'bark, bark canoe'.]
A bark canoe. [1847]

> **1953** A. RUSSELL, *Murray Walkabout*, 89. The bark canoe, or 'mungo', the only float known to the Murray-Darling aborigines … simply a sheet of bark stripped in one piece from a gum tree trunk and turned up a few inches at its ends and sides.

murrawirrie /mʌrəˈwɪri/
Also **murawirrie**.
[Diyari, around Lake Eyre, South Australia *mara* 'hand' + *wirri* 'throwing club'.]
A heavy boomerang-like club used for striking at an opponent. [1879]

> **1879** *Native Tribes of South Australia*, 288. Murawirrie … two-handed boomerang, from 6 to 14 ft long, and 4 in. broad.

mutting /ˈmʌtɪŋ/
Also **mutach** and **muton**. *Obsolete.*
[Dharuk, Sydney region *mudiŋ* 'multi-pronged fish spear'.]
A fish spear. [1790]

> **1892** R. HILL & G. THORNTON, *Notes on Aborigines of NSW*, 2. A blackfellow in his way, as a rule, is very clever … and with the mutting (four-pronged spear) … not easily surpassed.

nulla-nulla /ˈnʌlə-nʌlə/
Formerly also with much variety, as **nilla-nilla**, **nolla-nolla**, and **nullah-nullah**.
[Dharuk, Sydney region *ŋala-ŋala*.]

A hardwood club, used in fighting and hunting. [1790]

> **1808** *Sydney Gazette*, 6 November. A perhaps deadly stroke with a *nulla-nulla* ... [*Note*] This weapon is formed by affixing to the end of a club a circular piece of very hard wood, 8 or 10 inches in diameter, with a sharp edge, and of a mushroom form. It is frequently carried as a weapon of defence, but the natives seldom exercise it against each other.

tawarang /ˈtæwəræŋ/
Also **tourang** and **towerang**. *Obsolete.*
[Dharuk, Sydney region *dawarraŋ* 'wooden shield'.]
A shield. See also *hielaman*. [1790]

> **1798** D. COLLINS, *An Account of the English Colony in New South Wales*, I, 585. Ta-war-rang ... is about three feet long, is narrow, but has three sides, in one of which is the handle, hollowed by fire. The other sides are rudely carved with curved and waved lines, and it is made use of in dancing, being struck upon for this purpose with a club.

waddy /ˈwɒdi/
Also **waddi**, **waddie**, **wody**, and **woodah**.
[Dharuk, Sydney region *wadi*, 'tree, stick, club'.]
A war-club; a piece of wood used as a club. Note that *waddywood* is also the name for a type of tree (p. 145). [1790]

> **1832** J. BACKHOUSE, *A Narrative of a Visit to the Australian Colonies* (1843), 90. The chief instrument used in the chase by these people is a Waddy, a short stick about an inch in thickness, brought suddenly to a conical point at each end, and at one end a little roughened, to keep it from slipping out of the hand.

The word **waddy** is used in several other ways.

1. In Australian pidgin to refer to a tree, or a piece of wood.

> **1870** C. H. ALLEN, *A Visit to Queensland and her Goldfields*, 182. 'Fellow' is a very important word in their English vocabulary, and expresses number; as 'six fellow yarraman', six horses; 'big fellow waddy', a large quantity of wood; 'little fellow waddy', a small quantity.

2. As a name for a club or cudgel as used by a person other than an Aborigine.

> **1824** *Australian* [Sydney], 30 December, 3. On Sunday night, a book-binder residing in Phillip-street, named Welsh, while in a state of intoxication, was attacked by three soldiers, who with waddies beat him in a most dreadful manner.

3. In the phrase, **to take up the waddy,** 'to engage in vigorous defence' (comes from 'to take up the cudgels').

1907 *Bulletin* [Sydney], 7 February, 15. I beg to take up the waddy of disputation on behalf of 'Crossnibs'.

4. As a verb meaning 'to strike, beat, or kill' (an animal or person) with a waddy.

1833 *Launceston Advertiser*, 31 October, 3. The spearing and waddying are yet of too recent occurrence to be remembered with indifference by our settlers.

1840 *Sydney Gazette*, 10 September. We learnt … that three males and one female belonging to the brig *Maria*, had been waddied in the day time.

wadna /'wɒdnə/
Obsolete.
[Gaurna, Adelaide region *wadna* (related to *wanna*, see p. 185).]
A South Australian name for an implement, believed to be primarily used for killing large fish, and for climbing. Also widespread as a name for a digging stick similar to a crowbar. [1840]

1840 C. G. TEICHELMANN & C. W. SCHÜRMANN, *Outlines of a Grammar, Vocabulary and Phraseology … around Adelaide*, 51. Wadna … A stick for climbing, one end of which has a sharp point for entering the bark of trees.

1860 *Transactions and Proceedings of the Royal Society of Victoria* (1861), 170. The 'wadna' is a kind of weapon about three feet long, with a knee in the middle. It is never used as a weapon for fighting, but only for killing large fish.

weet-weet /'wit-wit/
[Wuywurung, Melbourne region, and related languages *wij-wij*.]
A weapon and toy, sometimes called *kangaroo rat* or *leaping kangaroo*. The first Australian cricket team to tour England, in 1868, consisted of Aborigines, who, as well as playing cricket, would give demonstrations of throwing spears, boomerangs, and weet-weets. [1839]

1904 *Bulletin* [Sydney], 11 February, 16. The 'weet-weet' … is still occasionally used by the blacks on the Coranderrk (Vic.) mission station … When well-thrown, this missile travels an astonishing distance.

1988 J. MULVANEY & R. HARCOURT, *Cricket Walkabout*, 123. Although modern cricketers might wish for an armoury of boomerangs with which to silence persistent barrackers, even with the Aborigines, such 'blood sports' were exceptional. Throwing the 'kangaroo-rat' was no exception. The name is misleading. Normally termed a 'weet-weet', this weapon consisted of a solid wooden or bone knob on a flexible handle about 60 centimetres in length. It was normally used for bringing down birds or small animals. After it had been swung rapidly backwards and forwards to gather momentum and flex the weapon, it was skimmed low along the ground with an underarm jerky motion. In an impressive display at the Oval one was hurled right across the arena.

wirri /ˈwɪrə/
Also **wirra**.
[Gaurna, Adelaide region *wirri*.]
A club used for fighting and hunting. [1839]

> **1860** *Transactions and Proceedings of the Royal Society of Victoria* (1861), 170. Another weapon, called 'wirra', is made of the stem of young trees, about one and a-half feet long, and barely an inch thick. The thin end, which serves for the handle, is generally notched, while towards the thicker end it is a little bent, somewhat in the shape of a sword … This weapon the natives use for killing kangaroo rats and other small animals.

> **1868** *Illustrated Sydney News*, 28 December, 108. The ease, the grace, and the sure aim with which the native throws his wirri, or waddy … are matters of surprize to the civilized white men.

wonguim /ˈwɒŋgwəm/
[Wathawurung and Wuywurung, southern Victoria *waŋgim*.]
A type of returning boomerang. [1839]

> **1886** F. COWAN, *Australia: a charcoal-sketch*, 24. His Won-guim: Boomerang of play: an Eucalyptus-leaf-like toy of wood.

woomera /ˈwʊmərə/
Also **wammara**, **womera**, **wommara**, **wommera**, and **womra**.
[Dharuk, Sydney region *wamara*.]
An implement used to propel a spear, sometimes known as a *spear-thrower* or *throwing-stick*. The name is also that of a town in South Australia. Also known as *meera* and *midla*. [1793]

> **1819** W. C. WENTWORTH, *A Statistical, Historical and Political Description of the Colony of New South Wales*, 116. The womera, or throwing-stick, which enables the natives of Port Jackson to cast their spears with such amazing force and precision, is not used by them [Tasmanian Aborigines].

> **1963** D. ATTENBOROUGH, *Quest under Capricorn*, 73. He also owned a few spears and a wommera or spear-thrower, a long slat of wood shaped into a handle at one end and fitted with a spike at the other. The spike slots into a notch on the end of a spear and the wommera virtually doubles the length of a man's arm, thus increasing the leverage on the spear and greatly augmenting the power with which he can hurl it.

Food collection and preparation

coolamon /ˈkuləmən/

Also **coolaman**, **cooliman**, and **kooliman**.

[Kamilaroi, east New South Wales, and nearby languages *gulaman*.]

A basin-like vessel of wood or bark used by Aborigines to hold water and other liquids, and for a variety of other purposes such as carrying a baby. Also called *pitchi*. *Coolamon* is the name of a town in New South Wales. [1845]

> **1845** L. LEICHHARDT, *Journal of an Overland Expedition in Australia*, 27 May (1847), 269. Three koolimans (vessels of stringy bark) were full of honey water, from one of which I took a hearty draught, and left a brass button for payment.

dilly /ˈdɪli/

Also **dilli**.

[Yagara, Brisbane region *dili*, 'coarse grass or reeds, a bag woven of this'.]

A bag or basket made from woven vine, grass, or fibre. Frequently **dilly-bag**. [1830]

> **1904** C. C. PETRIE, *Tom Petrie's Reminiscences of Early Queensland*, 106–7. Unlike a number of words that we white people have picked up believing them to be aboriginal, 'dilli' is the genuine name for the baskets or bags the blacks used … One dilli was made from the small rush found in freshwater swamps. These rushes grow about three feet high, and when pulled up the bottom end is white, then there is a red length, and the top is green. To prepare them for the dillies, the natives drew the lengths through hot ashes till quite soft, then they twisted them up on their thighs into round string. A loop of string the size of the dilli wanted, was got ready, then a gin sat down, and put her legs through the loop to hold it firm, while she worked the dilli on the loop … The inland women made dillies from a coarse, strong grass (which they called 'dilli') found in the forests. (Xerotes longifolia.) It is broad and tough, and grows in bunches here and there. The gins pulled this up, split it with their thumb nails to a certain thickness, then softened it with hot ashes, but did not twist it. These dillies were made with the help of a loop held on the big toe.

> **1930** F. HIVES & G. LUMLEY, *The Journal of a Jackeroo*, 75. His spouse would follow with two 'dilly-bags', one made from plaited lawyer cane, and the other of bark. These dilly-bags were generally beautifully made, symmetrical in shape and very strong. They were carried on the back, the weight being supported by a strip of lawyer-cane in the form of a sling, which passed around the forehead.

katta /ˈkætə/

Also **kiatta**. *Obsolete.*

[Gaurna, Adelaide region *gada*, 'digging stick, fighting stick'.]

A woman's digging stick. [1839]

> **1840** C. G. TEICHELMANN & C. W. SCHÜRMANN, *Outlines of a Grammar, Vocabulary and Phraseology … around Adelaide*, 11. Katta … a heavy stick to fight with; club. That of the females is longer, and used for digging up roots, &c.

pitchi /ˈpɪtʃi/
Also **pitchie** and **pittji**.
[Western Desert language (and neighbouring languages) *bidi*.]
A coolamon. [1896]

> **1936** C. CHEWINGS, *Back in the Stone Age*, 1. All the women and most of the young girls carried wooden trays, or *pittjis*, mostly … shallow … and twice as long as they were broad.

wanna /ˈwɒnə/
Also **wonna** and **wonnah**.
[Nyungar, Perth–Albany region (and other Western and South Australian languages) *wana* (related to *wadna*, see p. 182).]
A woman's digging stick. [1839]

> **1902** *Proceedings of the Royal Society of Queensland* (1903), 69. The ordinary yam-stick (wonna) was a rounded piece of wood, not quite as thick as a broom-handle, about 6 feet long, scraped, and hardened with fire at one extremity.

wirra /ˈwɪrə/
Also **wira** and **worra**.
[Western Desert language *wirra*.]
A small cup-like digging scoop, traditionally made of hardwood. Also used as a drinking cup and for collecting small berries. Note that *wirra* is also the name of a kind of tree (p. 147). [1935]

> **1969** A. A. ABBIE, *The Original Australians*, 78. If water supplies are scanty and undependable, the women collect what water they can in their wooden vessels (*wirras*, *pitchis*, *coolamons*) and carry these carefully on their heads throughout the day's march.

yandy /ˈyændi/
Also **yandi** and **yandie**.
[Yindjibarndi, Hamersley Range, Western Australia, and neighbouring languages *yandi*, 'winnowing dish'.]
A shallow (wooden) winnowing dish used to separate edible seeds from refuse, or particles of a mineral from alluvial material. Also called **yandy-dish**. [1903]

> **1914** *Register* [Adelaide], 30 July, 8. Moolyella has been a very rich tinfield … There are a number of aborigines in the locality, and the whites employ the gins to 'yandie' their tin—i.e. to clean it—which is done on a piece of wood hollowed out after the fashion of a butcher's tray, and described by natives as a 'yandie' … This contrivance is jugged [*sic*] by a peculiar motion of the wrist that impels the dirt in one direction while the tin goes the other. Only the gins do it.

The word **yandy** is also used as a verb, meaning 'to winnow'. A **yandier** is one who does this.

> **1933** C. FENNER, *Bunyips and Billabongs*, 158. When a gin has collected a coolamon (shallow wooden vessel) full of seed she has also a good deal of sand, dust, grass and leaves. But by shaking and twisting the coolamon in a particularly skilful way an almost perfect separation is made. This art of separation is called 'yandying'.

> **1997** T. EGAN, *Sitdown Up North*, 257. The best test to see if you can yandy is to mix tea and sugar, and then separate the tea from the heavier sugar.

> **1954** I. L. IDRIESS, *The Nor'-westers*, 165. A noted yandier, Mary Ann … yandied a whole bag of stream tin.

Musical instruments

There is a greater variety of Aboriginal sound instruments in the north of Australia than there is in the south. The didgeridoo is the best-known, but clap sticks, boomerangs and, occasionally, skin-drums are used to make music, mostly to the accompaniment of dancing and singing, as well as the clapping of hands and stamping of feet. Music is played either for entertainment or as part of sacred ritual. Musical instruments are frequently carved and decorated with designs of religious significance.

didgeridoo /dɪdʒəri'du/
Also **didjeridu**, **didjiridu**, and **didjerry**.
[Although it has been suggested that this must be a borrowing from an Australian language, it is not one. The name probably evolved from white people's *ad hoc* imitation of the sound of the instrument—see the two 1919 quotations, below.]
A wind instrument that was originally only found in Arnhem Land. It has in recent years spread and is now in use by Aboriginal people in every part of the continent. The didgeridoo is a long, wooden, tubular instrument that produces a low-pitched, resonant sound with complex, rhythmic patterns, but little tonal variation. It is also called *eboro* or *yidaki* or *drone-pipe*. [1919]

> **1919** *Huon Times* [Franklin], 24 January, 4. The nigger crew is making merry with the Diridgery doo and the eternal ya-ya-ya ye-ye-ye cry.

1919 *Smith's Weekly* [Sydney], 5 April, 15. The Northern Territory aborigines have an infernal—allegedly musical—instrument, composed of two feet of hollow bamboo. It produces but one sound—'didjerry, didjerry, didjerry—' and so on ad infinitum … When a couple of niggers started grinding their infernal 'didjerry' half the hot night through, the blasphemous manager decided on revenge.

1925 M. TERRY, *Across Unknown Australia*, 190. The didjiri-du … is a long hollow tube, often a tree root about 5 feet long, slightly curved at the lower end. The musician squats on the ground, resting his instrument on the earth. He fits his mouth into the straight or upper end and blows down it in a curious fashion. He produces an intermittent drone.

eboro /ˈɛbərou/

Also **eboro** and **ebroo**. *Obsolete*.
[Margu, Croker Island, Northern Territory, probably *baaru*.]
An older name for the *didgeridoo*. [1845]

1845 L. LEICHHARDT, *Journal of an Overland Expedition in Australia* (1847), 16 December, 534. They tried to cheer us up with their corrobori songs, which they accompanied on the Eboro, a long tube of bamboo, by means of which they variously modulated their voices.

yidaki /yəˈdaki/

[Yolngu languages, north-east Arnhem Land *yirdaki*.]
A didgeridoo. This name has been popularised through the success of popular music group Yothu Yindi, made up of Yolngu-speakers. [1974]

2001 *Koori Mail*, 30 May, 18. David Hudson, a world-renowned yidaki exponent and cultural teacher, of the Ewamin/Western Yalangi people of far north Queensland, said he was proud to give a taste of Aboriginal culture to the millions of American and global viewers who tuned in to the show.

Art

Aboriginal art is primarily religious and is rich in symbolism. There are usually several layers of meaning in every artwork, and the deepest and most important artistic symbols may only be revealed to initiated men, who must have a store of religious knowledge with which to interpret the symbols. Some art is purely decorative, and this tended to be executed on painted hunting implements, woven bags, and other objects that were in everyday use. See also *churinga*, *mimi*, *Quinkan*, and *Wandjina*, under Religion and Ceremony, above.

pirri /ˈpɪri/
Also **pirrie**.
[Arabana, northern South Australia, and neighbouring languages *birri*, 'fingernail, extended to anything pointed'.]
An engraving tool made of stone. [1924]

> **1961** *Proceedings of the Prehistoric Society* [Cambridge], XXVII, 75. A pirri is a symmetrical, leaf-shaped, uniface point, retouched over all or part of its upper surface, apparently by pressure flaking … Specimens vary in length from about 1 to 7 centimetres, and even the smallest are made sometimes from intractable quartz. This combination of superb craftsmanship with the production of aesthetically pleasing artefacts … makes the pirri one of the most distinctive items of prehistoric culture.

tula /ˈtulə/
Also **tuhla**, and **tula adze**.
[Arabana, northern South Australia, and neighbouring languages *dhurla*, 'small stone cutting tool'.]
A tool used for wood-working. [1930]

> **1981** J. MULVANEY et al., *Aboriginal Australia*, 70 (*caption*). Tula adze, or woodworking chisel, from Barrow Creek, Northern Territory … exhibits the characteristically curved and stout handle, with stone tip firmly fixed with *Triodia* cement.

wilgie /ˈwɪlgi/
Also **wilga**, **wilghi**, **wilgi**, and **wilgy**. Used chiefly in Western Australia.
[Nyungar, Perth–Albany region *wilgi*.]
A red ochre used to paint the body on ceremonial occasions. [1833]

> **1842** G. F. MOORE, *Descriptive Vocabulary of the Language … of Western Australia*, 76–7. Wilgi … An ochrish clay, which, when burned in the fire, turns to a bright brick-dust colour; with this, either in a dry powdery state, or saturated with grease, the aborigines, both men and women, are fond of rubbing themselves over. The females are contented with smearing their heads and faces, but the men apply it indiscriminately to all parts of the body. Occasionally they paint the legs and thighs with it in a dry state, either uniformly or in transverse bands and stripes, giving the appearance of red or particoloured pantaloons. This custom has had its origin in the desire to protect the skin from the attacks of insects, and as defence against the heat of the sun in summer, and the cold in the winter season. But no aboriginal Australian considers himself properly attired unless well clothed with grease and wilgi.

FEATURES OF THE ENVIRONMENT

Aboriginal communities have an extremely close bond with the land they inhabit. This relationship is reflected in their myths, their songs, their rituals, and their religion. The actions of ancestors in the creation of the physical world made the topography of the landscape rich with significance and meaning.

The environment is not only of religious significance. An intimate knowledge of features of the landscape is crucial for the survival of a hunting and gathering community. Aborigines know much about the actions of the sea, the sky, and the earth, and the richness of their vocabulary in this area is a reflection of that knowledge.

The European colonists of Australia found that there were a number of unusual aspects to the Australian landscape. A new settlement was often given an Aboriginal name (which might describe something that had happened to a dreamtime ancestor at that location). Aboriginal words were sometimes borrowed to describe peculiarities of the land and seascapes.

billabong /ˈbɪləbɒŋ/
Also formerly **billibang**, **billibong**, and **billybong**.
[Wiradhuri, south-west New South Wales *bilabaŋ*, 'a watercourse which runs only after rain'. Mitchell (see 1836 quotation, below) states that it was originally the name of the Goobang River near Condobolin, New South Wales, and the missionary James Günther [1840 mss] that it was the Bell River, but they are both probably incorrect.]
An arm of a river, made by water flowing from the main stream, usually only in time of flood, to form a backwater, blind creek, anabranch, or, when the water level falls, a pool or lagoon (often of considerable extent); the dry bed of such a formation. The term *billabong* has rich connotations in Australian literature, probably the best known use being in 'Banjo' Paterson's ballad 'Waltzing Matilda'. [1836]

> **1836** T. L. MITCHELL, *Three Expeditions into the Interior of Eastern Australia* (1838), II, 21. The name this stream receives from the natives here, is Billibang.

The word **billabong** is also used figuratively:

> **1950** G. FARWELL, *Surf Music*, 23. His life was a billabong, closed in upon itself, joining up with the outer world at rare floodtimes.

It is also used as a verb, meaning 'to follow a circuitous route in a leisurely fashion, to meander':

> **1908** MRS A. GUNN, *We of the Never-Never*, 1. It [*sc.* the train] was out of town just then, up-country somewhere, billabonging in true bushwhacker style, but was expected to return in a day or two.

A **billabonger** is a 'swagman'.

> **1954** T. RONAN, *Vision Splendid*, 217. They dispensed tactfully casual invitations for lunch or tea to billabongers who hadn't eaten a really square meal for months.

birrida /ˈbɪrədə/
Used chiefly in the coastal area north of Perth, Western Australia.
[Nhanta, Geraldton region, Western Australia *bidida*, 'long flat claypan, salt flats'.]
A gypsum claypan. [1999]

> **2003** *Landscope*, Winter, 19. The park and the rest of the peninsula is interspersed with gypsum claypans known as birridas. Most birridas were landlocked saline lakes when sea levels were much higher, and gypsum was deposited on the lake floors.

bombora /bɒmˈbɔrə/
Also **boombora** and **bumbora**.
[Possibly from Dharuk, the Sydney language *bumbora*, said to be the name of a current off Dobroyd Head, Port Jackson.]
A wave which forms over a submerged offshore reef or rock, sometimes (in very calm weather or at high tide) merely swelling, but in other conditions breaking heavily, and producing a dangerous stretch of broken water. The reef or rock itself is known by the same name. The term is mostly used in New South Wales, where there are several bomboras along the coast, usually close to cliffs. Also abbreviated as **bommie** and **bommy**. [1871]

> **1895** C. THACKERAY, *The Amateur Fisherman's Guide*, 21. At the mouth of Lake Macquarie and within coo-ee of Reid's mistake, a bumbora will be found, and alongside it tremendous black and red rock-cod.

> **1988** *Townsville Bulletin*, 3 June, 4. Only last week two trawlers were dragged off, doubtlessly causing a nice amount of damage, after running aground on coral bommies.

The word **bombora** is also used figuratively. See the quotation on page 217 and:

> **1979** D. MAITLAND, *Breaking Out*, 73. He married Shirley and inherited her bitch of a mother at Coogee, the Eastern Suburbs beach community … and got sucked into a deadly *bombora* of domesticity.

cowal /ˈkaʊəl/
[Kamilaroi, east New South Wales, probably *guwal* for 'gully'.]
See the quotations below. [1882]

> **1882** C. LYNE, *Industries of New South Wales*, 213. The homestead … is situated … not far from … the shores of a lake which in this part of the Colony is called, in the language of the aborigines, a 'cowall', or 'cowell'.

1910 C. E. W. BEAN, *On the Wool Track*, 251. If one gets bogged in a creek or a cowal (which is a small tree-grown, swampy depression often met with in the red country), the other will never leave him there.

gibber /ˈɡɪbə/

Formerly also **gibba**.

[Dharuk, Sydney region *giba*, 'stone'.]

A stone, a rock, or mass of stone; a boulder. In early use, applied chiefly to a large outcrop of rock or boulders. Now used specifically for 'gibber-stone' and colloquially for a stone of any size. [1790]

> **1833** *Currency Lad* [Sydney], 13 April, 2. As the hour appointed for the combat approached all the 'lads' from the 'gibbers [The Rocks, a district of Sydney] and Cockle-bay' repaired to a spot in the latter place where the mill was to come off.

> **1850** *Australasian Sporting Magazine*, 92. The great velocity and ease with which these creatures [rock wallabies] ascend or descend the huge gibbas, is truly astonishing.

The combinations **gibber country** and **gibber plain** refer to an arid, stony area of low relief in which the stones sometimes form a surface layer. The central area in the east of Western Australia and the Stony Desert of Charles Sturt are examples of gibber country.

> **2003** *Outback*, December, 22. Travelling bullocks were often cued in gibber country, to prevent them going lame.

> **1896** B. SPENCER, *Report on the Work of the Horn Scientific Expedition to Central Australia*, I, 12. Nothing could be more desolate than a gibber plain when everything is bare and dry, and the outline of the distant horizon is indistinct with the waves of heated air.

A **gibber stone** is a rounded, weather-worn stone of arid, inland Australia.

> **1932** I. L. IDRIESS, *Flynn of the Inland* (1965), 127. The country is strewn with gibber stones and suggests a gigantic cobble pavement.

The chat *Ashbyia lovensis*, which occurs in gibber country, is called **gibberbird**, **gibberchat** (or *desert chat*).

> **1952** A. M. DUNCAN-KEMP, *Where Strange Paths Go Down*, 162. The Gibba bird, also known as the 'paper bag' from its habit of rolling along like a small inflated brown paper bag when disturbed from its nest.

gibber-gunyah

See *gunyah*.

gilgai /ˈɡɪlɡaɪ/
Also **ghilgai, gilgi,** and **gilgie.**
[Wiradhuri and Kamilaroi, New South Wales *gilgaay,* 'waterhole'.]
Terrain of low relief on a plain of heavy clay soil, characterised by the presence of hollows, rims, and mounds, as formed by alternating periods of expansion during wet weather and contraction (with deep cracking) during hot, dry weather. This type of terrain is described as **gilgaied.** A single hole is known as a **gilgai,** or **gilgai hole.** Such holes are also known as *crab-holes, dead-men's graves,* or *melon holes,* country so characterised as *Bay of Biscay country.* [1867]

> **1898** E. E. MORRIS, *Austral English,* 160. Ghilgai … an aboriginal word used by white men in the neighbourhood of Bourke, New South Wales, to denote a saucer-shaped depression in the ground which forms a natural reservoir for rainwater. *Ghilgais* vary from 20 to 100 yards in diameter, and are from five to ten feet deep. They differ from *Claypans* … in being more regular in outline and deeper towards the centre, whereas *Claypans* are generally flat-bottomed. Their formation is probably due to subsidence.

> **1952** *Bulletin* [Sydney], 21 January, 13. The rain came. Before it, the gilgai holes were dry, dusty depressions. Within a week they were fairly teeming with small black and brown crabs.

gnamma hole /ˈnæmə hoʊl/
Also **amar, namma,** and **ngamar hole.**
[Nyungar, Perth–Albany region *ŋamar.*]
A hole (commonly in granite) in which rainwater collects. Also called *rock-hole.* [1837]

> **1948** M. UREN, *Glint of Gold,* 34. Gnamma holes are holes in rock with an impervious bottom and walls, and generally with a narrow neck. Natives enlarge the necks sufficiently to get their arms into the holes and dip out the water. The rock covering prevents the water from evaporating.

jingera /ˈdʒɪndʒərə/
[Possibly from a New South Wales language.]
Remote and mountainous bush-covered country. *Jingera* is also the name of a town in southern New South Wales. [1870]

> **1977** G. C. JOYNER, *The Hairy Man of South Eastern Australia,* 20. It was supposed to be in the Tinderry mountains, and what is known as the 'jingera' behind—the wild, rough country.

kopi /ˈkoʊpaɪ/, /ˈkoʊpi/
Also **copi.**
[Marawara dialect of Baagandji, junction of Darling and Murray Rivers, New South Wales *gabi.*]

A fine, powdery gypsum occurring near salt lakes in arid areas, and used in ritual Aboriginal mourning; a more cohesive, gypsum-rich mass, sometimes a rock, found where opal is mined. [1860]

> **1886** E. M. CURR, *The Australian Race*, II, 238–9. It was the practice of the women of the Marowera Blacks, on the death of a husband, to put a small net on the head and cover it with mortar one or two inches thick. This mortar consisted sometimes of gypsum and at others of pipe-clay. After being worn several days it became solid, and was removed unbroken by means of the net, so giving the cast of a considerable portion of the head of the wearer. After removal it was baked in the fire and laid on the tomb of the deceased ... These casts, which the Kulnine tribe call *kopi*, weigh sometimes as much as fourteen pounds.

> **1951** E. HILL, *The Territory*, 19. If you happened to call on a burial, you would see ... women of the dead men ... wearing heavy widows' caps of kopi, black man's plaster of Paris.

kwongan /ˈkwɒŋgæn/
[Nyungar, Perth–Albany region, *gwoŋgan*, 'plains country, sand plain'.]
A term used in Western Australia to describe an area of dry scrubland with woody evergreen vegetation, having leaves that are hard and tough, and usually small and thick, so reducing the rate of loss of moisture. [1851]

> **1989** K. BRADBY, *A Park in Perspective*, 33. Kwongan—this is a term brought into use in recent years to describe communities of low sclerophyll shrubland. It is similar to areas described in other Mediterranean climate areas such as maquis (French), macchia (Italian), chapparral (Californian), matorral (Chile), fynhos (South Africa).

mickery /ˈmɪkəri/
Also **mickeri**, **mickerie**, and **mickri**.
[Wangganguru, north South Australia *migiri* (a similar form occurs in neigh-bouring languages). See quotation for original meaning; after introduction into English, it was extended to cover soaks in a dry river bed.]
A soak, a hollow in (often) sandy soil where water collects, on or below the surface of the ground, specifically an excavated and formed soak, especially in a dry river bed. [1899]

> **1986** L. A. HERCUS, *Archaeology in Oceania*, XXI, 51. [The Wangkangurru] people got water from clay-pans after rains and spread out all over the country, then fell back on their permanent water-supply at the *mikiri* when the surface water had dried out. The *mikiri* were deep soaks or rather wells where water was obtained by clambering down through long narrow tunnels dug sometimes as much as seven metres into the ground.

min-min /ˈmɪn-mɪn/
Also **min-min light**.
A will-o'-the-wisp; a phosphorescent light seen on marshy ground, perhaps result-ing from the combustion of gases. [1950]
[This is said to be from a language in the Cloncurry area, but it does not appear in any of the materials for languages of the region, nor was it recognised by the last speakers of these languages.]

> **1956** H. HUDSON, *Flynn's Flying Doctors*, 115. 'We're catching up with the Min-Min.' 'What's that?' I asked. My mates explained that it is an Aboriginal name for a mysterious dancing light or will-o'-the-wisp that moves about on the plains. Some say it is caused by luminous gases or luminous insects, but the Aborigines believe it is an apparition of evil spirits, anyway nobody has ever caught up with a Min-Min.

mirrnyong /ˈmɜnyɒŋ/
Also **mirnyong**.
[Probably from a Victorian language.]
A mound of ashes, shells, and other debris, accumulated in a place used by Aborigines for cooking. Also known as *native oven* or **mirrnyong heap**. [1878]

> **1969** D. J. MULVANEY, *The Prehistory of Australia*, 168. Both the Western District and the Riverina Plains were dotted with 'mirrnyongs' or 'native ovens'—isolated middens up to 100 feet thick, often crammed with burials.

murrillo /məˈrɪloʊ/
Obsolete.
[Yuwaalaraay, north New South Wales *murrila*, 'rocky ground, pebbly ridge'. The materials on this language do not support the 1881 quotation in its statement that the word originally meant 'ant-hill'.]
See quotation below for definition. [1881]

> **1881** W. E. ABBOT, in *Journal and Proceedings of the Royal Society of New South Wales*, XV, 43. A conglomerate composed chiefly of waterworn quartz pebbles, called on the Barwon and Narran murrillo, but not known by this name in other parts of the country where the conglomerate is found. On making enquiries among blacks I found that in their language murrillo means ant-hill … These ant-hills are nearly always built on the highest ground in that part of the Colony, to avoid floods, and as the highest ground is generally that which is composed of the quartz conglomerate it is easy to understand how the word which first meant ant-hill came also to mean ridges on which the ant-hills are found.

narriwadgee /ˈnærəˈwædʒi/
[Possibly from an Australian language.]
A 'night well', a waterhole that fills with water during the night. [1923]

> **1923** *Bulletin* [Sydney], 25 January, 22. The mysterious waterhole … is no doubt a 'narriwadgee', or night well.

pindan /ˈpɪndæn/
[Bardi, north-west of Derby, Western Australia *bindan*, 'the bush'.]
A tract of arid, sandy country characteristic of the south-west Kimberley region, in northern Western Australia; the low, scrubby vegetation occurring on the sandy soils of such country; any of several plants typifying such vegetation, such as *Acacia tumida*. Also used in the compounds **pindan country** and **pindan scrub**. In north Western Australia, an inland Aborigine is sometimes called a **pindaner**. [1888]

> **1927** M. DORNEY, *An Adventurous Honeymoon: the first motor honeymoon around Australia*, 147. It is very similar to what is called 'desert country' in the Northern Territory, only that the sandy soil of the 'pindan' is loose and makes travelling very difficult, which is not the case with the hard red sandy soil of the 'desert' in the Territory.

tally-walka /ˈtæli-wɔkə/
Also **tally-walker**.
[Baagandji, Darling River, New South Wales *daliwalga*, name of a specific ana-branch of the Darling River which runs from Wilga Station to just south of Menindee, borrowed into English as a general term for 'anabranch'.]
An anabranch (a division of a river which rejoins it further on). [1886]

> **1947** M. MACLEAN, *Drummond of the Far West*, 92. Further along the road, we passed a 'tally-walker', which was a new one to us city folk. According to my informant, a billabong is a backwater of a river, or was so until the water receded and left the billabong isolated. He said a tally-walker is much the same thing, but it rejoins the river along again, when flowing sufficiently.

willy-willy /ˈwɪli-wɪli/
Also **whirly-whirly**, **whirly-wind**, **wurley-wurley**, etc.
[Probably from Yindjibarndi, Hamersley Range, Western Australia (or a neighbouring language) *wili-wili*.]
A name used to describe a whirlwind. [1894]

> **1898** R. RADCLYFFE, *Wealth and Wild Cats*, 70. 'Willie-Willies' … are water-spouts made of sand instead of water … They usually begin upon a very small scale … a dancing column of dust, dung, dead flies, and old paper. Give them time and they will show sport. But the 'willie-willie' has no perseverance; he lacks continued effort,

and the slightest opposition in the shape of a tin hut or a telegraph pole so destroys his symmetry that he dies of disgust in a small heap of refuse. But with plenty of room he becomes rampant. When he gets over fifty feet high his power is vast.

willy-willy is also used figuratively:

> **1939** K. TENNANT, *Foveaux*, 254. A willy-willy of words sprang up, a blown dust-spout in the path of an oncoming storm.

> **1974** C. THIELE, *Albatross Two*, 135. Andy ran his hands through his willy-willy hair. 'Aren't we poetic this morning?'

BODY PARTS

bingy /'bɪndʒi/
Also **bingey**, **bingie**, **binjie**, and **binjy**.
[Inland dialect of Dharuk, Sydney region *bindhi*, 'belly'.]
The stomach, the belly. [1791]

> **1892** *Truth* [Sydney], 19 June, 5. And each small boy went home and told his parents that he warn't going to be a butcher or a baker, but to be a member of Parliament, have a big binjie, wear a gold chain, and cut about among the toffs!

Hence **bingied**:

> **1913** H. LAWSON, *For Australia*, 159. They're patting their binjies with pride, old man, and I want you to understand, that a binjied bard is a bard indeed.

cobra /'kɒbrə/
Also **cobberra** and **cobbra**. Chiefly used in Australian pidgin, and now obsolete.
[Dharuk, Sydney region *gabarra*, 'head'.]
The head or skull. Note that *cobra* is also the name of a shipworm (p. 91). [1790]

> **1831** *Sydney Herald*, 14 November, 4. After a hard fought battle they parted good friends, some of their *cobberas* having sustained considerable damage.

mundowie /mʌn'doʊi/
Also **mundoey** and **mundoie**. Chiefly Australian pidgin.
A foot, a footstep. [1790]
[Possibly Dharuk, Sydney region *manuwi*, 'foot', or possibly Awabakal, Newcastle region *manduwaŋ*, 'foot'.]

> **1976** C. D. MILLS, *Hobble, Chains and Greenhide*, 11. We saw tracks about a mile from the hole, and though the big, splayed 'mundowies' meant nothing to me, Pebble could read them like a printed page.

CLOTHING

gina-gina /ˈdʒɪnə-dʒɪnə/
Also **jinna-jinna**. Used in Australian pidgin, chiefly in Western Australia.
[Possibly Mantjiltjara dialect of Western Desert language *jina-jina*.]
A kind of dress worn by Aboriginal women. [1927]

> **1955** F. B. VICKERS, *The Mirage* (1958), 187. The jinna-jinna dress was a shapeless scarlet colored bag with holes in it for the neck and arms. It had no trimmings, no finish, except the turned-in hems.

naga /ˈnagə/
Also **naga-naga**, **narga**, **nargara**, and **narger**.
[Wuna, east of Darwin *naga*, 'clothing, covering generally'.]
A loin-cloth (as worn by Aborigines). [1869]

> **1969** A. A. ABBIE, *The Original Australians*, 65. In northern Arnhem Land … where the first observers described the Aborigines as naked, contact with Indonesians over the past two or three centuries had led to the adoption of the naga, the common term for both the male breech-cloth and the female skirt.

DWELLINGS

There was variation across Australia in the style of dwellings built by Aborigines. As groups of people moved about frequently in search of food, it was unnecessary for them to build permanent, or even semi-permanent, buildings. Most buildings were shelters, which could be erected rapidly and required only readily available materials. The simplest were no more than windbreaks. More complex constructions were built in areas such as Arnhem Land, where there was frequent flooding; here huts stood off the ground on poles and were often large enough to hold several families.

Names for these temporary dwellings were borrowed from Australian languages in a number of localities; *gundy* and *gunyah* became current in New South Wales, *humpy* in Queensland, *mia-mia* in Western Australia and Victoria, and *wurley* in South Australia. Now the words have a wider distribution, effectively over the whole continent.

gundy /ˈgʌndi/, /ˈgʊndi/
Also **goondie**.
[Yuwaaliyaay and Kamilaroi, east New South Wales *gundhi*, 'house, hut'. Also Wiradhuri, south-west New South Wales *gunday*, 'stringybark, and a shelter made from this'.]
A gunyah. [1876]

> **1980** S. THORNE, *I've Met Some Bloody Wags*, 82. My mate Tom and I went there after a busy afternoon bending the elbow around at his gundy.

gunyah /'gʌnyə/

Also **gunya** and formerly with much variety as **guneah**, **gunneah**, **gunnie**, and **gunyer**.

[Dharuk, Sydney region *gañi*, 'house or hut'.]

A temporary shelter of the Aborigines, usually a simple frame of branches covered with bark, leaves, or grass. Gunyahs were usually built close together either in a row or in a semi-circle, with the more closely related families near to each other. Unmarried men often shared a hut that was built at some distance from the others. [1790]

> **1845** L. LEICHHARDT, *Journal of an Overland Expedition in Australia* (1847), 14 June, 290. We saw a very interesting camping place of the natives, containing several two-storied gunyas, which were constructed in the following manner: four large forked sticks were rammed into the ground, supporting cross poles placed in their forks, over which bark was spread sufficiently strong and spacious for a man to lie upon; other sheets of stringybark were bent over the platform, and formed an arched roof.

A shallow cave used as a dwelling or for shelter is called a **gibber-gunyah** (also *rock shelter*). [Dharuk, Sydney region *giba*, 'stone' + *gañi*.]

> **1836** *Tegg's Monthly Magazine* [Sydney], I, 136. I found the shepherd … safely ensconced from the scorching heat of the sun under the shade of a commodious *gibba gunya*.

Gunyah has also been used in other contexts:

> **1827** *Australian* [Sydney], 27 March, 2. At my friend L … 's *gunha*, the native name for house, our breakfast table was never without beefsteaks, roast wild duck, fried bream and potatoes, besides the more usual accompaniments of pancakes, eggs, cream, and bread superior to any out of Sydney.

humpy /'hʌmpi/

[Yagara, Brisbane region *ŋumbi*.]

A Queensland name for a gunyah. In recent use, **humpy** has been applied to 'any makeshift or temporary dwelling, especially one made with primitive materials'. Being unaccustomed to words that begin with /ŋ/, the English speakers who first borrowed the word changed it to *umpy* or *humpy*. [1838]

> **1853** *Moreton Bay Free Press*, 13 December, 4. These *humpeys* or *gunyahs*, as they are called, are constructed by placing a few young boughs or saplings tightly in the ground, in a semi-circular form, the upper parts are then woven or fastened together, and the framework of the structure is then completed.

mia-mia /'maɪə-maɪə/, /'miə-mie/, /'mai-mai/

Formerly also with much variety, as **mai-mai**, **miam**, **miam-miam**, **mi-mi**, **myam-myam**, **mya**, and **mya-mya**.

[Although this word was much used in Victoria (the earliest Victorian instance is 1838), it appears to have originated as *maya* or *maya-maya* in Nyungar, the language of the Perth–Albany region.]

A gunyah. In New Zealand, where it is pronounced /'mai-mai/, it is used for a duckshooter's hide. [1833]

> **1833** R. M. LYON, A *Glance at the Manners, and Language of the Aboriginal Inhabitants of Western Australia*. (*Perth Gazette*, 13 April 1833). *Mya*, a house … The term is applied indiscriminately to a small piece of bark of the Melaleuca made to hold small fishes, and frogs; or to a shelter made from small sticks, rudely stuck into the ground, and covered, with large pieces of the same material.

> **1838** *Historical Records of Victoria* (1983), III, 544. I went through the native mia-mias and managed to answer a question in the native language.

> **1842** G. F. MOORE, *Descriptive Vocabulary of the Language … of Western Australia*, 58. *My-a* … A house; the bark of the tea-tree; or paper-bark tree with which the natives cover their huts, which are in shape like a section of a bee-hive, about three feet high. They are formed of a framework of sticks stuck in the ground, and thatched with paper bark or grass-tree leaves, or small brushwood, or bark, or whatever is most easily found on the spot.

Like *gunyah* and *humpy*, **mia-mia** has also been applied to any temporary shelter erected by a traveller.

> **1861** *The Burke and Wills Exploring Expedition*, 29. This evening I camped very comfortably in a mia-mia.

wiltja /'wɪltʃə/
Also **wilja**.
[Western Desert language *wilja*, 'a shelter, shade, or shadow'.]
A shelter. [1950]

> **1950** V. E. TURNER, *Ooldea*, 136. There are three kinds of native homes—houses (karrpa), shelters (wilja) and breakwinds (yaw).

> **2000** *Sunday Mail* [Adelaide], 12 November, 51. When groups of children start trying to build wiltjas from branches, many automatically moved to four corners as they mimicked their familiarity with rooms with four walls. Gradually some figured out a triangular shape might be better, so the core branches support each other as more are added.

wurley /'wɜli/
Plural **wurlies**. Also **whirley**, **whirlie**, and **wurlie**, and formerly with much variety. Chiefly used in South Australia.
[Gaurna, Adelaide region (and other South Australian languages) *warli*, 'camp or hut'.]
A gunyah. [1839]

1854 W. SHAW, *The Land of Promise, or, My Impressions of Australia*, 209. They live in what are termed 'whirleys', which are fragile erections made of rushes or bark, disposed in a conical shape, and about the size of an oven.

yu /yu/
Also **yaw**.
[Western Desert language *yuu*, 'wind-break'.]
A shelter, specifically a wind-break. [1950]

1979 M. HEPPELL, *A Black Reality*, 144. The two traditional shelters of an Aboriginal camp are the yu (wind-break) and the wiltja (literally, shade). As their names imply, one is protection from the wind, the other is protection from the heat of the sun.

VERBS

Loans which are Verbs, Adjectives and Adverbs come predominantly from Dharuk, the Sydney language, plus a few from other languages spoken at or near other capital cities. Although used a good deal in the early days, many are now obsolete. However, a number— particularly *go bung* and *bogey*—have achieved wide currency.

bogey /'boʊgi/
Also **bogie**.
[Dharuk, Sydney region, intransitive verb root *bugi-*, 'to bathe or dive'.]
Used as a noun to mean 'a swim' or 'a bathe', and as an intransitive verb meaning 'to swim' or 'to bathe'. [1789]

1789 *Historical Records of New South Wales* (1893), II, 700. I have bathed, or have been bathing … Bogie d'oway. These were Colby's words on coming out of the water.

1996 M. MAHOOD, *Bunch of Strays*, 196. 'It'll do for yer bathroom fer the time bein', he said. 'Yer can stick the hose in at the side and syphon the water when yer want a bogey'.

1999 L. WALLACE, *Dad and Joey in Possum Gully*, 56. Mum followed Mavis and Bobby to the river for a bogey, but I reckoned the water'd be too hot anyway.

A **bogey-hole** is a 'swimming or bathing hole'.

1949 B. O'REILLY, *Green Mountains and Cullenbenbong*, 274. The 'bogie hole' was … a large basin three feet deep sculptured from the living granite.

boomalli /bu'mæli/
[Probably from an Australian language as the verb root *bu-m-*, 'to hit', is common throughout the languages of the continent. In Kamilaroi, *buma-* is the verb 'to hit, kill', and *bumali* is its future form.]

To beat (an animal). [1876]

> **1945** T. RONAN, *Strangers on the Ophir*, 99. A thousand head of bullocks, hungry and mostly thirsty, boomallied and knocked about as these had been, are hard to hold.

crammer /ˈkræmə/
Also **cramma**. Used in Australian pidgin and now probably obsolete.
[Dharuk, Sydney region, verb root *garrama*, 'to steal'.]
To steal (something). [1790]

> **1849** J. P. TOWNSEND, *Rambles and Observations in NSW*, 102. If he had been a good fellow, and had not 'crammered (stolen) corn'.

nangry /ˈnæŋgri/
Used in Australian pidgin, but now obsolete.
[Dharuk, Sydney region, verb *nan-ga (-ra)*, 'to sleep'.]
To sleep; to rest; to reside. Also used as a noun meaning 'a sleep'. [1790]

> **1830** R. DAWSON, *Present State of Australia*, 73. It was much too far without *nangry* (sleep, rest, or night).

patter /ˈpætə/
Also **patta**. Used in Australian pidgin, but now obsolete.
[Dharuk, Sydney region, verb root *bada-*, 'to eat'.]
To eat. Also as a noun meaning 'food'. [1790]

> **1851** J. HENDERSON, *Excursions and Adventures in New South Wales*, II, 114. When a gin has had intercourse with a European, and produces a half-caste child, they say, 'That been *patter* (eaten) white bread'.

> **1884** A. W. STIRLING, *Never Never Land*, 174. White men never eat these birds; the blacks, however, are not so particular, and even where food is plentiful say kites make good 'patter'.

pialla /paɪˈælə/
Also with much variety, as **pai-alla**, **pialler**, **pile**, **piola**, and **pyalla**.
Used in Australian pidgin, but now obsolete.
[Dharuk, Sydney region, verb *bayala*, 'to speak, talk'.]
To tell (news, etc.). Also, to talk. [1790]

> **1846** *Cumberland Times* [Parramatta], 25 April, 4. Hearing some alarm was felt in Sydney respecting them, they at once dispatched one of the tribe to Sydney, as a special Courier, to *pialler* news as to their whereabouts.

quamby /'kwɒmbi/

Also **quambi**, **quambie**, and **quomby**.

[Probably Wuywurung, Melbourne region, *guwambi*, 'a sleeping place'.]

To lie down, to camp. [1839]

The word **quamby** has also been used as an imperative, meaning 'stop!', and as a noun, meaning 'a camp, a temporary shelter'.

> **1843** J. COTTON, *Correspondence of J. Cotton, Victorian Pioneer*, Part 1, 22. In these woods it is customary for the blacks to visit the neighbourhood to quamby.

wongi /'wɒŋgi/

[The form *waŋga* (or some variant of this) is found in most languages of Western Australia and some from Central Australia, as a verb 'to speak, talk' (and sometimes also a noun 'language'). This borrowing may have originally come from Nyungar, Perth–Albany region.]

To talk, or to tell. *Wongi* is also used as a noun, 'a talk'. Note that *wongi*, with a different pronunciation, is also a regional term for 'an Aborigine' (p. 173). [1835]

> **1835** G. F. MOORE, *Diary of Ten Years Eventful Life of an Early Settler in Western Australia*, 5 July (1884), 271. Weeip ... asked me to 'paper wonga' the Governor about it.

> **1976** C. D. MILLS, *Hobble Chains and Green Hide*, 35. We used to 'wongi' in the dialect, and I owe most of my knowledge of it to his teaching. *Ibid.*, 103. This was the first chance I had to get close to the camp, and we 'wongied' with our toes in the ashes until late that night.

yabber /'yæbə/

Also **yabba** and **yabber-yabber**. Originally used in Australian pidgin.

[This may well be based on a form of the verb 'to talk' in an Australian language; a root commencing in *ya-* is found in Wiradhuri, from south-west New South Wales, and Waga-waga and Gabi-gabi from south-east Queensland, for example. The Australian word *yabber* was probably also reinforced by similarity to English *jabber*.]

To talk; to chat. [1841]

> **1969** *Kings Cross Whisper* [Sydney], LXIX, 1. Few Australians can speak English. Most have learnt from disc jockeys and yabber in an odd language called Strine.

The word **yabber** has been used in several other ways.

1. As a noun meaning 'talk, conversation, discussion, language'.

> **1987** G. FRANCIS, *God's Best Country*, 9. I agreed to let that mob camp in their old spot by the lagoon while the big yabber's on.

2. In the combination **yabber stick**, to mean *message stick*.

> **1942** L. & K. HARRIS, *Lost Hole of Bingoola*, 16. The notched stick, the yabber stick, was a letter and would give more news than the smoke signal he had wondered about.

3. As a verb meaning 'to say, to ask', and so as the verbal noun **yabbering**, 'talking, conversing'.

> **1873** C. H. EDEN, *The Fortunes of the Fletchers*, 168. 'That fellow yabber plenty questions?' asked George.

> **2001** B. MATTHEWS, *As the Story Goes*, 25. The mobile is profligate: talk on, it seems to say, articulate, verbalise. Yet there are some yabberings it won't tolerate.

yan /yæn/

Once used in Australian pidgin, but now obsolete.

[The verb root *ya-n-*, 'to go', occurs in many Australian languages, including Dharuk from Sydney.]

To go, to move. [1839]

> **1848** H. W. HAYGARTH, *Recollections of Bush Life*, 108. The phrase used by our tribe to signify a handsaw was taken from its motion when in action; they could never be persuaded to call it anything but a 'yan' (go) 'and come back again'.

ADJECTIVES AND ADVERBS

budgeree /'bʌdʒəri/, /'bʊdʒəri/

Also with much variety, as **boodgery**, **boojeri**, **boojery**, and **budgeri**. Australian pidgin.

[Dharuk, Sydney region, adjective *bujiri*, 'good, right'.]

Good, pretty, fine. [1790]

> **1790** D. SOUTHWELL, *Correspondence and Papers, 1788–90*. Boógĕrēē (boo-jĕ-ee), good handsome, comely, pretty.

> **1793** W. TENCH, *A Complete Account of the Settlement at Port Jackson*, 116. We were Englishmen, and Bud-yĕe-ree (good).

bung /bʌŋ/

Formerly also **boang**, **boung**, and **bong**. Originally Australian pidgin.

[Probably Yagara, Brisbane region *baŋ*, 'dead'.]

Originally **bung** meant 'dead', and the phrase **to go bung** meant 'to die'. The word is now used to mean either 'bankrupt, in financial ruin' or 'incapacitated, out of order, exhausted, broken'. The phrase **to go bung** now means 'to fail, to collapse'. [1841]

1885 *Australasian Printers' Keepsake*, 40. He was importuned to desist, as his musical talent had 'gone bung' probably from over-indulgence in confectionery.

1893 *Braidwood Dispatch*, 26 April, 2. A man was fined £3 at the Sydney Water Police Court on Monday for having injured a notice posted at the Savings Bank of New South Wales. He wrote the words 'Gone Bung' on the notice, and advised the crowd to look after their money.

cabon /ˈkɒbɒn/

Also **cawborn** and **cobborn**. Used as adjective and adverb in Australian pidgin, but now obsolete.
[Dharuk, Sydney region, probably *gabawan* or *gabawun* 'big']
As an adjective, **cabon** meant 'big' or 'great', as an adverb, 'extremely'. [1801]

1849 s. & J. SIDNEY, *Emigrant's Journal*, 311. He required a rig out, as a necessary preliminary that he might appear 'a cabon swell'.

cooler /ˈkulə/

Also **coola**, **coolar**, and **coolie**. Used as adjective, adverb, and noun in Australian pidgin, but now obsolete.
[Dharuk, Sydney region, adjective *gularra*, 'angry'.]
Angry; anger. [1790]

1845 J. O. BALFOUR, *A Sketch of New South Wales*, 18. I ... was told that they did not like my interference and that they would become 'coolie'; in other words, that there would be enmity between them and me.

jerran /ˈdʒɛrən/

Also **gerrund**, **gerun**, **jeerun**, **jerron**, **jerrund**, and **jirrand**.
Chiefly used in Australian pidgin, but now obsolete.
[Dharuk, Sydney region *jirran*, which might have been a noun, 'coward', or an adjective, 'afraid'.]
Afraid. Also used as a noun to refer to 'a coward'. [1790]

1867 A. K. COLLINS, *Waddy Mundoee*, 12. I'm a bit jerrund to stay out at Crowther's with nobody but my mate.

merryjig /ˈmɛridʒɪg/

Also **merejig**, **merrijig**, **merrygig**, and **merrjik**. Used in Australian pidgin, but now obsolete.
[Wathawurung, Geelong region, Victoria *mirrijig*, an exclamation meaning 'well done!']
Very good. *Merrijig* is the name of a small town in the Victorian Alps. [1838]

1839 *Historical Records of Victoria*, (1982) 2A, 119. They … clapped me on the back and exclaimed 'merryjik' (which is a barbarism introduced among them meaning very good).

mindic /ˈmɪndɪk/
Also **mendyk**.
Australian pidgin.
[Nyungar, Perth–Albany region, probably *mindij* or *mindik*.]
Ill; sick. [1839]

1929 W. J. RESIDE, *Golden Days, being Memoirs and Reminiscences of the Goldfields of Western Australia*, 164. She replied, 'Black fella welly mindic,' which meant that one of the tribe was sick. … Whether the chlorodine cured the 'mindic' native I never learned.

murry /ˈmʌri/
Originally used in Australian pidgin, but now obsolete.
[Dharuk, Sydney region *mari* or *maray*, which appears to have functioned as an adjective, 'great', an adverb, 'very', and a number, 'many'.]
Chiefly an adverb, meaning 'very', but also an adjective, meaning 'great'. [1793]

1793 W. TENCH, *A Complete Account of the Settlement at Port Jackson*, 65. They called him *Mùr-ree Mùr-la* (a large strong man).

1803 J. GRANT, *The Narrative of a Voyage of Discovery*, 90. You know me *murrey jarrin*, that is *much afraid*.

narang /nəˈræŋ/
Also **narangy** and **nerangy**. Chiefly used in Australian pidgin, but now obsolete.
[Dharuk, Sydney region, adjective *ŋarraŋ*, 'small, little, few'.]
Little. [1790]

1870 *Illustrated Sydney News*, 24 December, 2. The latter were occasionally met on the runs by shepherds, who gave them a 'narang' bit of tobacco, and they passed away without molesting anyone.

OTHER

baal /baːl/, /baɪl/
Also **bael**, **bail**, **bale**, and **bel**. Used in Australian pidgin, but now obsolete.
[Dharuk, Sydney region *biyal*, 'not, no'.]
Used to express negation, 'no' or 'not'. The word was also used as an adjective. [1790]

1828 *Sydney Gazette*, 2 January. Casting his eyes wistfully around him, and giving a melancholy glance at the apparatus of death, he said, in a tone of deep feeling, which it was impossible to hear without strong emotion, 'Bail more walk about', meaning that his wanderings were over now.

1848 *Atlas* [Sydney], IV, 121. Nay the aboriginal jabber is pressed into the service, as if the forty or fifty thousand words of the standard dictionaries of our language were inadequate to express or dissemble all our ideas '… payala, patter, bel', etc. are all reckoned elegances of a particular kind among certain classes of society.

borak /ˈbɔræk/
Also **borack** and **borax**.
[Wathawurung, Geelong region, Victoria *burag*, 'no, not'.]
Originally an adverb in Australian pidgin, used, like *baal*, to express negation, but now obsolete. The word is now used as a noun, meaning 'nonsense' or 'rubbish'. [1839]

The phrase, **to poke borak** (at a person), means 'to make fun of'.

1876 J. A. EDWARDS, *Gilbert Gogger*, 185. 'O! Hume, that is all borack … ' Borack: humbug. Thus it is a common saying amongst bushmen, when any person is attempting to make them believe something improbable. 'O! Don't poke borack at me!'

cooee /ˈkui/, /kuˈi/
[Dharuk, Sydney region *guuu-wi*, 'come here'.]
Originally a prolonged, shrill, clear call, used by an Aborigine to communicate with someone at a distance; later adopted by settlers, and now widely used as a signal, especially in the bush. [1790]

1793 J. HUNTER, *An Historical Journal of the Transactions at Port Jackson and Norfolk Island*, 149. We called to them in their own manner, by frequently repeating the word *Co-wee*, which signifies, come here.

1827 P. CUNNINGHAM, *Two Years in New South Wales*, II, 23. In calling to each other at a distance, the natives make use of the words *coo-ee*, as we do the word *Hollo* prolonging the sound of the *coo*, and closing that of the *ee* with a shrill jerk … [It has] become of general use throughout the colony.

1845 C. GRIFFITH, *The Present State and Prospects of the Port Phillip District of New South Wales*, 65. The cooey is a call in universal use amongst the settlers and has been borrowed from the natives. The performer dwells for about half a minute upon one note, and then raises his voice to the octave. It can be heard at a great distance.

1891 A. CONAN DOYLE, 'The Boscombe Valley Mystery' (in *The Adventures of Sherlock Holmes*) But 'Cooee' is a distinctively Australian cry, and one which is used between Australians. There is a strong presumption that the person whom McCarthy expected to meet at Boscombe Pool was someone who had been in Australia.

The word **cooee** is used in several other ways.

1. As a verb, meaning 'to utter a cooee'.

> **1988** *Age* [Melbourne], 5 September, 1. They applauded and cooeed until Dame Kiri had given three encores.

2. In the phrase, **within cooe** 'within earshot, within reach, anywhere near'.

> **1988** *Age* [Melbourne], 27 June, 1. And you're not going to come within cooee of John and Sally Byram for wealth, ostentatiousness or sheer over-the-top bad taste.

3. Figuratively:

> **1894** W. CROMPTON, *Convict Jim*, 28.

> An' the river is a banker, an' its current's running strong,
> An' I don't think I'll be waiting for Death's cooee very long.

4. In the combination, **cooee bird**, as a name for the large cuckoo *Eudynamys orientalis*, the Indian koel, a summer visitor from south-east Asia to northern and eastern Australia. The *cooee bird* produces a call that is very similar to the human *cooee*.

goom /gum/, /gʊm/

[Possibly a transferred use of *guŋ*, 'water, alcohol' from Gabi-gabi, Waga-waga, and Gureng-gureng, south-east Queensland.]
Methylated spirits (as drunk by a derelict); an immoral woman. A **goomy** (or **goomee**) is one addicted to drinking methylated spirits. [1967]

> **1994** *Songs of Dougie Young*, n.p. You'll find me beneath the old gum tree drinkin' goom and lemonade.

> **1999** M. LUCASHENKO, *Hard Yards*, 78. What'd he expect anyway, doing crime all the time, sleeping in parks, drinking with the goomies?

Moomba /'mumbə/

A carnival held annually in Melbourne from 1955.

> **1969** L. A. HERCUS, *The Languages of Victoria*, II, 371. *Mum*, bottom, rump. The jocular Healesville expression *mum ba*, 'bottom and …', has been given to the authorities in jest with the translation, 'let us get together and have fun', hence the Melbourne Moomba Festival. [Note: languages with *mum* for 'bottom, anus' include Wuywurung and Wemba-wemba.]

pink-eye /'pɪŋkaɪ/, /'pɪŋki/

Also **pink-hi** and **pinki**. Chiefly used in Western Australian pidgin.

[Possibly from Yindjibarndi, Hamersley Range, Western Australia *biŋgayi* 'holiday' which, according to F. Wordick, *The Yindjibarndi Language* (1982) 337, may ultimately relate to the verb *biŋga*, 'to hunt', in the neighbouring language Ngarluma. An alternative origin may be *binigayi*, 'go', from the avoidance language style of Panyjima, Tom Price region, Western Australia. This avoidance style is connected with male initiation, which would in recent times be held during the pastoral off-season or 'holiday'/'walkabout' period.]
A *walkabout* (see p. 236). [1899]

> **2002** D. PILKINGTON, *Under the Wintamarra Tree*, 10. Tjirama was encouraged to remain on the station until 'pink-eye' time. This was when all of the station workers had time off to attend their clan's traditional ceremonies.

pink-eye also means 'to go on a walkabout; to holiday'. A **pink-eyer** is a holiday-maker.

> **1919** *Smith's Weekly* [Sydney], 10 May, 11. Pearlers crowd away for a holiday … in the off-season, when the boats cannot operate. One such party happened to 'pink-eye' on a small island off the N.W. coast … The island soon disappeared, all but a rock or two, from which derisive crabs watched the shivering 'pink-eyers' steer for the mainland.

toa /ˈtoʊə/
[Diyari, Lake Eyre region, South Australia, probably *dhuwa*.]
An Aboriginal direction marker. For a full account, see P. Jones and P. Sutton, *Art and Land* (South Australian Museum and Wakefield Press, 1986). [1918]

> **1981** J. MULVANEY et al., *Aboriginal Australia*, 11. Very interesting examples of native constructions … are the little-known Aboriginal directional markers from the Lake Eyre region known as 'toas'. Made of an amalgam of gypsum, wood and feathers, they were stuck in the ground on departure from a camp to communicate the destination of a departing group to anyone able to read them.

towri /ˈtaʊri/
Also **taori**, **taurai**, **tauri**, **touri**, and **tyri**.
[Kamilaroi, east New South Wales *dhawuray*.]
'Country'; the traditional territory of an Aboriginal people. [1872]

> **1892** J. FRASER, *The Aborigines of New South Wales*, 36. It is well known that each tribe has its own 'tauri'—territory or hunting-ground—usually determined by natural boundaries, such as mountain ridges and rivers.

yackai /ˈyækaɪ/, /yæˈkaɪ/
Also with much variety.
[Wiradhuri, south-west New South Wales (and very many other languages) *yagaay*.]

A call used by an Aborigine to command attention or express emotion, such as pain or surprise. **Yackai** is also used as a verb to mean 'to utter such a call'. [1887]

> **1977** V. PRIDDLE, *Larry and Jack*, 70. In no time his brother Jack and three other searchers appeared and gave a 'Yakki' of delight when they saw Larry had the little girl.

> **1992** A. C. PAINE, *Bralgie*, 33. The other boys yelled and yackaied at him to come back.

yakka /ˈyækə/
Also **yacca**, **yacka**, **yacker**, and **yakker**.
[Yagara, Brisbane region *yaga*.]
Work; strenuous labour; especially in the phrase **hard yakka**; also as a verb, 'to work, to labour'. [1847]

> **1847** J. D. LANG, *Cooksland in North-eastern Australia*, 447. The word *yacca*, in the Moreton Bay dialect of the aboriginal language, is one of those unfortunate words that has more than double duty to perform. It signifies everything in the shape of service or performance, from the first incipient attempts at motion to the most violent exertion; and it usually takes its significance from the noun to which it is appended, as in the instance I have given above, *mooyoom-yacca*, to read, to write, or to cast accounts [relating to *mooyoom*, 'a book'].

> **1888** *The Boomerang* [Brisbane], 14 January, 13. The Brisbane wharf labourers are so accustomed to hard yakker that they can't be happy for a single day without it.

yohi /ˈyoʊʊwaɪ/, /yoʊˈwaɪ/
Also **youi**. Australian pidgin.
[Yagara, Brisbane region (and many similar forms in other languages) *yaway*.]
An affirmative reply, 'yes'. [1859]

> **1881** A. C. GRANT, *Bush-Life in Queensland, or John West's Colonial Experiences*, I, 236. 'You patter (eat) potchum?' 'Yohi' (yes) said John, rather doubtfully, for he is not sure how his stomach will agree with the strange meat.

4

The words in English

In the last chapter, we looked in some detail at each word that has been borrowed from an Australian language into English. In the present chapter, we will make some general observations about the process of borrowing, and draw some general conclusions about the history of the loan words once they became a part of the English language.

New objects or concepts can be given names in a number of ways. As early as 1798, the settlers at Sydney had sighted a sloth-like creature, which was known to the local Aborigines as *gulawañ* or, in a short form, *gula*. The first attempt to record the name in English spelling was *cullawine*. Over the next few years, it was written as *coola* or *koolah*; this was a fairly accurate representation of the Aboriginal word *gula* (which can be pronounced as *gula* or *kula*). Then another spelling arose, *koala*, which was probably a scribal error for *koola* (in the days before typewriters, everything was handwritten, and mistakes of this sort were fairly common). For much of the nineteenth century, the names *koola* and *koala* were both used until eventually *koala* became established and *koola* dropped out of use.

That ought to have been the end of the matter, but now another naming process came into operation. Some thought that the koala looked like a bear, a monkey, or a sloth, so the meanings of these words were extended and the koala was called *bear* (until as late as 1911), or *monkey* (at least until 1872), or *sloth* (until 1886). It was clear, though, that the koala was not really a kind of bear, or monkey, or sloth, so pairs of words were put together in a combined name to show both the similarities and the differences. This animal was also known as *native sloth* (until 1906), as *native bear* (as late as 1989), or as *monkey bear* (as late as 1980). During the twentieth century, a new factor came in. The advent of the koala as one of a number of creatures that peopled the bush in children's stories by May Gibbs and others, and as a cuddly toy, gave rise in 1917 to the name *koala bear*, which, while most commonly applied to the toy, is also used of the long-suffering animal.

Koala is one, admittedly spectacular, example of the unpredictability with which the naming process works. Elsewhere in this book, we suggest that an

Aboriginal word was preferred if the object being named was unfamiliar. But this was not always the case. Though in 1834 a traveller near Yass recorded *gogera* or *gogobera* as the local Aboriginal name for what is now the *kookaburra*, it was not until 1867 that *kookaburra* was used in English. Before that, and indeed for some years after, names were used which described characteristics of the bird's behaviour as these were perceived by settlers and travellers—names like *laughing jackass* (or just *jackass*) and *settler's clock* or *bushman's clock*.

The bird now commonly known as the *brolga* had been called by the picturesque name *native companion* for eighty-odd years before the Aboriginal word entered English. One small green and yellow parrot species was first called *love-bird* and only later *budgerigar*; despite the popularity of the Aboriginal name (with the familiar abbreviation *budgie*), it still endures competition from *shell parrot, warbling grass-parakeet, zebra parrot, canary parrot*, and *love-bird*. Conflicting naming principles are still in operation, as is evident from the 'bush tucker' pair *alunqua* and *bush cucumber*, the Arrernte (Aranda) word being first recorded in English in 1935, and the descriptive compound in 1937.

These examples show English responding to a new need, either by linking together existing words to make new compounds or by borrowing from another language. English has at all stages of its history been a borrower. During the centuries when it was spoken only in Britain, there were many loans from Norman-French and Latin, and later from Greek and Italian. In the period of colonial expansion, when English was transplanted into the far corners of the globe, it borrowed from many indigenous languages and from other immigrant European languages. In North America, for instance, English acquired words not only from American Indian and Inuit (Eskimo) languages but also from Dutch, French, German, Spanish, and Yiddish. In Australia and New Zealand, the situation was simpler: English was effectively the only immigrant language, and the only sources from which it could borrow were the indigenous languages.

In Chapter 3, we listed almost 440 words of Aboriginal origin which are (or have been) used in Australian English. This is not a large number, given that there are some 10,000 Australianisms recorded in the *Australian National Dictionary*. The number of borrowings clearly says something about the nature of contact between colonists and Aborigines, as does the breakdown of the words into areas of meaning. But it would be wrong to think that the Aboriginal contribution to Australian English, because relatively small, was insignificant. In fact, it provides the most distinctively Australian words of all—many of them refer to emblematic features of the country (*koala* and *kookaburra*), to features which can not adequately be described by any other name (*the mallee* and *the mulga*), and to other things of a uniquely Australian character, as various as the *dingo* and the *galah*, the *boomerang* and the *humpy*, the *billabong* and the *swagman on the wallaby*. Though comparatively few of these words would be recognised outside

Australia—and none compares in the extent of its world-wide adoption with the American Indian *potato* or *tomato*—a good number of them are part of the active vocabulary of all Australians, and are rich in their connotations for Australians.

The great majority of loan words from Australian languages are nouns. They are the names of animals and plants, of weapons and domestic implements, of features of the environment, and of aspects of Aboriginal culture and ceremony. They are the sorts of words which could be borrowed by explorers or travellers seeking to give a name to a species of flora or fauna not previously encountered, or to label some item which attracted an anthropological curiosity. More than half of the loans are names for species of flora and fauna, the next largest category being those words which have an application mainly in the description of Aboriginal life—the names of weapons and tools, for instance, and names for items of religious significance or ceremonial importance. Only the relatively small number of words from the early Australian pidgin which found a (usually short) life in the English of the colonists—words like *baal*, 'no, not', verbs *bogey*, 'bathe', and *patter*, 'eat', adjectives *budgeree*, 'good', and *cabon*, 'big'—are what one might expect from two races living together and sharing their daily lives. Borrowing was therefore fairly restricted, being mainly a response to the linguistic needs of the white settlers, and did not relate to any widespread cultural exchange or integration.

Most of the nouns are inert, in the sense that they were borrowed as the local names for particular animals, birds, or plants, not bringing with them the transferred or figurative meanings that they would have had in the source language. And they were accepted into English in varying degrees. Thus, some names for trees and other plants, like *bangalow*, *belah*, *bindi-eye*, *boobialla*, *brigalow*, *bunya*, and *burrawang*, are the accepted names for which there are no alternatives. But many other words follow the example of *koala*, and acknowledge synonyms, often descriptive compounds—like *bush cucumber* for *alunqua*, *bastard mahogany* for *bangalay*, *native mahogany* for *jarrah*, *ordnance tree* for *kurrajong*. In the case of animals and birds, there is no alternative for *kangaroo* and *wombat*, but *banded anteater* can be used in place of *numbat*, *bell magpie* for *currawong*, *little lorikeet* for *jerryang*, and *cockatiel* for *quarrion*.

Some animals and plants are only found in a limited area, and names for them, borrowed from Australian languages, are naturally only used in that region; this applied to *noolbenger* for the honey possum *Tarsipes rostratus*, from the south-west corner of the continent. There are other animals and plants with wide distribution for which an Aboriginal name is used in the English spoken in just one state—the sand goanna, *Varanus gouldii*, is known as *bungarra* only in Western Australia, and the golden perch, *Macquaria ambigua*, is called *callop* only in South Australia. Sometimes there are different names, each borrowed from an Australian language, in different regions—the mallee fowl, *Leipoa ocellata*, may be referred to as *lowan* in Victoria and as *gnow* in Western Australia, and the name *kylie* is used in Western Australia for what is called everywhere else (in Australia and overseas) the *boomerang*, an original loan from the Sydney language.

There are also examples for what were originally regional alternatives now being used as general synonyms, as with *adjigo* and *warran* for a native yam, *cooba* and *wirra* for an acacia, *parakeelia*, *junga*, and sometimes *munyeroo*, for a herb with succulent leaves, and *pituri* and *mingil* for what is also called *native tobacco*. As synonyms for the kind of shelter used by Aborigines, *gunyah*, a Sydney word, was joined by *gundy* from languages of inland New South Wales, *humpy* from the Brisbane language, *mia mia* from the Perth language, and *wurley* from the language spoken around Adelaide.

Many Aborigines dislike the use of 'Aborigine' or 'Aboriginal', preferring to use the word for 'person' from a local language. Hence *koori*, originally from languages on the north coast of New South Wales, is now used as an alternative to 'Aborigine' over much of that state, and also often in Victoria. Now non-Aboriginal newspapers and radio stations in Victoria have largely switched to using *koori*. Other terms are preferred in other regions—*murri* over most of south and central Queensland, *bama* in North Queensland, *nunga* in the southern portion of South Australia, *nyoongah* around Perth, and other terms in other areas (see pages 162–74).

Borrowing has inevitably been haphazard, taking place in the various colonies or states independently; it is possible that in the nineteenth century it was discouraged, perhaps partly by some awareness that there are many original Australian languages rather than a single tongue understood by all. The situation is more favourable now. Sometimes words come into standard usage because of a preference expressed by the indigenous people themselves. Other adoptions indicate an awareness on the part of white Australians of the cultural identity of Aborigines. *Makarrata* (p. 156) is an example of a word chosen for political reasons: its use as the name for a proposed treaty between the Aboriginal people and white Australians was indicative of a new-found respect for the original inhabitants and for their traditions; it is itself a gesture of goodwill. *Mimi*, *Quinkan*, and *Wandjina* owe their currency to a rapidly increasing interest in Aboriginal art. A definite preference to employ indigenous names for animals and plants, both in scientific nomenclature and popular usage, is developing. Two recently recognised species of wallaby are known as *nabarlek* and *monjon*; marsupial carnivores of the genus Dasyurus were for a considerable period called *native cat*, but the name *quoll* (recorded by Captain Cook from the Guugu Yimidhirr language, but then virtually forgotten for a century and a half) has recently been adopted, and is gaining in popularity.

From the mid-1960s, there has been a dramatic increase in the volume of autobiographical, literary, and socio-political writing in English by Aborigines, providing an increased opportunity for words of Aboriginal origin, and also the specifically Aboriginal senses of words like *business*, *clever* and *country*, to enter the English of white Australians (see chapter 6).

Words once borrowed begin a new life, becoming part of the receiving language and behaving according to its conventions. So a number of commonly used loans were shortened, in typical Australian style, or shortened and then supplied with a familiar *-ie* ending—*barra* from *barramundi*, *budgie* from *budgerigar*, *cunji* from *cunjevoi* (the sea-squirt), *kanga* and *roo* from *kangaroo*, *kooka* and *kooky* from *kookaburra*, *mowie* from *morwong*. Of these, *kanga* has acquired at least three further senses—as rhyming slang for *screw*, and hence used either of money or of a prison warder; as a trade name for a jack-hammer, and (most recently) in *kanga cricket*, describing a kind of cricket played with rules and equipment especially designed for young people. *Roo* is used in *roo bar* (otherwise *bullbar*), which is fixed to the front of a vehicle to protect the radiator and engine from damage in the event of a collision with a kangaroo (or with cattle) on an unfenced outback road.

When a word is borrowed into a language, speakers may sometimes reinterpret it as if it were a compound involving words familiar to them. The Middle French word *crevisse* was borrowed into Old English as *crevise*, but this gradually became written as *cray-fish*, because this crustacean is a water-dweller like fish (but in fact the last syllable of the word as it was borrowed is not related in any way to the word *fish* in English, or to *poisson* in French). Similar 'Anglicisations' happened with a number of loans from Australian languages—the Kamilaroi and Yuwaalaraay name *bindayaa* for a plant with barbed fruit became *bindy-eye*. More dramatically, the Yagara name *budinba* (or *bunba*) for a marine fish was at first taken over as *puddenba* or *puddinba*, but then reinterpreted as if it were a compound of two common English words, *pudding-ball*. Other examples are *gangabarri*, a name for a small shrub, being rendered as *conker-berry*, and *wijagala*, a name for the Major Mitchell cockatoo, becoming *wee juggler*. The fish nowadays called *nannygai* is said to have been originally *mura ngin a gai* or *moorra nennigai*, and was sometimes called *mother nan a di*. Sometimes a word gets provided with a 'false etymology' at quite a late stage—the Wiradhuri name *guwarrayiŋ* for a crested parrot was at first taken over as *quarrion*, and only later changed, by some speakers, to *quarry-hen*; and the name *badimaliyan*, for a small wallaby, became English *pademelon*, later written by some people as *paddy-melon*.

Other words, which were borrowed as nouns, behave like other nouns in English by developing a wider grammatical use. The most common practice is for them to be used like adjectives, to modify the meaning of another noun—in combinations like *bimble box, dillon bush, dilly bag, gibber country, gnamma hole, kangaroo bar, koala bear, min-min light, mulga scrub, mulga wire, parma wallaby*, and *yandy dish*. The combination sometimes indicates a degree of specification—a *gibber stone* is a particular shape and style of well-worn stone found in inland regions, a *gilgai hole* is a hole or hollow in a particular type of terrain, and *mulga scrub* is scrub country characterised by the presence of a particular kind of plant.

But sometimes the combination simply reinforces the meaning of an unfamiliar word—so *dilly-bag* means the same thing as *dilly*, and *min-min light* as *min-min*. Just occasionally, two loan words for the same thing are joined together—*colane* was borrowed from *galayin* in Wiradhuri, and *gruie* from *guray* in Kamilaroi, both as the name for the *emu apple*, *Owenia acidula*; and then they were combined as *gruie-colane*, another name (now obsolete) for this plant.

More interestingly, a word borrowed as a noun can be used as a verb. *Cooee*, the name of a call, very quickly became a verb meaning 'to utter such a call', and *boomerang*, borrowed as the name of a weapon which comes back to the thrower, came to be used as a verb 'to return like a boomerang' (as in a sentence like 'That fellow's ideas about creating redundancies boomeranged on him, and he got the sack himself'). *Jackeroo* is today as commonly used as a verb describing the occupation of being a jackeroo as it is as a noun. *Kangaroo*, as a verb, can either be used of the activity of hunting kangaroos, or of a movement which resembles that of a kangaroo—leaping or moving in bounds (or, when used of a car, in jerks).

Changes in form and function are one indication that a new word is fulfilling a need in the language; shift of meaning is another significant indication. *Kangaroo* is the longest-established loan from an Australian language; when, on 14 July 1770, Joseph Banks recorded *kanguru* in his diary, he was transcribing the name in Guugu Yimidhirr for the large, dark-coloured male of the species *Macropus robustus* (page 57). The Australian language pronunciation /gaŋurru/ or /kaŋurru/ became /kæŋgə'ru/ in English. When members of the First Fleet arrived at Port Jackson (where a quite different language was spoken) in 1788, they used *kangaroo* to describe any kangaroo-like creature (and others besides), so that it quickly became a loosely-used general term. In popular use, there is now a rough distinction between kangaroos and wallabies as larger and smaller members of the family Macropodidae. The ubiquity and utility of the animal led to two kinds of word combinations—those which distinguished one kangaroo from another by its colour or habitat, such as *brush kangaroo*, *bush kangaroo*, *great grey kangaroo*, *red kangaroo*, *hill kangaroo*; and those which referred either to the hunting of the kangaroo or to one of the products of this, such as *kangaroo hunt*, *kangaroo hide*, *kangaroo flesh*, *kangaroo skin*, *kangaroo leather*, and *kangaroo stew*. A further group of combinations gave names to species of flora and fauna which are associated with or resemble the kangaroo—*kangaroo apple*, *kangaroo grass*, *kangaroo fish*, *kangaroo rat*, and *kangaroo tick*.

More significant changes were afoot. The fact that the kangaroo was, for people overseas, the best-known and most unusual characteristic of Australia led to identification between the animal and the nation. In 1883, a cricket Test Match was described as a battle between 'Lion' and 'Kangaroo'. In the Boer War, Australian soldiers were sometimes known as 'Kangaroos' (as New Zealanders were later to be identified as 'Kiwis'). And in 1933, sporting journalists used 'Kangaroos' for members of the Australian international Rugby League team.

A range of unconnected associations firmed, giving compounds as various as *kangaroo bone*, a bone used by Aborigines either as a tool or as an item of personal adornment; *kangaroo camp*, a place where kangaroos often congregate; *kangaroo closure*, a term which originated in Britain for a method used in parliamentary committees for passing over some items on the agenda; *kangaroo court*, which originated in the United States, for an improperly constituted court; *kangaroo feather*, a jocular name for the emu plume worn by a member of the Australian Light Horse in the 1914–18 war; *kangaroo jack*, a heavy-duty, lever-action type of jack; *kangaroo paw*, a distinctively Western Australian plant; *kangaroo route*, a name invented by Qantas Airways for the Sydney–Singapore–London air route; *kangaroo start*, a jerking start of a car or truck; and *Kangaroo Valley* for the district of Earl's Court, in London, where many Australians lodge or live. Captain Watkin Tench was amused when, in 1788, the Sydney Aborigines used *kangaroo* of sheep and cattle, thinking that they had been taught an English word meaning something like 'large animals'. Speakers of Guugu Yimidhirr might be forgiven for thinking that some of today's users of the word have 'kangaroos in the top paddock'!

Wallaby, a word from the Sydney language, followed a similar but less adventurous course. Widely applied to smaller marsupials of the family Macropodidae, its reference was made specific by the addition of a distinguishing adjective—*agile wallaby, black-gloved wallaby, nail-tailed wallaby, red-necked wallaby* and *whiptail wallaby*, for instance. A second set of combinations recorded the pursuit of the animal and the use made of its products—*wallaby drive, wallaby hunt, wallaby trap, wallaby stew* and *wallaby rug*. For some reason, the path made by a travelling marsupial (kangaroo or wallaby presumably) was named as early as 1846 a *wallaby track*, and for some years before the appearance of the *swagger* (1855) or the *swagman* (1869), itinerant men in search of work in the country were described as being *on the wallaby track*. By 1867, this had been shortened to *on the wallaby*, and in 1869 *wallaby* itself was used as a synonym for *swagman*. Much later (in 1908), and probably influenced by the use of *kangaroo* for 'Australian', the Australian international Rugby Union team opted to be known as 'the Wallabies'.

A number of other loan words from Australian languages demonstrated the fullness of their absorption into Australian English by developing transferred or metaphorical meanings. The handpiece of a shearing machine looked to some people like the 'sleeping lizard', *Tiliqua rugosa*, which was known as *boggi* (from Wiradhuri *bugay*); *boggi* was also used for this handpiece. *Bombora*, probably from the Sydney language, was used for a wave breaking dangerously over a submerged rock, and then extended to describe other examples of 'commotion followed by uneasy calm' (see page 190); in 1990, a newspaper account of a plump singer's gown referred to 'a bombora of white frills between chest and neck'. *Bondi*, from the Wiradhuri word for a heavy club, was used in the phrase *to give someone bondi*, meaning 'to attack savagely'.

Borak, which meant 'not' or 'no' in the Geelong language Wathawurung (and was borrowed into pidgin, like *baal*, 'no, not', from the Sydney language) took on a meaning 'nonsense', 'rubbish' or 'gammon' (a British criminal cant word for 'pretence' or 'humbug', which is still used today in Queensland and Northern Territory Aboriginal English), and now survives in the phrase *to poke borak at*, meaning 'to make fun of'. *Bung*, which probably came from the Brisbane language and meant 'dead', was also used first in pidgin and later in Australian English, especially in the phrase *to go bung*, 'to die'; this was then transferred to the world of finance and came to mean 'to fail, to collapse, to become bankrupt'. And Miles Franklin followed her emblematic autobiographical novel *My Brilliant Career* with a sequel, *My Career Goes Bung*. *Bunyip*, the name of a fabulous amphibious monster supposed to inhabit inland waters, was borrowed in the 1840s and used to cast doubt on the pedigree of the *bunyip aristocracy* (in much the same way and at about the same time *geebung* was used as a derogatory term for an Australian whose interests lay more in material gain than in cultural enlightenment).

Dingo and *warrigal* were both early borrowings from Dharuk, around Sydney. Though they had contrasting meanings in the Australian language, *dingo* referring to tame members of the species and *warrigal* to wild ones, the settlers treated them as synonyms for the animal they also referred to as *native dog, wild dog*, and *native dingo*. But each word acquired a character of its own in English. By 1835, John Batman was writing of 'the cunning peculiar to the Australian dingo', and in 1869, 'E. Howe' wrote punningly of a bushranger, that 'he [might] well call himself Warrigal, the sneaking dingo!' From then on, the word *dingo* has been applied to a person whose behaviour betrays characteristics popularly attributed to the animal—that is, sneakiness, treachery, and especially cowardice. From the 1940s, *dingo* has been used as a verb, meaning 'to behave in a cowardly manner'.

Warrigal took a different course. Its primary sense remained 'dingo', but the characteristic of the dingo which attached to *warrigal* was its wildness. So, in the 1840s, the word was applied to an Aborigine living in a traditional fashion, as distinct from one who had adapted in some manner to white ways—a distinction made also by the contrastive use of *civilised, domesticated*, and *tame* to categorise those Aborigines who had made adaptations in their way of life. By the 1860s, *warrigal* (or *warrigal cabbage*) was being used as a name for the wild plant *Tetragonia tetragonoides*, which is also known as *New Zealand spinach*, having been first encountered by James Cook and Joseph Banks (who described it as 'a Sort of Wild Spinage'). By the 1880s, *warrigal* was being used of a wild or untamed horse. Both *dingo* and *warrigal* were only used as nouns in Dharuk; we have mentioned that *dingo* came also to be used as a verb in English. *Warrigal* developed within the new language to be an adjective, used from the 1840s of Aborigines, and from the 1880s becoming general in its reference. Ironically, through its application by whites—who made the tame/wild distinction concerning the race from one of whose languages it had come—*warrigal* regained something of its original meaning.

Galah is happier in its connotations. It was first recorded in 1862 and, probably as early as the end of the century, was preferred to the more cumbersome (or, as some said, more 'learned') *red-breasted cockatoo* and *rose-breasted cockatoo*. This bird had become notorious for its eccentric habits, so it was not surprising that in the 1930s the word came to be applied to a person whose behaviour was thought foolish (as of course was the name of another bird, the *drongo*, which was originally a loan word into English from the Malagasy language). Later, in what may or may not have been a separate development, the period of time on an outback radio network reserved for private conversations between women on isolated stations became known as a *galah session*.

The words we have just been looking at are loans from Australian languages which have undergone a shift or extension of meaning in response to new circumstances. They have not remained inert—like many of the names for species of flora and fauna, which are in a sense tied to the species they name—but have become living and vital parts of the language.

The words *mallee* and *mulga* demonstrate this very clearly, in that they have not only taken on new specific meanings but also gathered all sorts of connotations. Both began as the names of groups of trees of a certain genus, but quickly came to be used to describe areas of country which have communities of a certain kind of tree as their characteristic form of vegetation, as in *mallee country*, *mallee desert*, *mallee district*, and *mulga country*, *mulga flats*, *mulga paddocks*. Both came, with the definite article *the*, to stand independently for the type of country—*the mallee* and *the mulga*. The Mallee (with a capital letter) has been adopted as the official name for the mallee district in north-west Victoria.

Both words then took on something of the connotations of life in their respective types of country. Take *mallee*: 'Nobody knows who made the mallee, but the Devil is strongly suspected'; 'the usual barren wilderness termed the Mallee'; 'that dirty rabble of tin-roofed shanties I was born in, way out in the Mallee'. These quotations, from the *Australian National Dictionary*, bring out aspects of life when the mallee country was being opened up, and they give rise to compounds like *mallee cocky* and *mallee town*. Once cleared and farmed, the mallee redeemed itself in a way that the mulga did not. The *mulga* was country destined to remain sparsely populated, and so was equated with the outback or—in a contrast between the sophisticated city and an underdeveloped rural life—the bush. So, *Mulga Bill* is the archetypal bushie, a *mulga black* was an Aborigine from the remote inland, one who was *mulga-bred*. *Mulga madness* is an eccentricity attributed to living too long in the outback, and *mulga wire* is another name for 'bush telegraph'.

Fit as a mallee bull is as colourful and vigorous an Australianism as is *mulga mafia* as a nickname for the Country Party (now the National Party). *Mallee* and *mulga*, like some of the other words we have looked at in this chapter, have come a long way from their original specific meanings as names for kinds of trees, and have become an essential part of the creative fabric of Australian English. As Maori words have given a distinctive character to New Zealand English, so words from the native languages of Australia have helped establish the Australianness of the Australian variety of English, and perform an essential role in it because, quite simply, they do things that no other words can do.

5

Borrowings into
Australian languages

When two languages come into contact, speakers of one will borrow words from the other. This book is mainly concerned with loans from Australian languages into English, but in this chapter we mention some loans in the other direction. This is a considerable topic, about which a large volume could be written; all we attempt here is an outline of some of the more important factors.

Australian languages borrow freely from each other, as do the languages of Europe, Africa, and so on. Some rare and valued commodity, such as *pituri* (page 124), could be traded from tribe to tribe across hundreds of miles, and its name might go with it. A new song or ceremony, or a new principle of social organisation, could diffuse over a wide area, and the relevant words would be borrowed also.

The happiest encounter Aborigines had with outsiders involved fishermen from Macassar, in the southern Celebes (north-west of Timor), who came to the waters off Arnhem Land to catch bêche-de-mer, a sea slug which is a valued delicacy in China. They visited Australia each year from at least the middle of the eighteenth century (possibly earlier) until, in 1906, they were told to keep away by a federal government implementing a white Australia policy.

The Macassans treated Aborigines with respect. Some local people worked on the boats, and a few even went to live for a while in Macassar. A trade language (or 'pidgin') developed that mixed together words from Macassarese and from Australian languages, and there were a considerable number of loans into languages along the Arnhem Land coast. Several hundred are listed in a paper 'Austronesian loanwords in Yolngu-matha of northeast Arnhem Land' by A. Walker & R. D. Zorc, in *Aboriginal History*, Vol. 5, pp. 109–34 (1981), including:

Yolngu	From Macassarese
barlaŋu 'anchor'	*baláŋo*
dhamburru 'drum'	*tamboro?*

dhuumala 'sail'	*sómbala*?
jinapaŋ 'rifle'	*sinápaŋ*
balanda 'white man'	*balánda* 'Hollander'

The Macassans had had contact with Europeans at least since the Dutch established themselves at Batavia (modern Jakarta) in 1619; hence their word *balanda*, which was a loan from the Dutch *Hollander*, with *b* replacing *h*. Note that Yolngu, like almost all other Australian languages, has no *s*, and an *s* in Macassarese became *dh* before *u* and *j* before *i*.

Then came the English, with a multitude of new things, activities, and ideas. As Aborigines encountered clothing, iron and glass, strange foodstuffs, money, buying and selling, organised work and employment, they needed a whole new set of words. Sometimes an established word was given a new shade of meaning; sometimes a new word was made by putting together words or endings already in the language (similar to what happened when English made *skyscraper*); and sometimes an English word was adopted, cast into a phonetic shape appropriate to an Australian language.

Aborigines were used to being multilingual, and to picking up new languages. It was they who learnt the invader's tongue, rather than the other way round. As mentioned on pages 22–3, there was a pidgin used in the early days between settlers and Aborigines, with a mixture of words from English and (mostly) the Sydney language. It was the white people who spread this, as they pushed sheep and cattle into new pastures. The pioneer missionary E. R. B. Gribble commented (*Forty Years with the Aborigines*, Angus and Robertson, 1930, p. 99):

> In the early days of our work pidgin English was used by us all, and a beastly gibberish it was. As time passed, I determined that it should cease, and good English be used; and, strange to say, the people seemed to find it easier to avoid than did the staff, who had got so accustomed to its use that they found it extremely difficult to avoid addressing in pidgin English every black they met.

Aborigines were perfectly capable of learning standard English, if given any opportunity, but many white people somehow feel unable to address them in anything but pidgin. With the early spread of the pidgin, some words, such as *yarraman* 'horse' (pages 80–1), were borrowed into Australian languages over a wide area of the continent.

Things sometimes spread faster than people. Pieces of iron and suchlike were traded from tribe to tribe, and Aborigines in inland regions encountered white people's goods some time before they came face to face with the invader. Words could precede the things they named. On 8 January 1832, the explorer Thomas Mitchell encountered some Aborigines near the Gwydir River in northern New South Wales. Mitchell's party were undoubtedly the first Europeans the

Aborigines had seen, but, Mitchell states (*Three Expeditions into the Interior of Eastern Australia*, 1839, Vol. 1, pp. 71–2):

> We heard calls in various directions, and '*witefellow*' pronounced very loudly and distinctly. 'Witefellow', or 'white ma', appears to be their name (of course derived from us) for our race, and this appellation probably accompanies the first intelligence of such strangers, to the most remote, interior regions.

During a later expedition, on 19 August 1846, Mitchell met a group of Aborigines near the Belyando River in central Queensland, and reported (*Journal of an Expedition*, 1848, p. 279): 'It was remarkable that on seeing the horses, they exclaimed "Yerraman," the colonial natives' name for a horse.' News of this new animal, and its name, had preceded the actual movement of horses into the interior.

As Aborigines adapted to the European culture that soon surrounded them, they borrowed many words from English for use in their own languages—before these gradually dropped out of use, to be replaced by English. There are, however, a dozen or so Australian languages that are still in a healthy state. In the far north and in central Australia, Aborigines and white people are working together in areas like health care, using an Australian language as the main means of communication. This creates the need for a number of new words—some made up from elements already existing within the relevant Australian language, and some borrowed from English—for things like stethoscope, syringe, oxygen cylinder, cotton wool, and tuberculosis. We discuss these and other words in the sections that follow.

EXTENDING THE MEANINGS OF WORDS

In no language in the world is it usual simply to invent new words out of the blue. When this does happen, it is a notable occurrence, as when the Flemish chemist J. B. van Helmont coined the word *gas* about 1640. (But even that was not totally original, being suggested by the Greek *cháos* 'atmosphere'.) When confronted by something new, people tend to borrow a word from another language, or else extend the meaning of an existing word.

The most serious misunderstanding Aborigines had about Europeans—and this was repeated in many parts of the continent—was to think that they were the spirits of their ancestors, come back to look after them. The reason for this was partly physical appearance—after a corpse has been left for a few days, the top layer of skin peels off, exposing a whiter layer below—and it was partly that the way in which white people arrived and acted seemed somehow supernatural, the kind of behaviour one would expect of spirits. In many languages, the words 'spirit of a dead man' and 'spirit of a dead woman' were extended to cover 'white man' and 'white woman'. In Nyungar, the language from Perth, *jan-ga*, 'spirit of a dead person', took on a new meaning, 'white person'. The word was borrowed into Western Australian English in two forms, each related to one of its senses in Nyungar—*jingy*, 'devil or spirit' (page 153), and *djanga*, 'white person' (page 165).

Many new things were described by familiar words because they looked like something familiar. 'Money' is often called by the word for 'stone', 'paper' by that for 'bark', and 'tea' by the word for 'leaf'. In Nyangumarda, from north of Port Hedland, *minda*, 'gum, resin', is used to describe 'sago' and 'tapioca', presumably as they were served in a milk pudding. In Yadhaykenu, from the Cape York Peninsula, *muña*, 'saliva', had its meaning extended to cover 'beer', describing the froth on top. When the Dyirbal people first saw a white man putting on a shirt, it reminded them of a bandicoot going into a hollow log, and the word *maralu*, 'hollow log', is also used for 'shirt'. In the hospital at Kintore, where the Pintupi dialect of the Western Desert language is used, the word for 'cotton wool' is *wamulu*, whose original meaning was 'eaglehawk down'.

In Warumungu, from around Tennant Creek, *liwanja*, 'fish', is also used for 'jet plane', because of the similarity of shape; *wiring-kirri*, 'yellow', is used for 'curry powder', because of its hue; *karnanganja*, 'emu', has been extended to cover 'motor bike' because they both travel fast; and *jirriminmin*, 'dragonfly', is also the name for 'helicopter', because of the way they both move their tail and hover. In several parts of the continent, 'eaglehawk' is used to describe an 'aeroplane' since it flies so high. The Walmatjari word *ngurti*, which is a general term for any sort of coolamon or carrying vessel (page 184) has been extended to cover 'car' and 'boat', introduced means of transportation.

George Watson, an authority on the Mamu dialect of Dyirbal, once named the parts of a car for R. M. W. Dixon, in many cases extending the meanings of human body part terms—headlights are *gayga* 'eyes'; the bumper is *guwu* 'nose'; the battery is *wiŋgiñ* 'spark'; the air cooler is *walŋgamu* 'lungs'; and the accelerator is *walŋga* 'breath, soul'. In Yidiny, from the Cairns area, *buŋgu* means 'that part of something which, by moving, propels it along the ground'. It refers principally to 'knee', but also to the 'hump' on a snake's body as it moves along the ground, and nowadays also to 'wheel'. (Dixon tells the story of talking to Yidiny-speaker Dick Moses, who broke off to exclaim, in English, 'Look at that car, it's got a flat knee!', the loan translation greatly amusing his friends who were present.)

In Warumungu, the action of a car tyre going flat is described by the verb *minjja-jinta*, originally used of a boil going down. The new activity of writing is described in different ways in different Australian languages. Pintupi uses the verb *wakani*, 'spear, pierce', and Diyari *daka*, 'pierce with a sharp implement, punch, kick, butt' (probably through the intermediate stage 'make dots'); in Dyirbal, it is expressed through the verb *baŋga*, 'paint with the finger'; and in Yidiny through the compound *gijar* + *gunda*, 'paint in pattern', which links the noun *gijar*, 'mark, line', and verb *gunda*, 'cut'.

Sometimes a newly introduced activity or thing is named because of the effect it has. In Nyawaygi, the verb *maguli*, 'to work', is related to the adjective *magul*, 'tired', and literally means 'to become tired'. In Yidiny, opium and alcohol are referred to as *jama*, which means 'dangerous or bad thing', and was previously applied to poisonous snakes, centipedes, stinging trees, and the like. (In Nyangumarda, alcoholic drink is named according to its taste, as *kari*, 'bitter'.)

The way a new type of person is named can be revealing of the nature of culture contact. The anthropologist A. P. Elkin remarked (*Studies in Australian Linguistics*, p. 39, Oceania Monographs, 1937): 'The Broome district words for policeman tell their own story: in Karadjeri he is called *weder*, fierce, severe-looking; in Yauor, *lendo*, sour, salty; and in Djaru, *yawadaro wainowadji*, the chaining horseman.' In Dhurga, from the New South Wales south coast, one of the words for 'policeman' is *juŋga*, 'octopus'!

MAKING NEW WORDS

New objects can be named by using words and grammatical endings already in a language, and putting them together in new ways. For *typewriter*, English just combined *type* with *write* and *-er*. Australian languages make new words in similar ways. Captain Watkin Tench, writing about the early days in Sydney said (*Journals*, 1961 edition, p. 292):

> Their translations of our words into their language are always apposite, comprehensive, and drawn from images familiar to them: a gun, for instance, they call *Goòroobeera*, that is—*a stick of fire* ... Sometimes also, by a licence of language, they call those who carry guns by the same name. But the appellation by which they generally distinguished us was that of *Bèreewolgal*, meaning—*men come from afar*.

The Wiradhuri described a blacksmith as *burguin mudil*, 'beater out of tomahawks', and 'horse' in Gaurna, the Adelaide language, was originally *bindi nhandu*, literally 'European kangaroo' (page 68). In Kalkatungu, the word for gun was *nduu-mayi-ñjirr*, literally 'hole-make-er'. In Warumungu, 'rabbit' is *kuwarta junmarn*, literally 'ear long'.

In Nyangumarda, there is an ending *-pinti*, 'thing concerned with', which is used to make names for all sorts of new objects, including:

jina-pinti 'hobble (for horses)'	from *jina* 'foot'
waŋal-pinti 'electric fan'	from *waŋal* 'wind'
pajini-pinti 'tobacco'	from *paji-* 'to smoke'

The Nyangumarda ending *-mili*, 'belonging to', is used to make the word *ŋulʸa-mili*, 'soap', from *ŋulʸa*, 'washing'.

Warumungu has the ending -*kari*, which means 'belonging to' or 'associated with', and can be used to form names for new things in a similar fashion:

jina-kari 'shoe'   from *jina* 'foot'

warna-kari 'air conditioner'   from *warna* 'cold'

ñanjji-kari 'mirror'   from *ñamjji* 'seeing'

The Warumungu ending -*jangu*, 'having', is used in *kunapa-jangu*, the name for a Greyhound bus, which is literally 'dog-having'.

Pintupi has an ending -*kunu*, 'associated with', and this has been used by Aboriginal health workers to coin terms for medical equipment:

pina-kunu 'stethoscope'   from *pina* 'ear'

ngalypa-kunu 'oxygen cylinder'   from *ngalypa* 'breathing'

Warumungu people classify foodstuffs as 'bush' (i.e. traditional) and 'shop' (introduced by Europeans). They name some introduced foods in terms of their similarity to traditional foods, adding the English word shop, and ending -*wariñi*, 'inhabitant of, relating to':

- *manaji* 'native yam'
- *manaji shop-wariñi* 'European potato' (literally: 'shop yam')
- *tiika* 'fat'
- *tiika shop-wariñi* 'margarine' (literally: 'shop fat')
- *marnukuju* 'conkerberry'
- *marnukuju shop-wariñi* 'grapes' (literally: 'shop conkerberry')

ADAPTING THE SOUNDS

A word that is borrowed into a language has to be adapted to the phonetic system of that language. French has nasalised vowels, but English doesn't, and a word like French *coupon*, where the final vowel is nasalised, is taken into English with both vowels pronounced in a plain manner, without any nasalisation. We mentioned in Chapter 1 that *ŋ* occurs at the end of a word in English (it is the sound written 'ng' in *bang*), but not at the beginning. English has taken over a few words that began with *ŋ* in an Australian language—this has sometimes been replaced by *n* (*nulla nulla* from *ŋala ŋala*, pages 180–1) and sometimes by *h* (*humpy* from *ŋumbi*, page 198).

Australian languages have some sounds that English doesn't have—the two *r*-sounds, *rr* and *r*; retroflex sounds like *rd*, *rn* and *rl*, where the tongue tip is turned back in the mouth; and *dh*, *nh*, and *lh*, which are made with the blade of the tongue against the teeth. But most Australian languages don't have frica-tives or sibilants, the sounds written in English as *f, v, th, s, z, sh*; and—as we explained in Chapter 1—in most Australian languages, *p* and *b*, *t* and *d*, and *k* and *g*, are interchangeable, without affecting the meaning of the word. (It thus doesn't matter whether one uses *b*, *d*, *g*, as we did in Chapter 3, or *p*, *t*, *k* as do some of the sources we quote in this chapter.)

We can give rough, general principles for how English consonant sounds are treated in loan words in Australian languages. All the examples quoted here are from Dyirbal, but they are typical of what happens right around the continent:

i)   *p*, *b*, *f* and *v* all become *b*, e.g. *burranda*, 'verandah'; *biba*, 'paper'; *bigi*, 'pig'; *binana*, 'banana'; *bugu*, 'fork'; *bunarra*, 'bow and arrow' (this is a single word in Dyirbal, corresponding to a three-word phrase in English);

ii) *s*, *z*, *sh*, *ch*, *j* and *th* all become *j* (recall that *j* is pronounced as a much sharper sound than English *j*, more like *d* and *y* said together), or *dh* (like *d* but with the tongue touching the teeth), e.g. *juga*, 'sugar'; *jiya*, 'chair'; *biñjin*, 'petrol' (from *benzene*); *jarrjin*, '(police) sergeant';

iii) *d* usually remains *d*, e.g. *damba*, 'damper';

iv) *t* becomes *d* at the beginning of a word, but it often becomes *rr* in the middle or at the end of a word, e.g. *dawun*, 'town'; *bilayŋgirr*, 'blanket';

v)   *k* and *g* become *g*, e.g. *gabiji*, 'cabbage'; *gaygi*, 'cake'.

Other English consonants keep roughly the same pronunciation when taken into Australian languages in a loan word.

It is not just the sounds of a language which matter, but the ways in which the sounds can be combined. Australian languages allow two consonants to come next to each other in the middle of a word, but not as a rule at the beginning or at the end. If an English word beginning with two consonants is taken as a loan into an Australian language, either one of the consonants is dropped, or a vowel is brought in to separate them. In one dialect of Dyirbal, 'spoon' is *buwun*, dropping the initial *s* and making the word have two syllables by inserting *w* (this word can be pronounced *buun*), and in other dialects it is *jibun* (rendering the *s* by *j* in Dyirbal and inserting an *i* to avoid a sequence of two consonants). In Walmatjari, we find *tuwa*, 'store'; *jart*, 'start'; *kuul*, 'school' (in each of these, the initial *s* has been omitted); and also *kuriyip*, 'grape'; *purayi*, 'pray'; *gilayij*, 'glass' (in each of these, a vowel has been inserted between the first two consonants).

Only certain sounds may come at the end of words in Australian languages. Walmatjari does have stop consonants like *p*, *t*, *k*, and *j* at the ends of some words, but many languages do not permit this. What happens, then, is that an extra vowel is added on at the end, as in Dyirbal *bugu*, 'fork', and *gaygi*, 'cake'. In Pintupi, every word must end in a vowel, so we get *jaata*, 'shirt', *piitula*, 'petrol', and *juupa*, 'soap'.

In some languages, no word may begin with an *r*-sound or an *l*-sound, and an extra *yu-* or *yi-* may be put at the front of a loan word, e.g. *yurrapiti*, 'rabbit'; *yurrayilway*, 'railway'; *yilamu*, 'lamb'.

In most Australian languages, every word must begin with a consonant. If a loan word into Dyirbal would begin with an *i*, then *y* is put before it, e.g. *yiñjin*, 'engine'; if a loan word would begin with *u*, then *w* is put before it, e.g. *wulman*, 'old man'; and if it would begin with *a*, then *ŋ*—the sound that cannot come at the beginning of a word in English but is very common in that position in Australian languages—comes before the *a*, e.g. *ŋayan*, 'iron', *ŋarriñji*, 'orange', *ŋaŋgija*, 'handkerchief'.

As we mentioned on page 13, English spelling has many different ways of showing a single vowel sound; and vowels are pronounced in distinct ways in different dialects of English. The way an English vowel was represented in terms of the three vowels (*a*, *i*, and *u*) available in most Australian languages depended on exactly how that word was pronounced by the first white people in the area. It is impossible to give any general rules about this.

WORDS ONLY PARTLY ADAPTED

When any language accepts loan words from another, the new words are for a time felt to be foreign. After the Norman conquest of England, in 1066, many words were taken over from the French spoken by the Normans. A speaker of English in 1250 CE would have told you that *gentle, faith, carry*, and *battle* were not 'true English' words, but recent importations from French. Now, 700 years later, we regard them as bona fide English words.

Loans can extend the phonetic possibilities of a language. Old English had no *j* sound at the beginning of a word, for instance, and this was introduced into the language mainly through loans from French, words such as *jealous, jelly*, and *judge*.

The English language still borrows words from French (and, of course, the other way round). In recent centuries, we have accepted *restaurant* and *croissant*. These words are still felt to be a bit foreign, and some people pronounce them in a slightly French sort of way. They haven't yet had time to be fully assimilated into the language, but give them another 500 years and they'll probably feel as English as do *gentle* and *carry* today.

The same observations apply to loan words in Australian languages. Some words may have been taken into a language more than a century ago, were adapted to fit the traditional phonetic system, and are now felt to be fully a part of the language. Others have been taken in more recently and are recognised to be foreign elements; their pronunciation may have been only partly assimilated to the phonetic pattern of the borrowing language.

Tamsin Donaldson, in a piece called 'From speaking Ngiyampaa to speaking English' (*Aboriginal History*, Vol. 9, pp. 126–47, 1985) talks about early loans from English into Ngiyambaa, from central New South Wales. *Fox* became *pakutha* by applying the principles described above. The 'x' in English spelling represents a *k* followed by an *s*; *f* becomes *p*, *k* stays as *k*, and *s* is represented by *th* (a sound like *t*, but with the tongue touching the teeth). Ngiyampaa can't have *k* and *th* next to each other (it can't have a sequence of two stop consonants), and it can't have a word ending in *th*, so a vowel was inserted between *k* and *th* and another after *th*—hey presto, *pakutha*.

Recently the word *Vicks* (trade name for a medicinal 'Vapour Rub') has come into the language. By the same principles which made *fox* into *pakutha*, we should expect *Vicks* to become *pikutha*. It is in fact pronounced *piks*. The *v* becomes *p*, but the *s* (a sound foreign to olden-days Ngiyampaa) is kept. Here, a foreign word is being used in Ngiyampaa with its pronunciation only slightly adapted (it's a bit like *savoir faire* in English—people who use this usually pronounce it in a manner part-way between French and English).

We mentioned that Pintupi has coined new words for use in the health domain, including *pina-kunu*, 'stethoscope', and *ngalypa-kunu*, 'oxygen cylinder'. There are also established loan words from English—which have been fully assimilated phonetically—such as *pulangkita* 'blanket'. Some recent loans have also been adapted to fit the Pintupi system, including *tiipi*, 'TB, tuberculosis', *miijila*, 'measles', and *riñtyi*, 'syringe' (note that here the initial s is lost). Side by side with these, medical workers use *sickness*, *scales*, *medicine*, and *eye-drop*, pronounced almost as they would be in English—these are loans which have not yet been phonetically assimilated into Pintupi.

Many Australian languages are dropping out of use, and the last generation of speakers may mingle together bits of English and bits of their traditional language. It can then be hard to tell what is a loan word, and what is just a bit of another language being mixed in. But for a language like Pintupi, which is still actively spoken, one of two things will happen—either the pronunciation of words like *sickness* will be changed, with *s* being replaced by *ty* to fit the phonetic pattern of Pintupi, or else the phonetic system will change by admitting *s* as a Pintupi sound (just as English added initial *j*, in the first place through loans from French).

SHIFTING MEANINGS

Some loan words in Australian languages appear quite quaint, and reflect the way English was spoken in the nineteenth century, at the time the loan words were taken in. In many languages, the word for 'dress' is *gawun* (from *gown*), and in some *jalgi* (from *sulky*) is used for 'a cart or dray'. One very common loan is *mijiji* (or *mijij*, in languages that allow a word to end in *j*) for 'white woman'; this comes from *missus*.

When a word is taken into another language, its meaning may shift. It is easy to see how this can happen. Captain John Hunter (*An Historical Journal of ... Port*

Jackson, 1793, p. 460) described how, in September 1790, Bennelong thought that the word for 'wine' was *the King*, 'for as he had always heard his Majesty's health drank in the first glass after dinner at the governor's table, and had been made to repeat the word before he drank his own glass of wine, he supposed the liquor was named "the King"; and though he afterwards knew it was called wine, yet he would frequently call it King.'

Sometimes a new object may be named from a description, in the donor language, of its use or result. In Yidiny, the word for 'gun' is *judim*, from *shoot him*, and in Nyangumarda, it is *kilaman*, from *kill a man*.

A loan can have a wider range of meaning in the new language than that which it has in the old. In Dyirbal, *ŋandil* means 'handle' (the word on which it was based), but it is also used for 'steering wheel of a car'. In a number of languages, *wilbarra*, from *wheelbarrow*, is used for any sort of wheeled vehicle. In Diyari, a train is called *thurru wilparra*, literally 'fire vehicle'.

Some loans are used more widely in Australian languages than their originals are in English. These include *gaman* for 'pretend, trick' (from the semi-archaic *gammon*), *hambag* 'sham' (from *humbug*), and *tikili* (from *tricky*), which can be applied to anything complex and demanding, such as sacred activities and ceremonies.

A number of objects seem to be named from their sound, e.g. *diŋgildiŋgil* for 'bell' in Dyirbal; but this is probably because early settlers described it as a *tinkle-tinkle*. In Nyangumarda, 'cat' is *miñawu*, presumably from *miaow*.

One interesting fact about loan words from English is that they are scarcely ever taken into Australian languages as verbs, even if they come from verbs in English. Almost all loans are nouns, but they can be used as verbs by adding one of the regular grammatical endings in a given language which made a noun into a verb. In Dyirbal, there is *wagi*, 'working', to which the ending *-bin* can be added, forming an intransitive verb, *wagi-bin*, 'to work'; and *majurrim*, 'mustering', to which the ending *-man* can be added, forming a transitive verb, *majurrim-man*, 'to muster'.

This can be taken one step further. In an article on 'How Warumungu people express new concepts' (*Language in Central Australia*, No. 4, pp. 12–25, 1985), Jane Simpson reports that:

> when people use English or Aboriginal English words in Warumungu, they add Warumungu endings to the English words. When English verbs are used in Warumungu, the Warumungu ending *-jinta* is added if the verb is intransitive: *bog-jinta* 'to get bogged', *drink-jinta* 'to drink alcohol', *save-jinta* 'to be saved (by Jesus)', *work-jinta* 'to work'. If the English word is combined with a preposition, such as 'ring up', 'think about', then the Warumungu ending follows the preposition: *ringup-jinta* 'to ring up', *sinkabat-jinta* 'to think about'.

SOME COMMON LOANS

We give here just a selection of some of the most common loans from English into Australian languages (the spelling and pronunciation will, of course, vary a little from language to language).

Humans

'white man', *waybala, walpala, wabulya, wabela* (from *white fellow*)
'white woman', *mijiji, mijij* (from *missus*)
'English', *yingkiliji*
'policeman', *bulijiman, buliman, poligman*; *gandhibal* (from *constable*); *jayijin, jarrjin* (from *sergeant*)
'boss', *maja, mayaja, maatha* (from *master*)
'missionary', *mijinari* (meaning sometimes extended to cover 'teetotaller')
'nursing sister', *jija*
'publican', 'pub', *babuligan*
'old woman', *olguman, wultuman*
'old man', *onman, wulman*
'cousin', *kajin*
'part-Aborigine', *yapukaji, apakantha* (from *half-caste*)

Animals

'rabbit', *yurrapiti, yurraapat*
'cat', *pujikati, pujigan* (from *pussy-cat*); *miñawu* (from *miaow*)
'cattle', *bulugi, puluku, puliki* (from *bullock*)
'calf', *kapi-kapi*
'mule', *miyulu*
'donkey', *tangkiya*
'camel', *kamula, kamulpa*
'fox', *puwujuma, pakutha*
'pig', *pigi-pigi*
'sheep', *jiyipi-jiyipi*; *wulubua* (from *wool*)
'goat', *nanikutu, ñanigun* (from *nanny goat*); *biliguwun* (from *billy goat*)
'chicken', *juku-juku, jugi* (from *chook*)
'snake', *jinayiki*
'turkey', *jarge, tharraki*
'English bee', *yiŋgilibiy, yiŋgiliman* (from *Englishman*)

Material Objects

'gun', *makiti, majgad, mugadi, marrgin* (from *musket*); *rayipula* (from *rifle*)
'matches', *majiji, maja, lujipa* (from the brand name *Lucifer*)

'scissors, knife', *nipinipi* (from *nip*)
'saw', *juwa*
'knife', *nayib, naybu*
'bag', *bagi*
'iron', *ŋayan; jitipayini* (from *sheet of iron*)
'strap' *jorab, tharaap*
'ladder', *lada*
'rope', *rubu*
'box', *pukuju*
'calico', *kaliku*
'cotton', *gadin*
'glass', *gilaji*
'mirror', *mira*
'soap', *juwupu, tupu, juuba*
'money', *mani;* recently *dala* (from *dollar*)
'cents', *janti*
'book', 'letter', 'paper', *bugu, payipa*
'handkerchief', *aŋgaja, ŋaŋgija*
'pipe', *bayib, baybu*
'medicine', *mirrijin*
'store', *juwa, tuwa*
'window', *winda*
'mission', *mijin*
'mine', *mayini*
'hospital', *wajbil*
'town', *tawunu, dawun*

Transport and Communication

'wheeled vehicle', *wilparra, wilbarr* (from *wheelbarrow*)
'steamer', *jima*
'motor car', *murtaka, mutika, mudaga*
'truck', *turuki*
'bicycle', *pajingkili, bajigul*
'aeroplane', *yiripilayini; bilhan* (from *plane*)
'aerodrome', *yiritirami*
'street', *turiyat*
'train', *yurrayilway* (from *railway*)
'wire', *waya*
'telegraph wire', *jaligirri; jaligiram* (probably from *telegram*)

Clothing

'blanket', *bilayŋgirr, pilangkirr, pilangkiti*
'trousers', *jawoj, jarruja, tarruja*
'shirt', *jaad, judi*
'socks', *dhagin* (from *stockings*)
'wrap-around', *rapurantiyi*
'coat', *gawuda*
'dress', *duraj, gawun* (from *gown*)

Foodstuffs and Plants

'tucker', *taka*
'damper', *damba*
'flour', *buluwa*
'stew', *putu* (from *pot*)
'sugar', *juga*
'milk', *milgi*
'tea', *tiyi, dhii*
'breakfast', *pirnpaji, purrayipit*
'dinner', *dina*
'supper', *jaba*
'watermelon', *wartimili*
'peanut', *binarra*
'lemon', *laymun*
'orange', *ŋarriñji*
'cabbage', *gabaji, gabiji*
'pumpkin', *bamigin*
'potato', *burrirra*
'mango', *mayŋgu*
'pineapple', *banabul*
'bread', *burrin*
'salt', *juwul*
'beer', *biya*
'alcoholic drink', *gurugu* (from *grog*)

SOURCES: (other than those mentioned in the text): Rob Amery, 'Languages in contact—the case of Kintore and Papunya', *Language in Aboriginal Australia*, No. 1, pp. 13–38, 1986 (this contains the discussion of Pintupi medical terms); J. Hudson & E. Richards, *The Walmatjari: an introduction to the language and culture*, Summer Institute of Linguistics, Darwin, 1978, pp. 24–32, 79–82; G. N. O'Grady, 'New concepts in Nyaŋumada', *Anthropological Linguistics*, Vol. 2, pp. 1–6, 1960.

6
English words extended

When a language moves into a new land, it not only takes in loans from the languages already spoken there, it also extends the meanings of its existing word stock, and combines them in new ways, in order to describe aspects of the land, its flora and fauna, and its people. For example, *damson*, the name in England for plum fruits of the tree *Prunus domestica* ssp. *institia*, was applied in Australia to *Terminalia seriocarpa*. A variety of trees with incidental similarities to the *plum* and *apple* of Europe were called *brown plum, black plum, milky plum, Burdekin plum, crow's apple, Argyle apple, winter apple, broad-leaved apple*, and so on.

As mentioned in Chapter 4, a descriptive name in English was first adopted for some animals and plants, to be later supplanted by a loan from an Australian language. The brown and white kingfisher with a mocking cry, *Dacelo novaeguineae*, was first called *laughing jackass* (or just *jackass*, or *settler's clock*, or *bushman's clock*). *Kookaburra*, an anglicisation of its name in Wiradhuri, although first recorded in 1834, did not come into everyday use until the late nineteenth century, gradually ousting the designation *laughing jackass*. The name *koola* (later deformed into *koala*), from the Sydney language, Dharuk, was in use from the earliest days of white settlement, with *native bear* being an alternative designation; these were then blended into *koala bear*.

This chapter briefly surveys some of the ways in which English words have extended their meanings, and been put together in new combinations, to describe the life, habits and aspirations of the indigenous inhabitants of Australia. (It is by no means an exhaustive treatment.)

RELATIONS BETWEEN THE RACES

The early explorers and first settlers used the term **Indians** for the indigenous inhabitants of Australia, as of the Americas (where the name stuck); this label was still occasionally used in Australia until the 1840s. The continent had been named **New Holland** by Dutch navigators, and its inhabitants were called **New Hollanders** by the pirate-explorer William Dampier (in 1697) and in the early days of white settlement. But the name **Australia**—suggested by the explorer Matthew Flinders and adopted by Governor Lachlan Macquarie in the 1810s—began to supplant New Holland. As a consequence, the autochthonous inhabitants were referred to as **Australians** (in contrast to *Englishmen*, or *Colonials*, for settlers from Britain), from the 1810s. Then the term *Australians* came to be reserved for the white inhabitants, with the original people being designated **Aboriginal Australians** or **Aborigines** (or **Abos**, the abbreviation having a derogatory overtone). An alternative was to use **Aboriginal**—which is properly an adjective—as a noun; this odd use began in the late 1820s and continues until the present, but does show signs of diminishing.

The terms **natives** and **native blacks** were in common use for many years. For a while, from the 1820s, these terms contrasted with *native-born*, used to describe white folks who had been born in Australia (as opposed to those who were born in England or Ireland and later came out as *immigrants*).

In colloquial use, **blackfellow** was employed, with the complementary term **whitefellow**. An indigenous woman could be referred to as a **mary**. **Black velvet** referred to a mary as a sex object (and could also be used of the sex act). **Combo** (thought to be based on *combination*) was a whitefellow who lived with a mary, or who sexually exploited Aboriginal women.

In the face of the relentless incursion of European settlers into their traditional lands, Aboriginal people were faced with a number of alternatives. A **station black** worked as stockman on a cattle (or sheep) property, being provided with food and accommodation for himself and his family. Anyone who appeared to live in such as way as to repudiate their Aboriginal identity might be referred to as a **coconut**, allegedly because that fruit, when ripe, has a brown exterior but a white centre.

Many Aborigines in white employ would periodically leave for a few days or weeks **to go walkabout**, pursuing traditional beliefs and customs. This term has gathered in popularity and use across the globe. In the English *Church Times* of 25 April 1980, we read that 'On Saturday the Bishop met local people during a walkabout in the market.' Aboriginal people have their own way and pace of doing things. **Aboriginal time** refers to the habit of commencing some activity once everyone is ready, and continuing it until everyone is satisfied that it is complete (rather than starting and stopping at fixed times on the clock).

As pointed out in Chapter 1, Aboriginal society did not have anything like a 'chief'. Nevertheless, it suited white settlers and missionaries who came into contact with Aboriginal people to 'appoint' one person as **king**. This could be marked by the bestowal of a **king plate**, a metal breastplate to be worn on a chain around the neck, engraved with the name of the 'king' and of his tribe. The more appropriate term for senior men (and women) of authority is **elders**.

From the early nineteenth century until the middle of the twentieth century, many police stations would employ one or more **black trackers**, with expert skills in tracking both criminals and lost persons, in rural areas.

Many of those Aboriginal people who did not attach themselves to a cattle or sheep (or police) station were rounded up and placed in **missions** (the process being termed **missionisation**) or else in government **settlements**; the latter were often referred to as missions, though not run by a church. The land around such a mission or settlement was sometimes gazetted as a **reserve**, for exclusive use of Aboriginal people. Many such institutions implemented the **dormitory system** (referred to in Chapter 1) under which boys and girls were segregated in separate dormitories, to hinder contact between the sexes, and also to sequester children from their parents, so that traditional customs and languages should not be passed on to them.

Those Aborigines who remained on their traditional land were—if a local resident reported them to be a nuisance—likely to be hunted and killed by **native police** (or **black police**, but officially called the Native Mounted Force). These constituted a group of armed **native troopers**: Aborigines from some distant tribe (sometimes, from another state), commanded by a white officer. In reports of these officers, the word **disperse** was used as a euphemism—if so innocuous-sounding a word can be recruited for so dastardly a function—for 'massacre'. A. J. Vogan, on page 142 of his book *Black Police, a Story of Modern Australia* (Hutchinson, London, 1891) writes: 'A young "sub", new in the force … used the word "killed" in place of the official "*dispersed*" in speaking of the unfortunate natives left *hors de combat* on the field. The report was returned to him for correction in company with a severe reprimand for his careless wording of the same. The "sub", being rather a wag in his own way as things turned out, corrected his report so that the faulty portion now read as follows: "We successfully surrounded the said party of aborigines and *dispersed* fifteen, *the remainder*, some half dozen, succeeded in escaping".'

Some Aboriginal people moved into makeshift accommodation on the edge of a town, being referred to as **fringe dwellers**. However, until the 1967 referendum, they were not counted in the Australian census. And they were subject to severe restrictions under the laws of state governments. For example, Aborigines in Queensland were **under the Act**; that is, the 1897 Act for the 'Protection (sic) of Aborigines', under which they were not allowed to marry or cohabit with a non-Aborigine, not allowed to consume alcohol, and not allowed to have their own savings bank book (it had to be maintained by the local policeman, who was often not averse to purloining a share for himself). However, a white person could apply for an **exemption** from the Act in the case of an Aborigine whose good character they could vouch for.

It was put about that Aborigines were a primitive people with little culture (see comments on this, below) and not much of a language. Aborigines were said to have **dialects**, in contrast to people of European origin, who had languages (see the 1994 newspaper quotation, on page 162). In fact, there were about 250 distinct **languages** in Aboriginal Australia, each not intelligible with the others, being as different as are Italian and Welsh. As mentioned in Chapter 1, most languages—especially those spoken over a wide territory—had a number (between two and twenty) of distinct dialects, as different as Australian, American and British varieties of English. Whitefellows would refer to an Aboriginal language as blackfellow's **lingo**, often with disdainful overtones.

Until quite recently, books on Australian history had little or no mention of Aborigines, what anthropologist W. E. H. Stanner called (in his 1968 Boyer lectures, *After the Dreaming*) the **Great Australian Silence.** Recently, they referred to Australia, at the time of the European invasion, by the Latin phrase **Terra Nullius**, literally 'nobody's land'. This implied that the Aboriginal inhabitants, despite their having been in Australia for tens of millennia, had no rights or interest in the country they inhabited.

ARTEFACTS AND SUCHLIKE

Some Aboriginal weapons were similar enough to those in other parts of the world for familiar terms to be retained. On pages 174–88, we note the loan words used for a number of clubs, and also *gidgee* and *mutting* for types of spear, *mogo* for stone axe, and *hielaman*, *malka* and *tawarang* for shield. But these were all local terms, some of which soon fell into obsolescence. Generally, both races use in their English familiar terms such as **spear**, **(stone) axe** (or **tomahawk**), and **shield**. A long, pointed stick used (typically by women) for extracting root vegetables is called a **digging stick** or **yamstick**.

A piece of hard timber would be rapidly twirled in the groove of a flat bottom piece, to generate sparks that set fire to some adjacent dry grass or shredded bark—these are collectively known as **firestick** (this term was also used for a smouldering taper carried when travelling). A **message stick**, carved with conventional symbols, could be sent to another community to invite them to an inter-tribal corroboree (Dixon was told that, for its bearer, the message stick acted as a kind of passport, or permission for safe conduct through alien territory). Two hard polished pieces of timber banged against each other for musical accompaniment are known as **clapsticks**.

The established term **sword** was used of wooden weapons fairly different from the familiar cutting and thrusting rapiers of Europe and Asia. For example, in 1909, W. E. Roth described the single-handed duelling sword prevalent in the rainforest country of north-east Queensland: 'It is from four and a half to five feet in length, and always used with the one hand stretched over the shoulder, the weapon hanging behind the back, and brought forward from above down with a more or less sudden jerk; well-directed, a blow from it can split a man's skull' (*Records of the Australian Museum*, Vol. 7, page 210).

The boomerang was unlike anything seen elsewhere, so that it could *only* be accorded a name from an Australian language (see pages 175–7). Another unusual artefact was a longish stick with a hook at one end, which fitted into a hole at the distal end of a spear; this acted like an extra limb on a thrower's arm and enabled a spear to be thrown a great distance. It was called a **throwing stick**, by Captain Cook and a number of later observers; but *woomera*, a loan word from the Sydney language, Dharuk, gained greater usage.

Vessels for movement over water were of familiar type—a **bark canoe**, with the ends sewn up and sealed with beeswax or tar, and a **raft** made by lashing together a number of lengths of light timber. An Aboriginal shelter could be called a *humpy*, a *mia-mia*, a *gunyah*, a *wurley* (see pages 197–200) or a **bark hut**. A natural source of water, used by Aborigines, was a **native well**.

The explorer Edward John Eyre explained how 'the **native oven** is made by digging a circular hole in the ground, of a size corresponding to the quantity of food to be cooked. It is then lined with stones in the bottom and a strong fire made over them, so as to heat them thoroughly, and dry the hole. As soon as the stones are judged to be sufficiently hot, the fire is removed, and a few of the stones taken, and put inside the animal to be roasted if it be a large one. A few leaves, or a handful of grass, are then sprinkled over the stones in the bottom of the oven, on which the animal is deposited, generally whole, with hot stones, which are kept for this purpose, laid upon the top of it. It is covered with grass, or leaves, and then thickly covered over with earth, which effectually prevents the heat from escaping' (*Journal of an Expedition of Discovery into Central Australia ...*, Vol. II, page 289, 1845).

This method of 'earth oven' cooking is typically described in North Queensland by a word which is often spoken but seldom written down, so that, when an attempt is made to write it, different spellings abound: *kupamari*, *kapamari*, *kapmari*, *cover-muri*, *cup-murray* among them. (It has been suggested that this word may come from a Pacific Island language, but no plausible etymology has yet been found.)

Bush tucker refers to traditional Aboriginal foodstuffs—vegetables, fruits, nuts and roots (it generally does not extend to flesh foods). Similarly, **bush medicine** covers a variety of plants and suchlike used to treat medical conditions. The only really sweet item on the traditional menu was honey from any of a variety of native bees; **sugar bag** is used for the honey, and sometimes also for the bee and its nest.

ABORIGINAL ART

During recent decades, there has been great national and international interest in **Aboriginal art**, noted for its originality and excellence. It exists in varied modes. **Stencil art** involves an object (typically a hand) placed on a rock surface with liquid pigment being sprayed around it from the mouth. **Rock art** and **cave art** refer to engravings, paintings or stencils executed on rock, either under a sheltered overhang or within a cave. Several adjacent designs are collectively referred to as a **rock art gallery**. Where paint was involved, the artworks would from time to time be touched up and renewed.

Bark painting, practised in Arnhem Land, involves a sheet stripped from a stringybark eucalyptus tree, bent flat over a fire and then under stone. The rough external surface is stripped off and the inner surface of the bark smoothed in readiness for painting with red and yellow ochres and pipeclay. One variety is **X-ray art**, depicting not only the external features of the depicted human, spirit or animal but also internal features such as spinal column, heart and lungs. Paintings on bark utilise designs and stories belonging to particular groups; some are of a sacred nature and are used in ritual. Today, bark paintings are included in major collections worldwide. They are now produced as **tourist art**, increasingly using canvas rather than bark, but often maintaining the artistic style associated with bark.

In desert regions, **sand drawings**—made with the hand or a stick—would include abstract designs of ritual significance. These are now being executed on wood or canvas, often using acrylic colours (hence **acrylic art**). They typically involve coloured dots in lines and clusters (hence the name **dot paintings**), which may portray the travels of dreamtime beings.

There was also **ground art**, which can refer to arrangements of stone and earth, as a bora or corroboree ring (pages 149–52), or this label can be used of sand drawings. Today, people of Aboriginal descent pursue a wide range of artistic styles and techniques, which may or may not have a connection with traditional designs; these are collectively referred to as **urban art**.

TRADITIONAL LIFE AND RELIGION

When Europeans came to Australia, they observed that Aboriginal boys (and sometimes also girls) went through a number of puberty **rites** that could appropriately be called **initiation**. This had a number of manifestations. Typically, the skin would be cut in such a way that the raised scar tissue left a pattern of a particular shape, called (**tribal**) **marks** or **cicatrices**. In a large, central swath of the continent, pubescent boys underwent **circumcision**, in which the foreskin was cut off (an operation much like that in other parts of the world). And in some tribes that was followed by an operation unlike anything reported from elsewhere. As described by W. E. Roth (*Ethnological Studies among the North-west-central Queensland Aborigines*, 1897, page 177), this 'aims at the permanent opening up of a more or less considerable extent of the penile portion of the urethra by incision commencing at the external urinary meatus'. Roth coined the name

introcision for this operation, which had previously been called 'the terrible rite'. But Baldwin Spencer and F. J. Gillen, in *The Native Tribes of Central Australia* (1899, page 263) offered an alternative, **subincision**, and it is this term which has gained general currency.

Most Aboriginal tribes are organised into a number of social divisions which constrain who may marry who. Some have two divisions, which are called **moieties** (employing a term already used by anthropologists for similar systems of social organisation in other parts of the world). A man belonging to moiety A must marry a women from moiety B, and vice versa. In a patrilineal society, a child belongs to the same moiety as their father, and in a matrilineal one to the moiety of their mother.

Other tribes have four divisions. In the early days of anthropological work on Aboriginal society, these were called **classes**. Then, in the 1920s, the term **section** was introduced, probably by A. R. Radcliffe-Brown. A man in section A must marry a woman from section B. Their children, who are in section C, must marry someone from section D. If descent is patrilineal, the son of a man in section C (the grandson of a man in section A) will be again in section A. 'A still more complex system is that in which the tribe has eight sub-divisions. These will be called *subsections*, since they can be shown to be subdivisions of the sections of a four-section system'. It appears that the term **subsection** was introduced in this quotation from page 8 of Radcliffe-Brown's *The Social Organization of Australian Tribes* (1931). In non-technical parlance, the term **skin** (or **skin name**) is used for moiety, section or subsection (whichever is appropriate for that tribe).

Typically, some (or more than one) animal or plant or natural object is associated with each moiety, or section, or subsection, and is known as its **totem** (a term earlier employed in relation to Indians of North America), something towards which they have a special responsibility. The term **meat** is sometimes used to refer to totem (or in place of 'skin').

Aboriginal society is characterised by considerable ritual. There may be a number of **sacred objects** (pages 150–1), employed in male or in female ceremonies, sometimes called **men's business** and **women's business** respectively. One such is a flat and elongated piece of smoothed wood, with a string attached to one end, which is whirled around so that it emits a howling sound. The term **bullroarer**, originally used for the playthings of country boys in English, was adopted as the name for this sacred object.

Aboriginal religion involves belief in **ancestral beings**, whose **(ancestral) spirits** continue to the present day. They shaped the world, provided foodstuffs and the like, and established the moral code, that which is now called the **customary law** (or just the **law**). In the Arrernte language from Central Australia the time of ancestral beings is called *aljerreŋe* (*alcheringa* in English, page 149) which was translated as **dreamtime**, a term now in common usage. **Dreaming** is used for a place or thing of special spiritual significance; one can have a **dreaming site**, or a **dreaming story**, or a **dreaming path** (or **track**) along which **dreamtime ancestors** travelled.

Each tribal group has its own panoply of spirits, but there is one that recurs across the continent (and is much feared): the **rainbow serpent**. George Davis recounted the Yidinyji legend concerning this spirit. At one time, the rainbow— who had the form of a snake—secreted the only fire in the world; all the animals (who were dreamtime people) sat around feeling cold and eating raw food. After many attempts to capture the fire, it was eventually snatched away by the satin bird. The people then shouted out to the rainbow that he could never again have fire, but must go to live in water, the opposite of fire and incompatible with it. He might come out and bask in the sun sometimes when it is raining, which would be as close as he could ever get to the fire he once owned. This spirit is said to live in the pool at the bottom of a waterfall, making this a dangerous place to bathe; a small rainbow is often seen dancing in the spray of a waterfall. (See pages 103–6 of *Words of Our Country*, by R. M. W. Dixon, 1991; and the survey article, 'The rainbow serpent myth of Australia', by A. R. Radcliffe-Brown, on pages 19–25 of the *Journal of the Royal Anthropological Society of Great Britain and Ireland*, Vol. 56, 1926.)

Aboriginal people feel a special attachment to their own **country**; the manner in which they care for it is often called **custodianship**. It may be believed that a person's spirit comes from a particular place, known as their **conception site** (and that the spirit will return there on their death). Certain places of high religious significance are known as **sacred sites**; these must not be disturbed. Places which have powerful associations, and perhaps should only be visited on special ceremonial occasions, may be called **danger places**.

Dreamtime legends were handed down through a mix of story and associated song. A full **song cycle** typically takes many hours to perform, the leading performers being known as **songmen**. There is likely to be accompanying dance; one recurrent style is known as **shake-a-leg dancing**, which involves rapid in-and-out movement of the knees. A song cycle might recount the travels of dreamtime ancestors, the 'map' thus laid out being **songlines** (as described in Bruce Chatwin's 1987 book with this title).

Traditionally, there was no fixed period of schooling for an Aborigine. Instead, they would continue learning all their life, building up a cumulative knowledge on matters spiritual and practical. A man in late middle-age, who was respected for both traditional knowledge and skill in hunting, would become an acknowledged authority, who was believed to have the power to induce and remove illness, and to cause death. The term *shaman*, used in other parts of the world, appropriately describes such a person, but for some reason this name has never been applied in Australia. There have instead been uneasy labels such as **medicine man**,

clever man or **doctor** (or, pejoratively, **witchdoctor**). One well-known method of projecting death is (oversimplifying things radically) by **pointing a bone** towards the victim. It had to be a particular type of bone (ideally, one taken from the body of a dead person), handled with great care so that its power should not rebound on the manipulator.

In traditional belief, all deaths (save those of the very young, the very old and people recognised to have a chronic condition) are believed due to sorcery. Various steps are followed to identify the perpetrator of a death, and then to snare them, as a **payback** (this can sometimes be delayed for years, until a suitable opportunity arises).

Aboriginal law was, essentially, self-controlling. Anyone who—either inadvertently or purposely—violated the social code would feel deep **shame**, which was generally considered sufficient punishment. In a regular Australian schoolroom, Aboriginal children find it hard to know how to behave. Anyone who pushes themself forward is said to 'have no shame'; but to do otherwise is to miss out on teacher's attention. The adjective **sorry** also has a special meaning in Aboriginal society, referring to the strong emotion experienced on losing a friend, or being separated from one's country. After a death, relatives may gather in a **sorry camp** for the **sorry business** of lamenting and mourning (often including songs, dances and bodily decoration or scarification).

REGAINING PRIDE, AND LAND

In the years after the white incursion into Australia, the number of full-blood Aborigines remaining in the well-settled areas decreased at a steady rate. (This varied from area to area, but generally it halved each generation, in some cases each decade.) It was truly believed that Aborigines would soon die out, and people talked of **smoothing the pillow of a dying race**; that is, making life bearable for the remnant members of once mighty tribes. However, many white men had taken indigenous women as partners, and their children, being treated like Aborigines, identified as Aborigines.

In the middle of the twentieth century, the official policy became **assimilation**. By this was meant that Aborigines should be integrated into mainstream Australian society, having the same responsibilities and following the same customs as the rest of the population. It was implied that, in the fullness of time, intermarriage would so dilute Aboriginal blood that people would no longer be able to—or would want to—identify Aborigines as a distinct ethnic or social group.

For almost 200 years, Aborigines had been told that they—and their customs and languages—were inferior to those of Europeans. It is difficult not to believe a doctrine declaimed with such force. Then, in the 1960s, things did begin to change. Indigenous people became proud—and said and showed they were proud—of their **Aboriginality**, of doing things the **Aboriginal way** (that is, in a way that relates, at least in part, to traditional life).

And they began to assert themselves in new ways. In 1965, the Gurindji people employed at Wave Hill cattle station in the Northern Territory staged a **walk off**, demanding a small portion of land on which to found their own Aboriginal community. That same year, a group of Aboriginal and white university students, calling themselves **freedom riders**, conducted a 3,200 kilometre bus ride through north-west New South Wales, investigating claims of racial discrimination and protesting against it.

Euphemisms were shed. Some people began to talk of the white **invasion** of Australia, rather than 'settlement' or 'colonisation'. Australia Day, January 26th, celebrates the arrival of the First Fleet in 1788. To Aborigines and their sympathisers, this became **Invasion Day** or **Day of Mourning**. On Invasion Day 1972, a tent was erected on the land outside Parliament House in Canberra, labelled the **Aboriginal Embassy**, protesting that Aborigines were being treated like foreigners in their own land. The tent was torn down by police and then re-erected, a large procession of white Australians marching from the centre of Canberra to Parliament House in support.

The **Aboriginal Flag**, designed by indigenous artist Howard Thomas, is divided horizontally into equal halves of black (representing the autochthonous people) and red (for the earth, and ochre) with in the centre a yellow sun, as the constant renewer of life. This flew for the first time at Victoria Square, Adelaide on 12 July 1971, National Aborigines Day, and later on the Aboriginal Embassy tent in Canberra.

In 1979, a group of prominent white Australians formed themselves into a committee campaigning for a **treaty** (also known as *makarrata*, page 156) between the federal government and its indigenous citizens. This served to focus attention on injustices, but no treaty was forthcoming, with the committee being wound up.

The main point of issue for these movements was **land rights** for Aboriginal people. They had been **dispossessed** in colonial times and were now demanding **native title** for some small portions of their traditional territory. During the 1970s, a legal mechanism was set up through which an Aboriginal group could make a **land claim** to a specially constituted court. Lawyers and anthropologists were employed aplenty, to try to prove or dispute that a certain group were the **traditional owners** of the land they claimed (and had a **special attachment** to it). Many, although not all, of these claims have succeeded, with Aborigines being granted limited title. (There were also claims by coastal people for **sea rights**, and by riverine dwellers for **river rights**.)

But being granted limited title was not enough. What was needed was a judgment that the indigenous people have *prior* title to the land, which title could not have been abrogated by the British king in 1788. Eddie Mabo, from the Murray Islands in the Torres Strait brought a case to the High Court in 1982 that his people were entitled to possession of 'lands of the Murray Islands'. On 3 June 1992, the court handed down a positive decision, and **Mabo** came into the language to refer to this landmark decision (although Eddie himself had passed away during the protracted legal manoeuvres). The Mabo judgment recommended a process of **reconciliation** between the races; indeed, a Council for Aboriginal Reconciliation had been established under legislation passed unanimously by both Houses of Parliament in 1991.

In a number of regions where Aborigines were in a majority, several groups had typically gathered together (or been gathered together) at one central location, generally a mission or government settlement. Then, in the 1970s, there began the **outstation movement** (or **homeland movement**), in which smallish bands would establish themselves on an **outstation** (better called **homeland centre**) on their traditional land, with regular links by truck—or by plane—to the central settlement. In some places, there is a **keeping place** or **keeping centre**, effectively a community centre with the purpose of keeping traditional culture (at least in part) alive.

Aboriginal people sought **self-determination**, the right to make their own decisions, in their own way, about themselves and their land. What the government did was establish a number of regional **(Aboriginal) land councils**, which had limited authority (and to which one should apply for entry to an Aboriginal reserve). Land councils were also responsible for distributing income from mining on Aboriginal land.

Until quite recently, the same vocabulary was used for referring to different degrees of racial mixing as pertains elsewhere in the world: **full-blood** and **part-blood**, which can be more fully specified as **half-blood, quarter-blood**, etc. (**Half-caste** was a less friendly term for any variety of part-blood.) But then part-blood Aborigines mounted a campaign against these labels, so that they came to be deemed politically incorrect. Now, according to imposed etiquette, anyone with any degree of Aboriginal descent must simply be termed an Aborigine (or an **Indigenous Australian**). Technically, a person is an Aborigine if (1) they are of Aboriginal descent, (2) they identify with Aboriginal people, and (3) they are accepted as a member of an Aboriginal community.

Tribe is a decent respectable label, used all over the world and most certainly appropriate to describe socio-political groupings amongst the indigenous inhabitants of Australia. But then anthropologists began to shy away from use of the term; without however suggesting an alternative (which does make things difficult). However, most Aboriginal people are happy—and indeed proud—to say which tribe they belong to. (A colloquial alternative is **mob**.)

Aboriginal Australians have worse housing, schooling, health, and life expectancy than any other group in the community. They also have by far the highest proportion of members in jail (sometimes for serious but often for trivial offences, for which a white person would have been let off with a caution). There was an outcry at the high number of Aboriginal **deaths in custody**, resulting in an official enquiry.

As part of the assimilation strategy, many state governments would take part-blood (and sometimes also full-blood) children away from their parents and foster them with a white family (the Aboriginal parents were sometimes told that the child had died). These children were referred to as the **Stolen Generations** by Peter Read in a 1984 book with that title (and subtitle: *The removal of Aboriginal children in New South Wales, 1883 to 1969*). In 1980, an organisation called **Link-Up** (more fully, Link-Up (NSW) Aboriginal Corporation) was established to try to help the stolen children (by now adults) re-establish contact with their Aboriginal parents and communities.

There was a 'National Inquiry into the Separation of Aboriginal and Torres Strait Islander Children from their Families'. Its report (in 1997) recommended that a process of reconciliation between the races should be embarked on, and this could appropriately commence with an **apology** being proffered for this (and other) wrongs. However, the federal government has thus far declined the invitation to apologise.

A National **Sorry Day** was inaugurated on 26 May 1998, one year after the tabling of the report into the Stolen Generations. 'The Day offers the community the opportunity to participate and be involved in activities to acknowledge the impact of the policies of forcible removal on Australia's indigenous population.' What is needed is for white people to feel 'shame', in the way that an Aborigine would.

FURTHER READING

Additional examples (and further detail on some topics) will be found in Chapter 6 (pages 125–52) of *Lexical Images: The Story of the Australian National Dictionary*, by Bill Ramson (Oxford University Press, 2002), and 'Australian English and Indigenous Voices', by Bruce Moore, pages 133–49 of *English in Australia*, edited by David Blair and Peter Collins (John Benjamins, 2001). See also the standard texts in anthropology, listed at the end of Chapter 1.

Index

This is an index of some of the more important terms from Chapter 6, of the names of Australian Aboriginal languages (or dialects), and of loan words from Australian languages (including some words of uncertain origin and some, like *picaninny*, wrongly thought of as Aboriginal in origin). Variant spellings are indexed either in their alphabetical place or in parentheses after the most usual spelling. References given in bold type are to the main discussion of a loan word or language.

Other Books on Australian English by OUP and the Australian National Dictionary Centre

The Australian National Dictionary Centre at the Australian National University is the major centre for research into Australian English. Its publications include:

Aboriginal English: A Cultural Study   J.M. Arthur

Australian Aboriginal Words in English: Their Origin and Meaning
R.M.W. Dixon, W.S. Ramson, and Mandy Thomas

Convict Words: Language in Early Colonial Australia   Amanda Laugesen

Diggerspeak: The Language of Australians at War   Amanda Laugesen

Gold! Gold! Gold! The Language of the Nineteenth-century Australian Gold Rushes
Bruce Moore

Lexical Images: The Story of The Australian National Dictionary   Bill Ramson

Tassie Terms: A Glossary of Tasmanian Words   Edited by Maureen Brooks and
Joan Ritchie

Voices of Queensland: Words from the Sunshine State   Edited by Julia Robinson

Who's Centric Now? The Present State of Post-colonial Englishes   Bruce Moore

Words from the West: A Glossary of West Australian Terms
Edited by Maureen Brooks and Joan Ritchie